Microsoft SQL Server 2008 R2 Master Data Services

Manage and maintain your organization's master data effectively with Microsoft SQL Server 2008 R2 Master Data Services

Jeremy Kashel

Tim Kent

Martyn Bullerwell

[PACKT] enterprise 88

PUBLISHING

professional expertise distilled

BIRMINGHAM - MUMBAI

Microsoft SQL Server 2008 R2 Master Data Services

First published: July 2011

Production Reference: 1110711

Published by Packt Publishing Ltd.
32 Lincoln Road
Olton
Birmingham, B27 6PA, UK.

ISBN 978-1-849680-50-9

www.packtpub.com

Cover Image by Artie Ng (artherng@yahoo.com.au)

Credits

Authors
Jeremy Kashel

Tim Kent

Martyn Bullerwell

Reviewers
Marc Delisle

Shashank Pawar

Valentino Vranken

Foreword
Ian Ahern

Acquisition Editor
Kerry George

Development Editor
Neha Mallik

Technical Editor
Sakina Kaydawala

Project Coordinator
Leena Purkait

Proofreader
Aaron Nash

Indexers
Rekha Nair

Monica Ajmera Mehta

Graphics
Geetanjali Sawant

Production Coordinator
Alwin Roy

Cover Work
Alwin Roy

Foreword

It is not customary to start a foreword with an admission that the writer of the foreword has only recently come to personally know the author of the book. I started hearing about Adatis, the company for which Jeremy works, a few years ago. The context was always around Business Intelligence implementations in the United Kingdom, always made with a positive context whether it was from someone working at Microsoft, a customer, or an industry analyst. So it was after being introduced to Jeremy by my friend and valued business partner in the UK, Ian Maclachlan, who has headed up European operations for the last two companies I founded around Master Data Management, I started a deeper investigation of both the author and the company he is part of. Starting, as we all do, with their website, I immediately found a kinship with the firm and the author. Their pragmatic approach echoed on almost every web page and blog entry made me realize that I had met another team like ours. Adatis focus on real-world problems and the direct solution of the problem instead of surrounding their projects with reams of expensive strategic and business consulting. Since then my conversations with Jeremy have re-enforced my earlier research. He knows MDS very well indeed.

As the founder of Stratature, the company which delivered +EDM, Enterprise Dimension Manger, to the market nearly ten years ago, it is naturally very gratifying to see four years after Microsoft acquired my prior company, Master Data Services is now doing so well in the market. With the release of MDS in SQL Server 2008 R2 last year, it has taken this long for the market to embrace the new release of SQL Server, due mainly, as far as I can ascertain, to IT approval and software maintenance and update cycles. As this book goes to press, we are seeing unprecedented levels of MDS adoption, so as they say, "timing is everything". As I started Profisee focused on extending MDS as an ISV and partner of Microsoft, I was struck by how long it took to bring MDS to market.

After all, as I was very aware, the technology was already successfully delivered into the market with many customers in production prior to Microsoft's acquisition. "What in the world could be taking three years ?", was often asked at our board meetings. With time I have come to appreciate how much effort and time went into strengthening MDS with its new Services architecture and internationalization. More subtle, but equally important improvements in rules processing and other key server capabilities have made the core MDS engine better than ever. Microsoft is due much credit for this transition of EDM into MDS and I'd like to take this opportunity to thank Kirk Haselden and John McAllister as the two key individuals for making this happen. Their vision and execution are to be commended. Both are still with Microsoft, but now working on other initiatives. These two gentlemen had a vision for master data management which extended well beyond my own, and I can't help myself in hoping they may, one day, return to the MDS team to once again lend their weight of experience to Microsoft's Master Data Management vision.

With the upgrade to R2 we are seeing unparalleled interest and adoption of MDS for all sorts of applications. It is interesting that with the consolidation in the MDM marketplace and the major bets and commitments to MDM of companies such as SAP, Oracle, and IBM; that Microsoft has effectively reduced the cost of a base MDM software platform to zero by including it as part of SQL Server Enterprise Edition. As far as I can determine, whereas the cost of the master data software platforms and applications from the other original MDM vendors has done nothing but escalate under their new found mega−vendor owners; Microsoft's approach of including MDS as part of SQL Server has allowed the floodgates to open. This means that companies looking to tackle the big business domains of Customer, Product, Location, Employee, Suppliers, and Partners can do so at a price point previously unavailable. In addition, because every Enterprise Edition of SQL Server now contains MDS; many, many more applications which are suited to the concepts and capabilities of a master data platform are being developed using the platform. After all, the concepts of master data entities, entity relationships, domain lists can be applied much more broadly than Customer or product. I find not a month goes by without a new MDS customer describing a novel new application of MDS. I am often chastised for describing MDS as "free". So to clarify: Yes, it depends on the customer obtaining a SQL Server license. And it must be Enterprise Edition or higher. But in my experience, regardless of the type of license an organization has with Microsoft, most IT directors and CIOs do, for the most part, fully understand the value of a committed investment and want to leverage these commitments as far as possible.

Therefore, in my experience, these same managers understand their adoption of the MDS platform to be a net-zero incremental cost from MDS software license perspective. This doesn't, of course, eliminate the cost of skills acquisition, application implementation, or maintenance, but this is where Microsoft deliver another major advantage. The sheer size of the Microsoft partner ecosystem around the world has proven time and time again that it regulates pricing with a downward trend in price. Just compare how easily and more cost effectively you can acquire skills for SharePoint and Analysis Services technologies for a business intelligence application. MDS has only been in the market as a fully released product from Microsoft for a year and already the cost of ownership for complete, enterprise grade master data management has dropped dramatically. This can only be good news for organizations looking to implement MDM applications in the toughest budget climate.

Another topic worth addressing is the adoption of MDS for specific domains. Microsoft's approach, as far as I can tell, is to focus on a single MDM platform and allow partners like Profisee to deliver specific applications or extensions to functionality suited for key MDM tasks. We may be the first in delivering Master Data Maestro as the world's first software built specifically for MDS, but we will certainly not be the last. I am aware of several application companies developing using MDS and several of the world's largest consulting companies are building comprehensive Master Data practices centered on MDS and custom MDS related MDM project methodologies.

As the original founder of the company which created the technology behind MDS, I am often asked how the market will react to MDS. Drawing on my own personal experience, I point to the introduction of Analysis Services by Microsoft well over 10 years ago. At the time, I was leading a BI team making a living from two of the then leading BI technologies. The market, especially led by Microsoft's competitors and those with invested skills and experience in those competitor's products did everything possible to dismiss Microsoft's first real entry into the BI market. Also included as part of SQL Server and at no additional cost to the SQL Server license, Analysis Services has gradually increased its market share to where most analysts now indicate Analysis Services holds the largest segment of market share in terms of installed BI applications. As one leading BI analyst shared with me, this has always resulted in one problem for Microsoft. Without a separately licensed SKU for products like Analysis Services and Master Data Services it is hard for Microsoft or the analysts to fully understand adoption, revenue contribution and consequently to allocate appropriate levels of investment amongst these software products. Based on my observation of the interest and adoption of MDS this past year alone I predict, that similar to Analysis Services, Master Data Services will in less than 10 years from its initial release be the leading, adopted master data technology in the world in terms of the number of installed applications.

It is with this background and belief in MDS that I formed Profisee and agreed to write this foreword. Making as much information available around the MDS product and implementing MDS applications is a necessity to helping Microsoft partners and customers alike obtain the information they need to attain self-sufficiency in the MDS and MDM skills necessary to succeed with their initial MDM projects.

There are already other books on the topic of MDS, so what makes this book different? The pragmatic style of the author comes through in almost every chapter. It seems to me this book is written ideally for the analyst or developer coming to MDS for the first time. The book lays out the ideal path for taking your first steps with MDS and culminates in excellent coverage of Security and the API which are both areas every new IT specialist wants to understand more thoroughly than the currently available documentation allows.

In conclusion, I'd like to thank Jeremy for taking the time to write this book which will assist many in coming to grips with their first Master Data Services application. Taking the decision to write a good technical reference is a major commitment in time and energy and I'm certain Jeremy has given up much this past year to bring this book to you.

Ian Ahern
Profisee Inc

About the Authors

Jeremy Kashel is a Principal Consultant with Adatis, a UK-based Microsoft Gold Partner, specializing in the Microsoft Business Intelligence stack. Jeremy has over 10 years' experience in delivering SQL Server Business Intelligence projects, for a variety of UK and international clients. Jeremy is also a keen blogger, and has spoken at a number of Microsoft events.

Jeremy authored Chapters 1, 2, 3, 4, 5, 7, 8, and 10.

First of all, I would like to thank Tim Kent for the constant input he's given across all of the chapters; this book couldn't have been delivered without his help. In addition, Martyn Bullerwell has helped out massively by writing a great chapter on the API, which I know took a while, and personally I think adds a great deal of value to the book.

A huge thanks also goes to Neil Dobner for the many hours he unselfishly put in on the BizTalk section. Neil carried this in his own time, in the middle of delivering a large project for one of our clients, so he put himself out to help, and it's very much appreciated.

I would also like to thank Sacha Tomey and David Morrison for the input they've provided, as well as Ian Ahern for writing the foreword.

In addition, I must also thank the technical reviewers, Valentino Vranken, Marc Delisle, and Shashank Pawar. Their comments and suggestions have helped improve the quality of the book, and have resulted in additional content that makes the book broader.

Finally I would like to thank the Packt team for the guidance given throughout the whole process. Thank you to Kerry George, Neha Mallik, Leena Purkait, and Sakina Kaydawala.

Tim Kent is one of the owners of Adatis and is also involved in project delivery and QA for the Microsoft Business Intelligence stack. Tim was first awarded the MVP for SQL Server in 2009, and has been specializing in SQL Server and the Microsoft BI stack for over 10 years. Tim is also an active member of the SQLBits SQL Server conference organizing committee, and has also been involved in speaking at the event.

Tim authored Chapter 6.

Martyn Bullerwell is one of the owners of Adatis, and is involved in project delivery for Adatis' larger clients, including multi-terabyte data warehouses. Martyn has led projects in a number of different clients and sectors, including media, oil and gas, and banking.

Martyn authored Chapter 9.

About the Reviewers

Marc Delisle is a system administrator at Cegep de Sherbrooke, Québec, Canada. He started to contribute to the open source project phpMyAdmin in December 1998, when he developed the multi-language version.

Marc authored the first ever *Packt Publishing* book — *Mastering phpMyAdmin for Effective MySQL Management*, and its revised editions. He also wrote *Creating your MySQL Database: Practical Design Tips and Techniques*, again with *Packt Publishing*.

Shashank Pawar, a SQL Server Technology Specialist at Microsoft Australia, is a database professional with over 10 years experience in the support, design, development, and usage of SQL Server database technology. His experience covers both OLTP and OLAP applications, with a specialty in high availability, troubleshooting, and performance improvement. With the release of SQL Server 2008 R2 he has been also working on self service BI implementations with PowerPivot and helping enterprises resolve Master Data Management issues with Master Data Services (MDS). He has been involved in MDS projects at government departments such as Health, Education, and also private financial services organizations.

Ever since **Valentino Vranken** graduated in 1998, he has been developing software. Development experience ranges from thick clients in VB6 to server applications in Java to web applications in .NET.

Almost right from the start of his career, besides developing software, he has been working with databases. Thanks to an always-present interest in databases—mainly SQL Server—he has been focusing more and more on designing and developing databases. Lately he has shifted his focus to Business Intelligence creating integration and data warehousing solutions.

Valentino works for Ordina—a consultancy company working for large corporations in Belgium and abroad—as a Senior SQL Server BI Consultant, where he's active in two Competence Centers (Data Intelligence and Business Data Optimization).

On certification level, he's holder of one MCITP and three MCTS certificates on SQL Server 2008.

In his free time, he's active as Core Member of the Belgian SQL Server User Group (`http://www.sqlug.be`) and blogs at `http://blog.hoegaerden.be` where he shares his knowledge with the world. Some of his articles are also posted on well-known specialist sites such as SQLServerPedia, Experts Exchange, and SSAS-Info. One of his articles has been elected as the winner in the first-ever SQLServerPedia Awards, in the Business Intelligence category.

You may encounter him on local SQLUG, VISUG, and Microsoft evenings and events where he likes to hear about other people's experiences.

Occasionally he gives a SQL Server-related presentation for his Ordina colleagues and customers.

I'd like to thank my wife Saskia, and my two daughters Rune and Sterre, for letting me spend some precious free time reviewing this book.

---

www.PacktPub.com

Support files, eBooks, discount offers and more

You might want to visit www.PacktPub.com for support files and downloads related to your book.

Did you know that Packt offers eBook versions of every book published, with PDF and ePub files available? You can upgrade to the eBook version at www.PacktPub.com and as a print book customer, you are entitled to a discount on the eBook copy. Get in touch with us at service@ packtpub.com for more details.

At www.PacktPub.com, you can also read a collection of free technical articles, sign up for a range of free newsletters and receive exclusive discounts and offers on Packt books and eBooks.

PACKTLIB©

http://PacktLib.PacktPub.com

Do you need instant solutions to your IT questions? PacktLib is Packt's online digital book library. Here, you can access, read and search across Packt's entire library of books.

Why Subscribe?

- Fully searchable across every book published by Packt
- Copy and paste, print and bookmark content
- On demand and accessible via web browser

Free Access for Packt account holders

If you have an account with Packt at www.PacktPub.com, you can use this to access PacktLib today and view nine entirely free books. Simply use your login credentials for immediate access.

Instant Updates on New Packt Books

Get notified! Find out when new books are published by following @PacktEnterprise on Twitter, or the *Packt Enterprise* Facebook page.

Table of Contents

Preface

Microsoft SQL Server Master Data Services (MDS) enables organizations to manage and maintain business data used to make critical business decisions. MDS is a Master Data Management (MDM) application, which standardizes and streamlines the critical data entities of an organization, centralizing your master data.

A focused, practical tutorial, this book will show you how to manage and maintain your organization's master data and improve data quality with Microsoft SQL Server 2008 R2 Master Data Services. Using credible techniques and an end-to-end approach, this book will take you through the steps required to implement Master Data Management, enabling business users to standardize and streamline their business data.

The book starts with an overview of Master Data Management, before moving on to an overview of Microsoft SQL Server 2008 R2 Master Data Services (MDS). Subsequent chapters then dive deep into topics such as installing, configuring, and maintaining Master Data Services, creating and using models, version management, business rules, and importing data into Master Data Services.

A comprehensive guide to Microsoft SQL Server 2008 R2 Master Data Services, which uses an end-to-end approach showing you how to implement Master Data Management on the Microsoft platform.

What this book covers

Chapter 1, Master Data Management, provides the reader with a foundation in understanding what Master Data Management (MDM) is, and how it can help to solve business problems. Different MDM architecture approaches are covered, as well as an illustration of different usage scenarios. The chapter will finish by covering a typical Master Data Management project, touching on areas such as data quality and data governance amongst others.

Chapter 2, Master Data Services Overview, gives an overview of SQL Server 2008 R2 Master Data Services (MDS), outlining the main features of the product as well as covering the architecture.

Chapter 3, Installing and Configuring Master Data Services, will get the user up and running with Master Data Services, guiding them through the installation and configuration process, as well as the installation of the sample models.

Chapter 4, Creating and Using Models, starts with introducing the reader to the concept of creating a Model within the Master Data Manager front-end, which will be beginning of an example solution that will run for the rest of the book. Each of the different objects within the MDS object hierarchy will be covered, guiding the reader on how to build a model up step-by-step.

A sample script will be provided that will populate the user's newly created model, and the user will then be guided through the process of editing and creating members using the front-end.

Chapter 5, Version Management, moves into the second part of the Master Data Manager front-end, which is Version Management. The reader will discover how to create and control versions, as well the understanding the transactions with a version.

Chapter 6, Importing Data into Master Data Services, looks at how to load data into Master Data Services using the SQL Server Staging tables and how to automate common MDS tasks using T-SQL and SQL Server Integration Services (SSIS). Sample T-SQL scripts are provided as well as walk-through of creating a SSIS package that will provide a sound pattern for loading any MDS model.

Chapter 7, Business Rules and Workflow, looks at one of the more powerful features of MDS, namely the MDS business rules. We will see how to create a series of business rules, which will include building and publishing a SharePoint workflow.

Chapter 8, Extracting Data from Master Data Services, is split into two parts. The first part will focus on creating the MDS objects that are needed in the data extraction process. The second part of the chapter introduces BizTalk Server, and shows how BizTalk can be used to deliver master data to a subscribing system by walking through a detailed example.

Chapter 9, Application Programming Interface, focuses on how to interface with MDS using the API. We discuss retrieving all model data through the provided web services, as well as using the DLL's to access MDS directly. We will also follow on from *Chapter 7*, expanding the SharePoint workflow example by using the API to update data in MDS.

Chapter 10, Master Data Services Security, will look at securing Master Data Services models. We will run through a series of examples, covering the various different options to ensure that user permissions are set correctly.

What you need for this book

To follow all of the examples in this book, we recommend that you have a PC with the following software installed:

- Microsoft SQL Server 2008 R2 Enterprise or Developer Edition, including:
  - ° Database Engine
  - ° SQL Server Integration Services (SSIS)
  - ° SQL Server Client Tools

- Microsoft Visual Studio 2010 Professional
- Microsoft SharePoint Server 2010 or Microsoft SharePoint Foundation 2010
- BizTalk Server 2010 Standard Edition

Who this book is for

If you are a business and systems analyst or database administrator who wants to manage and maintain your business master data and improve data quality with Microsoft SQL Server Master Data Services, then this book is for you. A basic understanding of Microsoft SQL Server is required.

Conventions

In this book, you will find a number of styles of text that distinguish between different kinds of information. Here are some examples of these styles, and an explanation of their meaning.

Code words in text are shown as follows: "The `MethodInvoking` method of `createTask2` is very similar to the task we created."

A block of code is set as follows:

```
SET @User_ID =     (SELECT ID
                    FROM  mdm.tblUser u
                    WHERE u.UserName = @UserName )
```

When we wish to draw your attention to a particular part of a code block, the relevant lines or items are set in bold:

```
SET @Model_ID = (SELECT Model_ID
                 FROM mdm.viw_SYSTEM_SCHEMA_VERSION
                 WHERE Model_Name = @ModelName)

EXECUTE mdm.udpValidateModel @User_ID, @Model_ID, @Version_ID, 1
```

New terms and **important words** are shown in bold. Words that you see on the screen, in menus or dialog boxes for example, appear in the text like this: "Select the **Integration Management** function from the MDS home page."

> Warnings or important notes appear in a box like this.

> Tips and tricks appear like this.

Reader feedback

Feedback from our readers is always welcome. Let us know what you think about this book—what you liked or may have disliked. Reader feedback is important for us to develop titles that you really get the most out of.

To send us general feedback, simply send an e-mail to feedback@packtpub.com, and mention the book title via the subject of your message.

If there is a book that you need and would like to see us publish, please send us a note in the **SUGGEST A TITLE** form on www.packtpub.com or e-mail suggest@packtpub.com.

If there is a topic that you have expertise in and you are interested in either writing or contributing to a book, see our author guide on www.packtpub.com/authors.

Customer support

Now that you are the proud owner of a Packt book, we have a number of things to help you to get the most from your purchase.

Downloading the example code for this book

You can download the example code files for all Packt books you have purchased from your account at http://www.PacktPub.com. If you purchased this book elsewhere, you can visit http://www.PacktPub.com/support and register to have the files e-mailed directly to you.

Errata

Although we have taken every care to ensure the accuracy of our content, mistakes do happen. If you find a mistake in one of our books—maybe a mistake in the text or the code—we would be grateful if you would report this to us. By doing so, you can save other readers from frustration and help us improve subsequent versions of this book. If you find any errata, please report them by visiting http://www.packtpub.com/support, selecting your book, clicking on the **errata submission form** link, and entering the details of your errata. Once your errata are verified, your submission will be accepted and the errata will be uploaded on our website, or added to any list of existing errata, under the Errata section of that title. Any existing errata can be viewed by selecting your title from http://www.packtpub.com/support.

Piracy

Piracy of copyright material on the Internet is an ongoing problem across all media. At Packt, we take the protection of our copyright and licenses very seriously. If you come across any illegal copies of our works, in any form, on the Internet, please provide us with the location address or website name immediately so that we can pursue a remedy.

Please contact us at `copyright@packtpub.com` with a link to the suspected pirated material.

We appreciate your help in protecting our authors, and our ability to bring you valuable content.

Questions

You can contact us at `questions@packtpub.com` if you are having a problem with any aspect of the book, and we will do our best to address it.

1
Master Data Management

Before covering Master Data Services (MDS) itself, we will start off by covering what Master Data Management (MDM) actually is, and looking at why it can be of benefit to an organization. This includes an examination of the different approaches to MDM, as well as listing the various components that make up an MDM initiative.

This chapter is therefore the foundation of the whole book, and aims to be largely technology agnostic by explaining why MDM is needed and what is actually required in order to implement MDM.

In this chapter, we will cover the following topics:

- Master data
- The need for Master Data Management
- Master Data Management overview
- Data quality
- Operational and analytical Master Data Management
- Different approaches to Master Data Management
- Data governance
- Data stewardship
- Politics and organizational changes

Master data

Before we start managing anything, we need to define what master data actually is. Master data can quite simply be thought of as electronic data that represents any noun belonging or related to the business.

Examples of these nouns are:

- Products
- Customers/clients
- Projects
- Employees
- Properties
- Accounts
- Suppliers
- Vendors
- Stores

Looking at the aforementioned list, we're clearly not mentioning sales data, or inventory data, for example. Instead, master data is the non-transactional data that gives the transactional data some context. For example, our sales system records a transactional sales amount, but this sale is given context by the Product and Customer.

A subject area of master data, such as Customer or Product, is known as an *entity*. If we take Product as an example, we can derive a number of characteristics about the product, which are known as *attributes* of the entity. When we think of any average product, such as an item of clothing, that product will typically have a color, a size, a brand, and so on.

In fact, a product may actually have more attributes than you may think. A more complete picture of what a product entity and its attributes might look like is shown next:

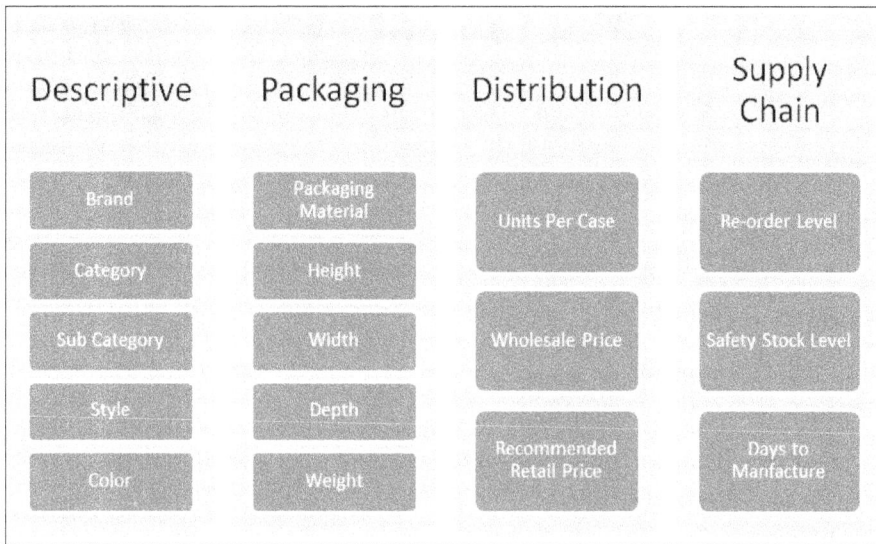

The entity and its attributes define a clear and robust structure for our Product master data subject area. However, a structure is nothing without data itself. The data in the case of the Product entity comes from a collection of *members*, which can be thought of as the physical instances of a given entity.

Each member of the entity will be different from every other member in some sort of way. This is usually achieved through the use of a code or unique identifier (such as the Product's SKU—which stands for Stock Keeping Unit—a unique identifier for items that are for sale in a retail store or other business), but it could easily be from a combination of attributes. An example of the different members for the Product entity is as follows:

SKU	Description	Category	Sub Category	Color
J10001	Men's Regular Fit Jeans	Clothes	Jeans	Blue
J10002	Men's Loose Fit Jeans	Clothes	Jeans	Blue
J10003	Men's Loose Fit Jeans	Clothes	Jeans	Black

The above concepts of entities and attributes are very similar to dimensions, attributes, and members in dimensional data warehouse design and Online Analytical Processing (OLAP) systems, for readers familiar with these concepts.

The need for Master Data Management

Unfortunately, no business of any significant size can run on just one piece of software—businesses need different software to carry out specific tasks. There is never just one user interface and one database to deal with the different functions that need to be carried out.

Large enterprises will always have more than one of the following list of systems that will require the business master data in some way:

- Financial / Accounting
- Sales / e-commerce
- Enterprise Resource Planning (ERP)
- Customer Relationship Management (CRM)
- Human Resources (HR)
- Budgeting and Forecasting
- Admin systems
- Data warehouses

The problems, and the need for MDM, arise because all of the above systems need some or all of the business master data. As these systems generally aren't explicitly linked, it means that each system normally maintains its own copy of master data in order to function correctly. All the systems have their own local database, each containing tables that hold the master data entities needed by the individual application. Therefore, separate copies of an organization's master data are scattered around the enterprise.

This creates a challenge as to how the master data can be passed from system to system. For example, if the Sales Order Processing system is the place where customers get created, then how are these customers made available to the CRM system, which needs to log new sales opportunities for existing customers? Furthermore, what if the CRM system needs to create its own set of potential customers? A situation could arise whereby the CRM creates a potential customer, who, after a few months, becomes a real customer. How is this new customer now entered into the sales system when they place an order? A likely scenario is that the new customer will simply be manually entered into the Sales Order Processing system, with different information than what was entered in the CRM system.

Situations like the one above can cause serious problems within an organization. We may now have a customer called 'Contoso' in our Sales Order Processing system, but our CRM system holds the very same customer as "Contoso Systems".

All this makes it very difficult to obtain a single version of the truth for customer data, meaning in this case that the analysis of the combined sale and cost of sale for reporting purposes will be difficult to obtain.

The overriding problem is that master data changes slowly over time. Inserts, updates and deletes should be applied across all systems at the same time, but due to the way that the individual systems were implemented this is not easily achieved, or in some cases it may actually not be possible. The result is that master data existing across disparate systems in the organization can very quickly become out of sync if not managed correctly. Further examples of how this can happen are as follows:

Manual updates

Sometimes master data can be initially fed from the original system of record to another system, but then no effort is made to keep the two systems automatically synchronized. This approach is typically used when the data that needs to be taken from the system of record is not volatile. An example of this is replicating Cost Centers from the Accounting system to the Budgeting and Planning system. The creation of a new Cost Center may be such an infrequent event that it's acceptable for the Planning administrator to manually re-create the cost center in the Budgeting and Planning system. Accountants and Planners tend to know the Cost Center codes well, meaning it's quite easy for them to make the change. The problem arises of course when other more subtle attributes of the Cost Center, such as perhaps the Cost Centre category, get updated in the Accounting system; then the updates wouldn't be passed to the Budgeting and Planning system, which could cause problems.

Different descriptions for the same attributes

It's quite possible that different systems may need the same attributes of a given entity, but that there is no standardization of the possible attribute values across the different systems. For example, the sales system for a clothing company will have some sort of Product entity, which could have an attribute of Product Category. The sales system may hold the Product Categories of 'Jeans', 'Chinos', 'Sweatshirts', 'Belts', and so on. However, when the marketing system was implemented, the categories were slightly different, being entered as 'Casual Pants' instead of 'Jeans' and just 'Sweaters' for 'Sweatshirts'. When sales figures and marketing costs by Product Category are needed on the same report, there will be no alignment between the Categories of the products.

Mergers and acquisitions

If an organization has grown by mergers or acquisitions then there's a good chance that the once separate companies that now form a group all sell to the same customers. This means it's possible that one of the companies holds a customer called "Contoso USA" and that another company holds a customer called "Contoso North America", which in fact in the fictitious example happens to be exactly the same customer. They've both historically sold to the customer, but have just internally given the customer a different name and have probably assigned different attributes. The end result is that any group level reporting on customer data will not be accurate due to the duplicates that exist.

Master Data Management overview

So what is Master Data Management and how can it help with the problems that we've now seen?

> Master Data Management is a set of tools and processes that aim to deliver a single clean and consistent view of each master data entity that exists within the organization.

In other words, we want each system across the organization to use exactly the same set of master data, in terms of entities, attributes, and members, as long as of course the system actually needs them.

As you might expect, this is easier said than done. Each system will have its own local database, possibly different meanings for different entities or attributes, and its own set of users who are highly accustomed to seeing their data in a certain way.

In order to achieve the above, there is a high-level plan that can be followed for implementing an MDM program:

- Getting executive sponsorship — You need to do this with any large IT project, but it's especially necessary with MDM. Someone will need to sell the benefits of MDM to the various group company heads or department heads who may prove to be an initial barrier to implementing MDM.
- Defining the scope — Your MDM project needs to have a clearly defined scope so that you know how many systems currently use a given entity, what involvement you will have with these systems, and therefore defining the overall objectives of your MDM program.

- Designing a solution — No IT project should ever just launch into the development stage, and the same applies for MDM. It is necessary to thoroughly analyze each source system, using data profiling amongst other techniques, in order to understand the behavior of each entity and attribute that is used.

- Develop a model — A standardized model must be created per entity that is capable of housing the entity in the best possible way. This includes choosing the correct names and data types for attributes, all of which is driven by the analysis of the various data sources.

- Extract data — Master data from the various legitimate sources must be extracted and loaded into the model. Whether or not this process also occurs on a continuous basis depends on the chosen MDM architecture, which is covered later in this chapter.

- Publish data — Once the model has been populated, a method must be devised to allow systems to use data from the newly defined master data model. As with extracting data, how this actually happens depends on the architectural choices.

By going through these steps, each system that falls under the scope of the new MDM program will require some changes in one way or another. These changes may be at the data level, or they may even require architectural/code changes to the system. Given the potential scale of getting each system on board, a sensible approach is to tackle each system in turn, on a piecemeal basis, instead of attempting a big bang approach.

Data quality

If effort is going to be made to distribute a single copy of master data across the organization, then it stands to reason that the data should be of high quality.

It is the responsibility of the MDM solution to ensure data quality - it cannot simply be left to chance that data coming from multiple data sources, or even a single source, will be immediately fit for consumption. Instead, it is likely that one or more of the following problems will need to be corrected:

- Lack of consistency — The existence of different attribute values across two or more members when the true attribute values are semantically the same. For example, the CRM could hold the Customer Genders as "Male" and "Female", whereas the ERP could hold the Genders as "M" and "F".

- Incomplete data—NULL or blank data for a given entity attribute. For example, the Sales Order Processing system could hold the Customer's First Date of purchase. In some systems, this would be calculated and could therefore be relied upon without problems. However, if it's a manually entered field, then having it as NULL or blank would mean any systems that want to use that field for analytical purposes would not be able to do so.

- Format issues—Data that is entered and stored in an incorrect format. For example, customer names being entered in upper case, rather than title case.

- Out of range—Numerical attribute values that are outside the bounds of what the business deems acceptable. For example, a stationary manufacturer may sell pens between the range of $5 – $20. Therefore, if a product price of $500 is encountered for a pen, then it is definitely incorrect.

- Complex data issues—A situation that can occur whereby an attribute value is correct by itself, but incorrect in the context of the member's other attribute values. For example, a Product Recommend Retail Price may well be correct at $1, but not if the Cost of Manufacture is $5.

- Data duplication—The existence of duplicate members for a given entity. As we've seen in one of the previous examples, this can arise due to different systems holding the same information, resulting in us getting two customers with slightly different names that are in fact exactly the same customer.

Data cleansing should be applied to the data before it enters the MDM database, according to a set of pre-defined business rules that check for the specific problems that can occur with the data. The results of any data cleaning should be logged so that reports can be created in order to meet compliance or auditing requirements.

Prior to the development of the data cleansing routines, a detailed data analysis, known as data profiling, should be carried out on the source data to anticipate where the problems may lie. This should be combined with discussions with users and source system experts to understand any additional data quality issues not uncovered by the data profiling.

All the major vendors, such as Microsoft, IBM, and Oracle, produce ETL (Extract Transform Load) tools that contain functionality to assist with data cleaning and data profiling. In addition, there are some more specific tools on the market that are able to assist with the sometimes complex area of de-duplication, especially for areas such as Customer names and addresses.

Operational and analytical Master Data Management

If we think of the places across the organization that need master data, there will be two broad categories that spring to mind, namely:

- Analytical systems, for example, Data Marts and Data Warehouses

- Operational systems; for example, Sales Order Processing, Finance, ERP, and CRM to name a few

The tasks involved in delivering master data are fairly different for analytical systems versus operational systems. Due to the differences, there are two separate categories or uses for MDM, which are known as Analytical MDM and Operational MDM.

Analytical MDM

Analytical MDM is the focus of delivering clean, conformed and consistent master data to data warehouses, cubes, and other business intelligence applications. The process is to extract data from the various operational source systems, and integrate that data into the MDM master entities that have been defined. As with any robust form of data integration, rules are applied to only allow valid data to enter the MDM environment.

Once in the MDM environment, users may interact with the master data via a suitable front-end. One of the key analytical maintenance tasks that users may be required to do is to supply additional entity attribute values for reporting purposes. It's quite likely that if, for example, Customer data has been sourced from the ERP system, then the master data entity that gets populated will contain Customer attributes such as names, address and telephone numbers. But what about a customer attribute such as 'Industry Classification'? In our example, senior management wish to see a report of customer sales that must include Customer Industry Classification, but as it happens there is no such customer attribute in the ERP.

Forgetting MDM for the moment, and depending on how mature the organization's Business Intelligence actually is, Excel may currently be involved to solve the above problem. It's not unheard of for someone to take a data feed from somewhere, and then manually adjust in Excel before delivering some sort of manual excel dashboard to the executive in question.

Another solution to this problem could be to create a new attribute in the ERP. This may be a good choice, but it could take time to implement and could be technically difficult, depending on which ERP product the organization has implemented.

MDM tools can offer a quicker and more robust solution, as they're highly specialized to deal with this kind of situation. As each new customer is detected by the MDM tool, a user can be alerted, and then prompted to fill in the Industry Classification for the new Customer. As you would expect, it's also possible to alter the new attribute value for existing Customers as well.

Due to the huge data volumes involved in some data warehouses and BI tools, the delivery of master data to these systems tends to happen in batch, for example, over-night.

Operational MDM

Operational MDM is a little more complex than Analytical MDM. With Analytical MDM, the data travels one way, from the source, via MDM in the middle, into the data warehouse. Operational MDM is altogether different, as the members of the master data entities that are controlled and improved by the MDM process actually become the members that get used directly by the source systems.

By addressing the overall data quality in the operational systems via a central program, the issues outlined earlier in this chapter can be addressed. For example, a situation could occur whereby users of a marketing system need to send out a promotion to a group of existing customers. They take a feed of customer contacts from the Sales system, which to them seems sensible enough. However, the salespeople who frequently call a range of existing customer contacts have discovered that a few contacts have recently left. This means that the marketing users will be sending promotions to out-of-date contacts and is a waste.

With operational MDM in place, updates to a central repository of customers would ensure that the Marketing users in the example above can send their promotional advertising to a list of customers that will be more likely to respond.

Often, in order to prevent the kind of problems that can occur at the operational level, data needs to be made available to the operational systems in near real time. This is in stark contrast to the kind of latency that is often acceptable in a data warehouse. There are several architectural design patterns that can help address this situation, as we will see in the next section of this chapter.

A final point is that there is some debate on Operational versus Analytical MDM in the industry. This centers around the point that if an entity is to be managed by MDM, then all systems, whether they are analytical or operational, should be using the very same master data.

One thing is certain: the tasks involved getting the operational and analytical systems to participate in the MDM program are different. Operational MDM may need to operate in real time, in order to detect source system changes, deal with them, and then synchronize them back to get users using the correct data as soon as possible. The normally over-night batch loading of a data warehouse is easier to undertake, as no-one will be using the system, and the integration will likely happen into a set of de-normalized tables, which are easier to understand for a developer when compared to the entire normalized structure of an off-the-shelf ERP database, for example.

Different approaches to Master Data Management

As could be said for a lot of IT solutions, there are several different architectural approaches to choose from when implementing MDM: three to be exact, each with their own advantages and disadvantages.

The three approaches to choose from are:

- Transaction Hub
- Registry
- Hybrid

Each approach is explained in turn next.

Transaction Hub

The Transaction Hub approach is the simplest of the three approaches to explain, but it's probably fair to say that it's probably the hardest to be able to implement.

The idea behind the Transaction Hub approach is to have a single repository of master data that all applications can connect to directly in order to retrieve the master data that's needed. A diagram of this approach is shown below:

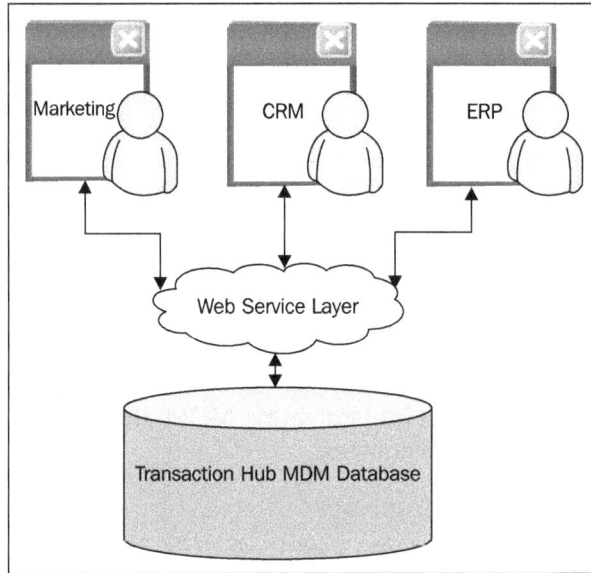

Allowing each application to directly retrieve from a single database involves altering all applications to make their database connections to the central database. For example, the CRM application may be set up to take customer data (such as Full Name, Street Name, State, and other attributes) from a SQL table called 'Cust' in a database called 'CRM'. Implementing a Transaction Hub approach to MDM would mean that the application would have to take customer data in a potentially different structure (perhaps First Name and Surname instead of Full Name) from a table called 'Customer' in a Transaction Hub MDM repository database called 'MDM', for example.

Prior to the existence of the MDM program, the business applications would have been able to insert, update, and delete records as much as they wanted. This is still allowed with the Transaction Hub approach, with the original application user interface facilitating the change, but the data part of the change being sent to the central database. A locking strategy is often employed to ensure that users cannot update the same record at the same time.

The advantages and disadvantages of the Transaction Hub approach are immediately obvious. By forcing all systems to retrieve data from a single database, the problem of having duplicate entries across different databases is eradicated.

The problem with the Transaction Hub approach is that it is probably not going to be possible for most organizations to be able to alter the data tier level of their operational applications. Altering the database connection string is one thing, but having to alter the whole data tier of an off-the-shelf application is very difficult to achieve.

For these reasons, the Transaction Hub approach is seen more as an idealistic approach to MDM, whereas other methods are more realistic to achieve.

Registry

The Registry approach involves the creation of a single database that maintains a mapping system in order to return a single, unique view of a given master data entity. This can be used for reporting, or for any operational reasons that need to obtain a view of a master data entity, such as a mail shot to all customers. The solution typically includes some sort of front-end application that connects to the registry application in order to maintain the mapping.

For each entity that is managed by the Registry, the database holds the following information:

- Member key/unique identifier
- One or more corresponding source system keys
- Optional metadata and business rules for survivorship

No additional attributes of the entities (for example, Name, Address in the case of a Customer) are held in the Registry system. Instead, these attributes are actually retrieved from the source systems directly, based on looking up the source system key value that is now held in the Registry. An example of how this would work for managing Customer master data derived from two Customer source systems is shown below:

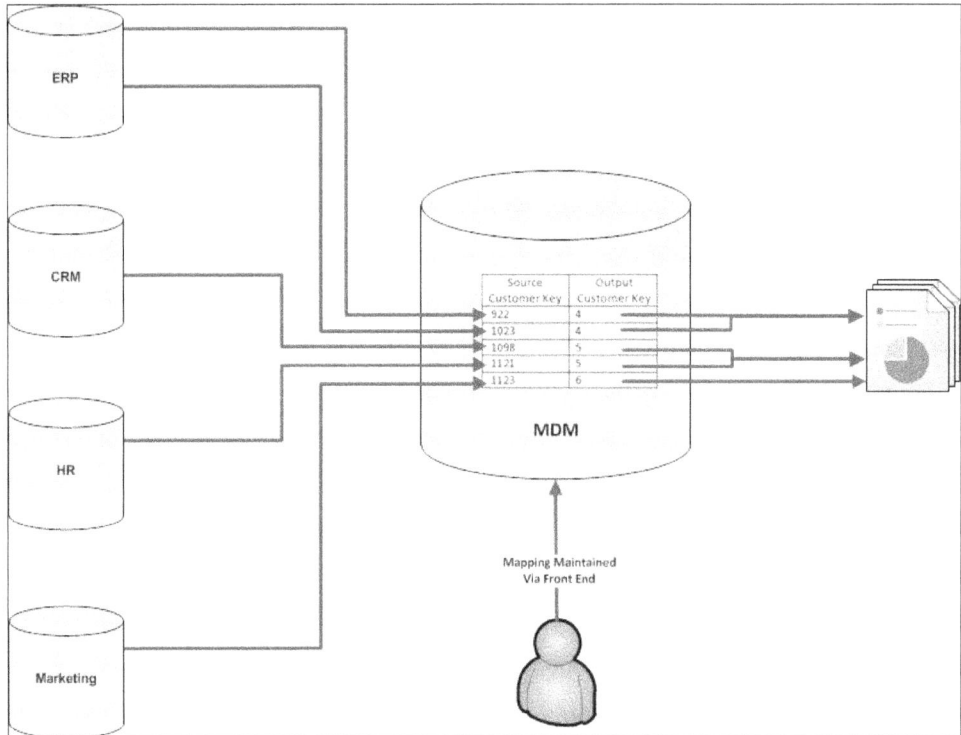

When a given master data entity must be queried or extracted by a downstream system, a distributed query must be executed, which is initiated from the MDM database, as shown. This query must join each system together by using the unique member key that is maintained in the registry mapping.

Given that the non-key attributes of the entities reside in the original different line of business systems, the registry approach typically delivers a *read-only* master data solution. As it only maintains a mapping, there is no interface or mechanism for allowing a user to update a given attribute (such as a Product Category, for example), before distributing that update back to the source systems.

The fact that updates are not allowed simplifies the implementation of a Registry system, although the approach is not without complication. If we have two legitimate sources that update Customer data (such as the Sales Order Processing System and the CRM), then there is a possibility that we will encounter duplicates. A set of business rules should be set up to deal with this eventuality, by picking a single surviving record when a duplicate has been found. The *survivorship* process of removing the duplicates happens in the distributed query, which returns the single merged record, but there is no process of pushing the corrected changes back to the source systems.

The advantage to the registry approach is that it's possible to extract a real time view of a given master data entity without interfering with the various source systems. It's also relatively easy to set up, given that there are a variety of relational databases that are capable of issuing distributed queries.

The main problem with the registry approach is that the large, cross-database queries that are required in order to combine the data are often slow to execute, especially if the data sets are large.

In addition, any time a new system is created or purchased, the distributed queries will have to re-written to incorporate the new source.

Hybrid

The Hybrid is a blend of the other two architectural styles, including a separate database as per the Registry style, but also including all, or most, of an entity's attributes as seen with the Transaction Hub approach.

The aforementioned database is the core of the Hybrid solution, and contains the following data per entity that is to be managed:

- Member Key/Unique Identifier
- The full set of entity attributes that must be shared across different applications
- Metadata and business rules for survivorship and data cleaning

The key concept behind the Hybrid model is that the line of business applications continue to connect directly to their original data stores, as they did before the MDM program existed. In some cases, the original applications update the local data stores directly; carrying out inserts updates and deletes for master data entities.

The role of the Hybrid MDM database is to connect to the individual application databases and to detect changes in the sources for the master data entities that are being managed. The changes that get detected are physically propagated to the MDM database, which maintains a separate, clean and conformed copy of the data.

Once data has been picked up from the application database, a number of operations may be applied to the data:

- Data quality checks and business rules will be run on the data to correct any problems that can be automatically fixed

- De-duplication and survivorship may occur so that an entity such as Customer gets conformed from multiple data sources

- Nominated users may enrich the data to add additional attribute values that are not present in the original data source

At a high level, the above will ensure that the new MDM database now contains a clean set of members that meet the data quality and structure rules as defined by the business.

Now comes the task of distributing the data out to any system that needs it, which from an operational system perspective can be somewhat of a challenge. We know that with the Hybrid approach, all applications continue to connect to their own data sources. The complication arises if the source applications are continuing to insert and update data. It may be possible to prevent, or lock, users out of updating entities directly in the source applications, but this will not always be the case. Therefore, when data gets sent back to the source applications, updates to the source application master data must be made, with the understanding that update conflicts could occur.

An overview of the Hybrid approach is shown below:

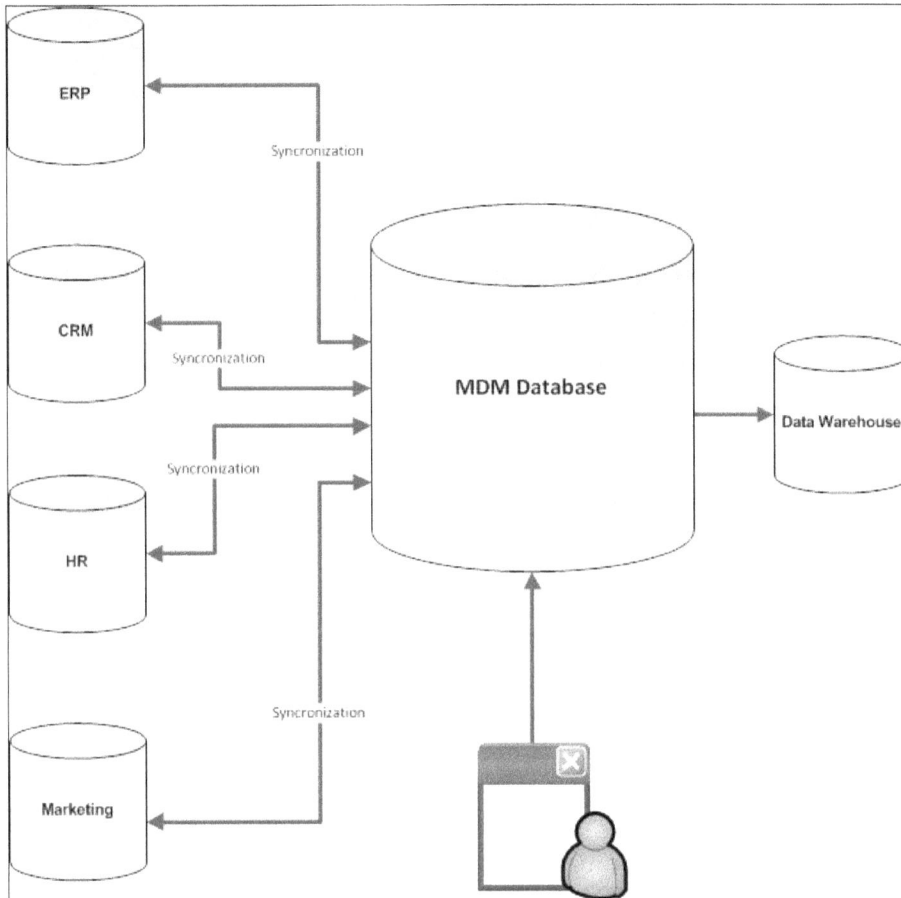

New applications that get implemented can either source master data from the MDM database, usually via web services, or simply fit into the same synchronization approach that is indicated above. The choice of whether to connect a new application directly will largely depend on whether it is developed in-house or purchased.

The Analytical MDM scenario that was presented earlier in the chapter of adding an extra Customer attribute, namely Industry Classification is dealt with elegantly by the Hybrid approach. Attributes that are needed by the source systems are sent back to the source systems, whereas in this case the Industry Classification would only be sent to the data warehouse.

Incidentally, the Transaction Hub approach also deals with the "extra attribute problem", but is likely to be less appealing to most organizations when compared to the Hybrid approach. The Hybrid approach has its challenges, but they are around pushing data into source applications, rather than re-architecting those applications.

Data governance

As we've seen, an MDM solution can incorporate some sophisticated automated functions to assist in delivering master data to the business. However, technology alone cannot ensure the success of an MDM program. Processes must be followed in order to ensure that the MDM solution doesn't fall into the same trap that required its creation in the first place. Data Governance is the method for ensuring this—a framework that defines how master data can be used within the organization.

The idea behind using data governance for MDM is to ensure that the use of master data follows specific rules, policies, and procedures that tie in with the organization's overall strategic objectives. The rules that are set in place typically cover the following areas of the MDM program:

- Data ownership—Defines who has overall responsibility for a given master data entity.

- Change management—Defines the approval process for changes to the use of master data, or changes to the MDM technology solution itself.

- Data access—Who can access the master data? This will include procedures for adding new users to the MDM solution.

- Data modification—A set of rules that govern how inserts, updates and deletes can happen for master data. This may also dictate what is to happen in the event of an update conflict.

- Data quality standards—Defines and monitors the overall data quality standards for the MDM program.

- Disaster recovery—A set of procedures for defining how the master data repository is made available in the event of a disaster. As the MDM program gains traction in the organization, this is a key area to address, as the MDM solution itself becomes a key operational system.

- Data privacy and retention—States how confidential and sensitive data is managed and how long data is retained.

The physical deliverable for data governance in MDM is a set of documents that clearly define the above rules and standards. These documents should be made available to the relevant people in the organization, according to the organization's standard document management policy, for example, SharePoint.

MDM policies and procedures are set up and enforced by a group within the organization known as the *Data Governance Board*. The Data Governance Board is working group within the organization that will meet on a regular basis to make decisions according to the policy. For example, the organization may be developing a new in-house Marketing system that will assist with campaign management. The stakeholders of this system wish to take a feed of Customer data from the MDM database, which must be approved via the Data Governance program.

Data stewardship

The Data Governance Board appoints one or more *Data Stewards* to implement the Data Governance policies. Each master data entity must have a data steward appointed, who is a subject domain expert responsible for maintaining the entity on a continuous basis.

The data stewards typically perform the following functions:

- Respond to any alerts (for example, an automated e-mail) generated by the MDM system
- Take corrective action on master data entities in order to over-ride the "best guess" made by the automated processes
- Monitor and recognize data quality issues with a given entity
- Continually improve an entity's data quality by suggesting enhancements to the data quality process

The data steward is typically a business user who possesses enough knowledge of the source data to make the important business decisions that ultimately result in the whole business consuming a given entity in one way as opposed to another. We can go back to earlier in the chapter to see a good example of this, where we had a Customer entity, sourced from the ERP, but the 'Industry Classification' attribute did not exist in the ERP, meaning it had to be added in the master data model. It would be the responsibility of a data steward to interpret the other Customer attributes, and then pick an appropriate Industry Classification. Although picking an Industry Classification is a simple task, the effect of getting it wrong could, for example, mean that any BI reports by Industry Classification would be incorrect.

Due to the important nature of ensuring high quality master data, the data stewardship process often involves workflow. In this situation, the data steward continues to maintain the master data entity, but certain actions may be pushed to another user to approve or reject the decision taken by the data steward.

Even though data stewards are typically business users, they will often have expert knowledge of the source data, as well as how to interpret it in a business context. This is often the case in businesses or departments where the production of reports is not from a central data warehouse, but through an expert user using Excel to arrange and clean the data. Given the data stewards, high level of knowledge, they should be involved in the requirements and design of any data capture processes in an MDM program right from the start.

Politics and organizational changes

Earlier in the chapter, we gave a one sentence definition of Master Data Management, which included the phrase 'tools and processes'.

The 'processes' part of MDM is a very key point. While this book is obviously about a technology product—you will not get far with implementing an MDM program by just focusing on MDS as a product. The same could probably be said to an extent for implementing any product, but it's particularly important when implementing Master Data Management.

The reason that the processes part of an MDM program are so important is due to the sheer number of systems and people that are used to interacting with the master data entities in the way that is relevant to their own need and use.

As we saw in the overall plan for an MDM program, one of the tasks is to produce a standardized entity model which will be initially fed from a number of different source systems. When this is carried out, the entities and the attributes will be conformed and standardized to mean the same thing. This could be for the actual names of entities and attributes, or for the actual attribute values. For example, the Customer entity may have an attribute of 'Industry' in one system, and this may be renamed in the new master data model as 'Market Segment'. Users who have been used to seeing an attribute called 'Industry' in their applications may not be happy with the renaming of the attribute. In a similar vein, the actual values of the attributes will be standardized, so users of the same application could see the segment of 'IT and Communications' change to a segment of 'IT', with a new segment added called 'Communications'.

As these issues have the potential to cause unrest in the organization, strong sponsorship at the executive level is needed to sell the benefits that an MDM program can bring.

Summary

In this chapter, we've learned the following key points:

- Master data can quite simply be thought of as electronic data that represents any noun belonging to or interfacing with the business

- Master Data Management is a set of tools and processes that aim to deliver a single clean and consistent view of each master data entity that exists within the organization

- There are two difference uses for MDM in an organization—namely Analytical MDM and Operational MDM

- There are three different architectural approaches to MDM, namely the Transaction Hub, Registry, and Hybrid approaches

- Data governance is set up to provide control over the valuable master data asset, by defining a number of policies and procedures

- Data stewards are subject domain experts who maintain the master data according to the practices set out by data governance

- An MDM project needs strong leadership to ensure that the whole organization buys into the MDM program

In the next chapter, we will introduce SQL Server 2008 R2 Master Data Services itself, and take a high level look at the features it has to aid with an MDM initiative.

References

Loshin, D (2009). MDM Paradigms and Architectures. Master Data Management (pp 166-171). Burlington, MA, USA: Morgan Kaufmann Publishers.

2
Master Data Services Overview

In this chapter, we will provide an overview of SQL Server 2008 R2 Master Data Services (MDS), outlining the main features of the product as well as covering the architecture. In addition to covering the architecture, the purpose of this chapter is to get the reader comfortable with navigating around the main MDS interface, namely **Master Data Manager**, before we launch into the detailed modeling topics in further chapters.

In this chapter, we will cover the following:

- Master Data Services overview
- Master Data Services architecture
- Master Data Manager

Master Data Services overview

Master Data Services is Microsoft's Master Data Management product that ships with SQL Server 2008 R2. Much like other parts of SQL Server, such as Analysis Services (SSAS) or Reporting Services (SSRS), MDS doesn't get installed along with the database engine, but is a separate product in its own right.

Unlike SSAS or SSRS, it's worth noting that MDS is only available in the Enterprise and Data Centre Editions of SQL Server, and that the server must be 64-bit.

MDS is a product that has grown from acquisition, as it is based on the +EDM product that Microsoft obtained when they bought the Atlanta-based company called Stratature in 2007. A great deal of work has been carried out since the acquisition, including changing the user interface and putting in a web service layer.

At a high level, the new product has the following features:

- Entity maintenance—MDS supports data stewardship by allowing users to add, edit, and delete members. The tool is not specific to a particular industry or area, but instead is generic enough to work across a variety of subject domains.

- Modeling capability—MDS contains interfaces that allow administrative users to create data models to hold entity members.

- Hierarchy management—Relationships between members can be utilized to produce hierarchies that users can alter.

- Version management—Copies of entity data and related metadata can be archived to create an entirely separate version of the data.

- Business rules and workflow—A comprehensive business rules engine is included in order to enforce data quality and assist with data stewardship via workflow. Alerts can be sent to users using e-mail when the business rules encounter a particular condition.

- Security—A granular security model is included, where it is possible, for example, to prevent a given user from accessing certain entities, attributes, and members.

Master Data Services architecture

Technically, Master Data Services consists of the following components:

- SQL Server Database—The database holds the entities such as Customer or Product, whether they are imported from other systems or created in MDS.

- Master Data Manager—A web-based data stewardship and administration portal that amongst many other features allows data stewards to add, edit, and delete entity members.

- Web Service Layer—All calls to the database from the front-end go through a WCF (Windows Communication Foundation) web service. Internet Information Services (IIS) is used to host the web services and the Master Data Manager application.

- Workflow Integration Service — A Windows service that acts as a broker between MDS and SharePoint in order to allow MDS business rules to use SharePoint workflows.
- Configuration Manager — A windows application that allows key settings to be altered by an administrator.

The following diagram shows how the components interact with one another:

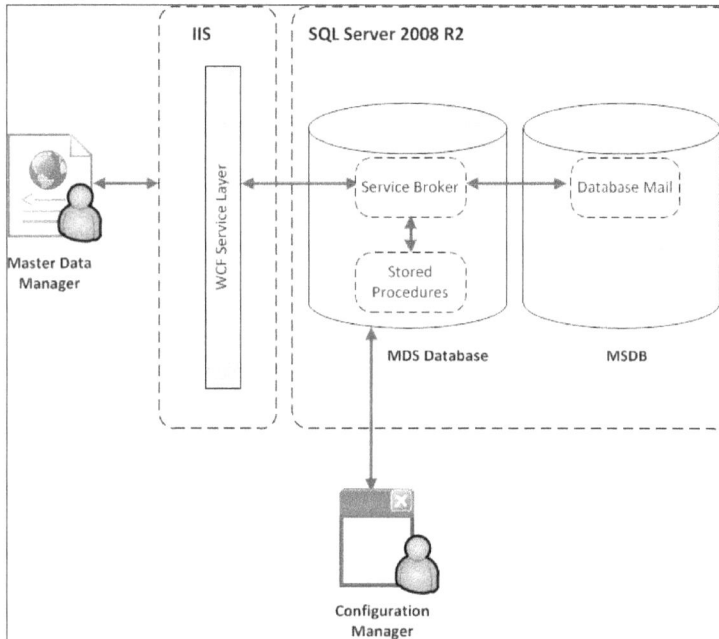

MDS SQL Server database

The MDS database uses a mix of components in order to be the master data store and to support the functionality found in Master Data Manager, including stored procedures, views, and functions.

Separate tables are created both for entities and for their supporting objects, all of which happens on the fly when a new object gets created in Master Data Manager. The data for all entities across all subject areas are stored in the same database, meaning that the database could get quite big if several subject domains are being managed. The tables themselves are created with a code name. For example, on my local installation, the Product entity is not stored in a table called "Product" as you might expect, but in a table called "tbl_2_10_EN".

> **Locating entity data**
>
> The exact table that contains the data for a particular entity can be found by writing a select statement against the view called `viw_SYSTEM_SCHEMA_ENTITY` in the mdm schema.

As well as containing a number of standard SQL Server table-valued and scalar functions, the MDS database also contains a handful of .Net CLR (Common Language Runtime)-based functions, which can be found in the **mdq** schema. The functions utilize the `Microsoft.MasterDataServices.DataQuality` assembly and are used to assist with data quality and the merging, de-duplication, and survivorship exercises that are often required in a master data management solution.

Some of the actions in MDS, such as the e-mail alerts or loading of large amounts of data, need to happen in an asynchronous manner. Service Broker is utilized to allow users to continue to use the front-end without having to wait for long running processes to complete.

Although strictly outside the MDS database, SQL Server Database Mail, which resides in the system **msdb** database, is used as the mechanism to send e-mail alerts to subscribing users.

In addition to the tables that hold the master data entities, the MDS database also contains a set of staging tables that should be used when importing data into MDS. Once the staging tables have been populated correctly, the staged data can be loaded into the master data store in a single batch.

Internet Information Services (IIS)

During the initial configuration of MDS, an IIS Web Application will get created within an IIS website. The name of the application that gets created is called "MDS", although this can be over-ridden if needed.

The Web Application contains a Virtual Directory that points to the physical path of `<Drive>:\<install location>\WebApplication`, where the various components of the Master Data Manager application are stored.

The MDS WCF Service called `Service.svc` is also located in the same directory. The service can be exposed in order to provide a unified access point to any MDS functionality (for example, creating an entity or member, retrieving all entity members) that is needed by other applications. Master Data Manager connects to the WCF service, which then connects to the database, so this is the route that should be taken by other applications, instead of connecting to the database directly.

Master Data Manager

Master Data Manager is the primary mechanism for accessing all the Master Data Services functionality and is therefore the focus of the earlier parts of this book. We will introduce Master Data Manager in this section, before covering the detailed functionality in further chapters.

Accessing Master Data Manager

With the default installation settings, Master Data Manager is accessed in a web browser by typing `http://<servername>/MDS/`. This takes us to the front page, as shown in the following screenshot:

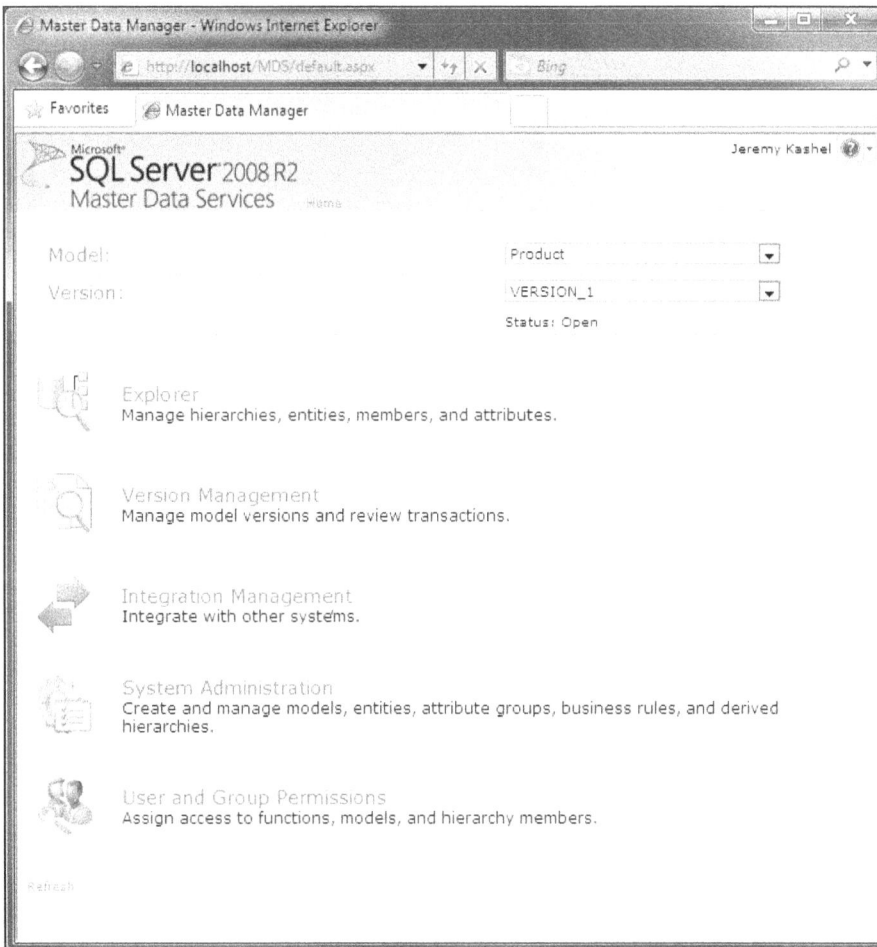

As indicated in the previous screenshot, Master Data Manager has five functional areas that users of the application may access, namely:

- **Explorer**
- **Version Management**
- **Integration Management**
- **System Administration**
- **User and Group Permissions**

We will now look at each of these functions in turn, and explore how they can help with an MDM initiative.

Explorer

The Explorer part of the application will be the primary interface used by data stewards as it allows a user to carry out the following:

- Add, edit, or delete entity members.
- Manage hierarchies.
- View transaction details, for example, who added a particular member and when.
- Reverse transactions that have previously been made.
- Run business rules.
- Export data to Microsoft Excel.
- Create and manage collections, which are user-defined groups of members that exist within an entity. Collections will be explained in detail in *Chapter 4, Creating and Using Models*, along with hierarchies and other objects that are key to MDS.

Clicking on the **Explorer** item on the front page takes us to the **Model View** screen, which gives an overview of the MDS view of our current subject area, for example, **Product**. The **Model View** of the sample **Product** model is shown next:

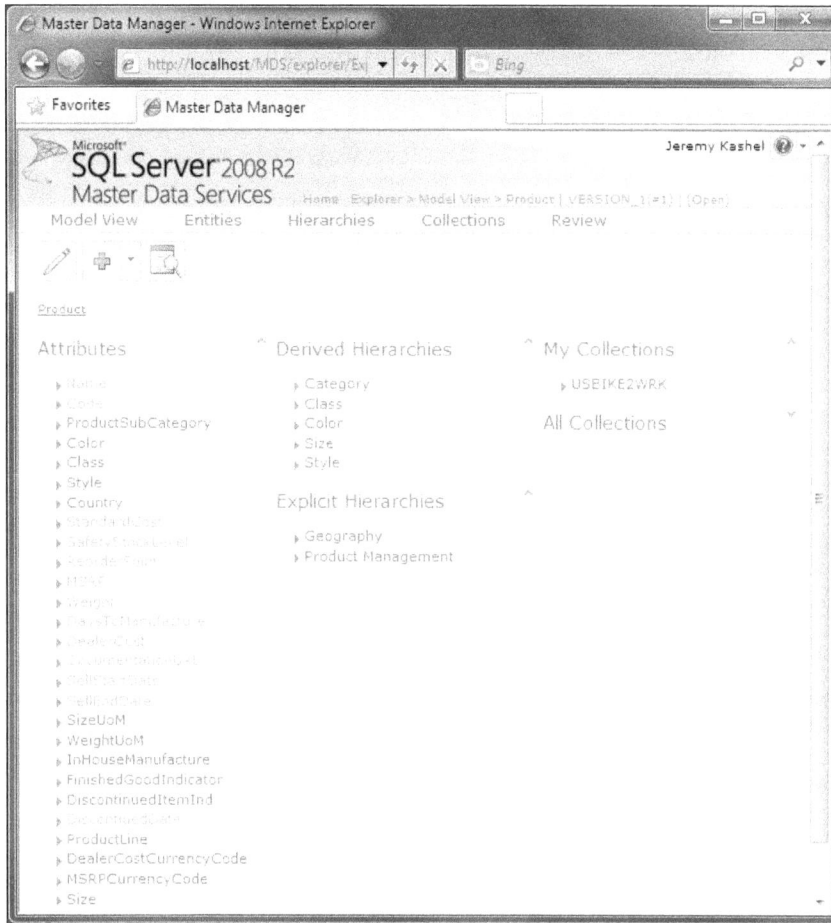

The above screenshot shows all the objects that are used by **Product**, namely a number of attributes, hierarchies, and collections. We can click on some of these objects to take us to the object itself. For example, clicking on the hierarchy called **Category** will take us to the hierarchy itself. Alternatively, we can also navigate to the various items using the menus shown at the top of the screen.

One of the most common tasks for a data steward to carry out will be to go to the Explorer Grid, which is a table structure that shows all the members in the chosen entity. Clicking on the "pencil" icon at the top of the screen is the next step to carry out:

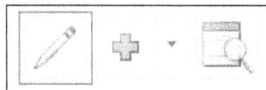

Once this has been carried out, we will get to the Explorer Grid page, as shown in the following screenshot:

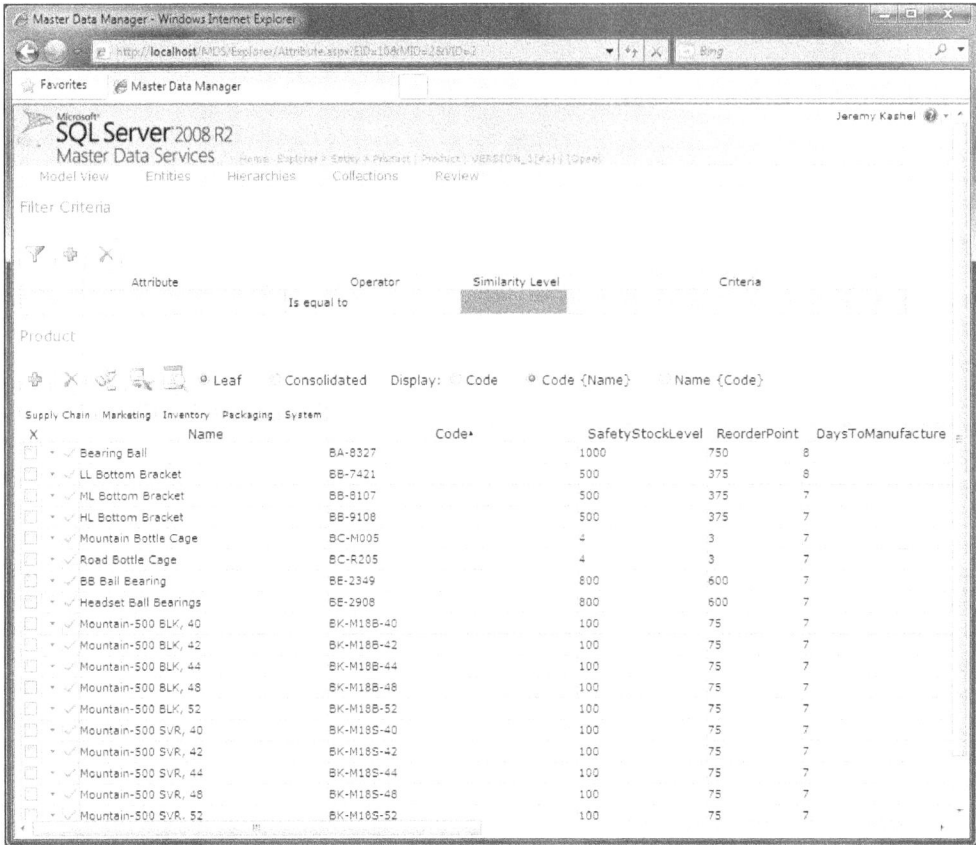

The **Filter Criteria** section at the top of the screen allows us to filter on a chosen entity attribute, in order to make searching easier, whereas the grid at the bottom of the screen contains the members themselves.

Within the grid, the columns are the attributes of the **Product** Entity, such as **Name** or **ReorderPoint**, whereas the rows are the members.

It is within this grid that the adding, editing, and deleting of members can be carried out.

Version Management

Clicking on the Master Data Services logo in the top right-hand corner takes us back to the Master Data Manager home page. From here, if we pick the **Version Management** option, we're taken to the **Manage Versions** page, as shown in the following screenshot:

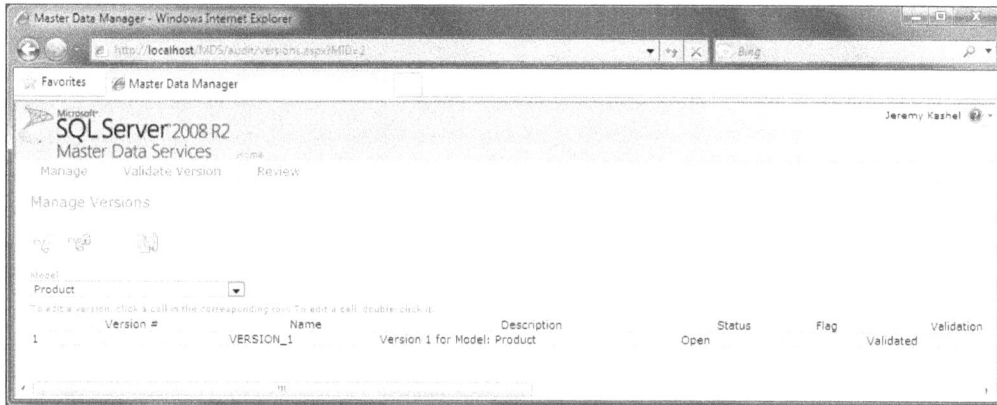

With **Version Management**, it is possible to carry out the following:

- Create a copy of an entity and its associated data, which is known as a version
- Control access to the version
- Validate the version
- Review any issues with the version
- View and reverse transactions that have occurred against a specific version

Versions provide an easy mechanism to create physical copies of all the members that exist within a given entity. This may be useful in an MDM program in order to record the historical changes to master data at a given point in time or to record a major data change, such as organizational realignment.

A new version is created by copying an old version. At this point, MDS can be configured to ensure that only the new version is available for editing, to prevent alterations to historical data.

Versions also contain the concept of validation. If a version is validated, then it meets the business requirements for the given master data entity, and can be safely extracted by any downstream systems that need the master data. Business rules run when a version is validated and will fail if their conditions are not met.

Validation is a key concept within Master Data Services and is covered in detail in *Chapter 5,.Version Management*.

Integration Management

The third option available on the front page of Master Data Manager is Integration Management. Within Integration Management it is possible to:

- Import data into MDS
- Export data out of MDS

Clicking on the **Integration Management** option defaults the screen to the **Import** page, as shown in the following screenshot:

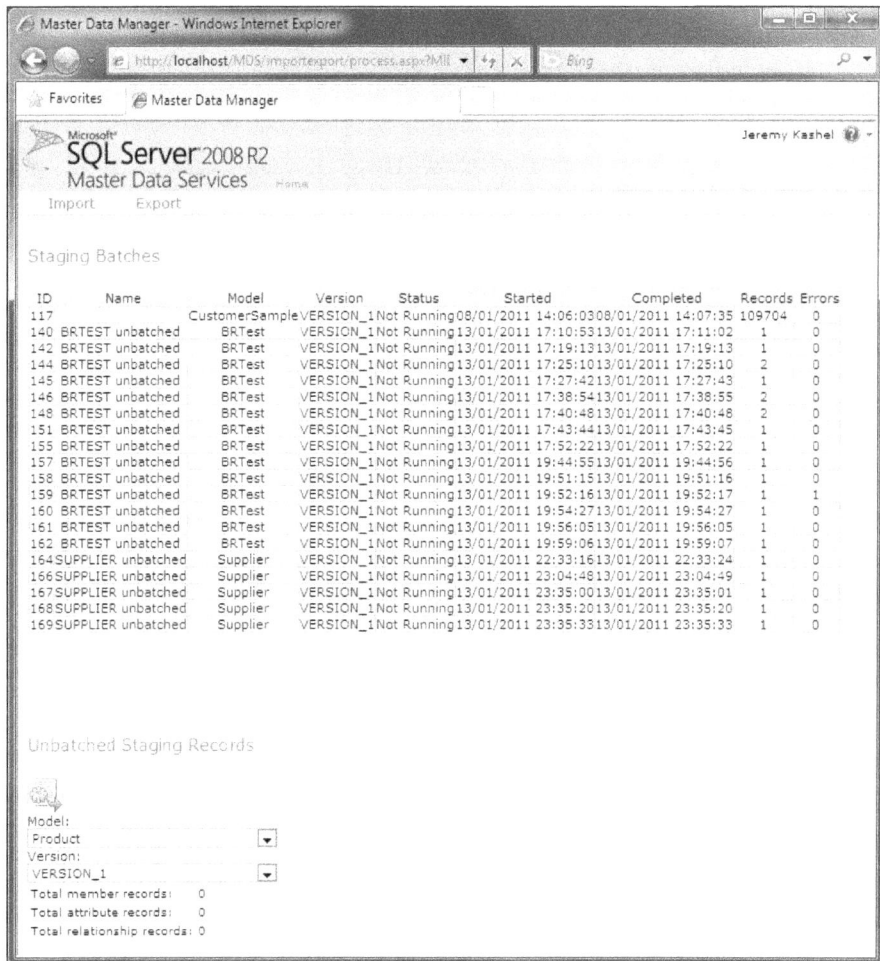

The grid at the top of the screen, under **Staging Batches**, shows the historical data that has been imported into the MDS database, as well as any data that is currently importing or is queued to import.

Importing is initiated by the button at the bottom of the screen. This causes Service Broker to kick off the loading of any data that exists within the staging tables, whereas the user can monitor the load of data by refreshing the grid at the top of the page.

Unlike the **Import** page, the **Export** page does not actually export master data to subscribing systems, but instead allows the creation of objects that external systems can connect to.

It is therefore entirely down to the solution architect as to how master data gets propagated to systems that need it. Depending on the MDM architecture style that needs to be used, subscribing systems may need to store a local copy of the data.

If data does need to be transferred to external systems, then another product within SQL Server is a good choice to help with this requirement. SQL Server Integration Services (SSIS) is Microsoft's ETL (Extract Transform Load) tool and it contains specific functionality for moving large volumes of data from a source to a target.

Integration Services is covered in more detail in *Chapter 6, Importing Data Into Master Data Services.*

System Administration

System Administration is the place within Master Data Manager where the MDS entities and all their related objects actually get created. For those of you who have developed operational or BI solutions using SQL Server, it may come as a surprise that this is not carried out in SQL Server Management Studio or Visual Studio.

Clicking on the **System Administration** option gives the following screen:

The **System Administration** screen provides two ways in which to manage the entities and their related objects. This can either be carried out by navigating the above tree or by utilizing the **Manage** menu item at the top of the screen.

The various sub screens that exist within **System Administration** allow for the creation, editing, and deleting of the MDS objects. As shown next, the familiar plus and pencil icons are used to add and edit objects respectively:

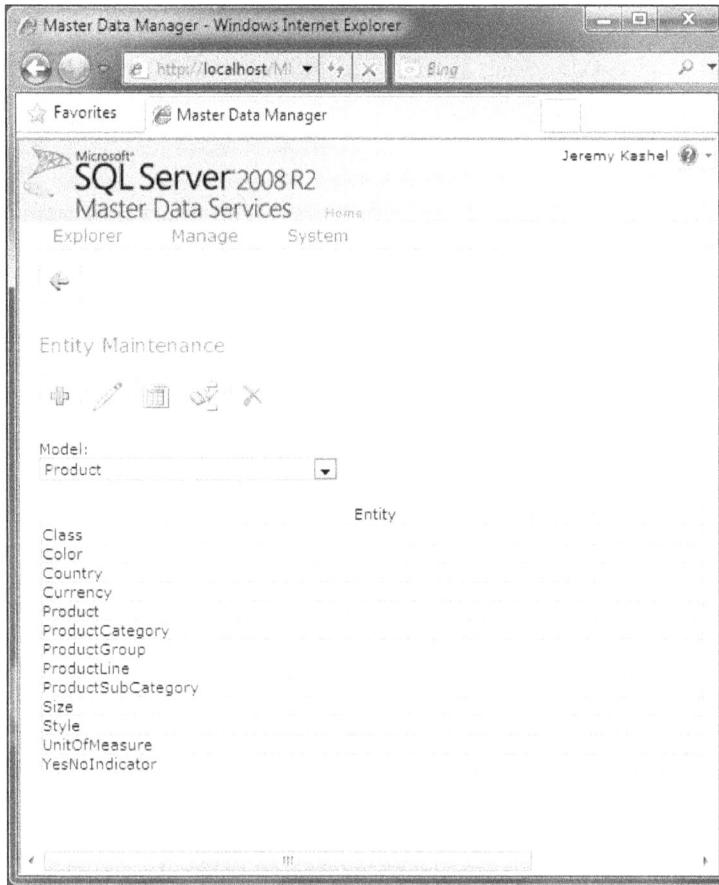

Finally the System menu option that's shown in the above image is the place whereby a deployment package can be created. Deployment packages are useful for deploying the entity structures from a test to a production environment, for example.

User and Group Permissions

As master data is one of the organization's prime data assets, it stands to reason that there should be some way of securing this data. This process is carried out within Master Data Manager by clicking on the **User and Group Permissions** option, the result of which is shown below:

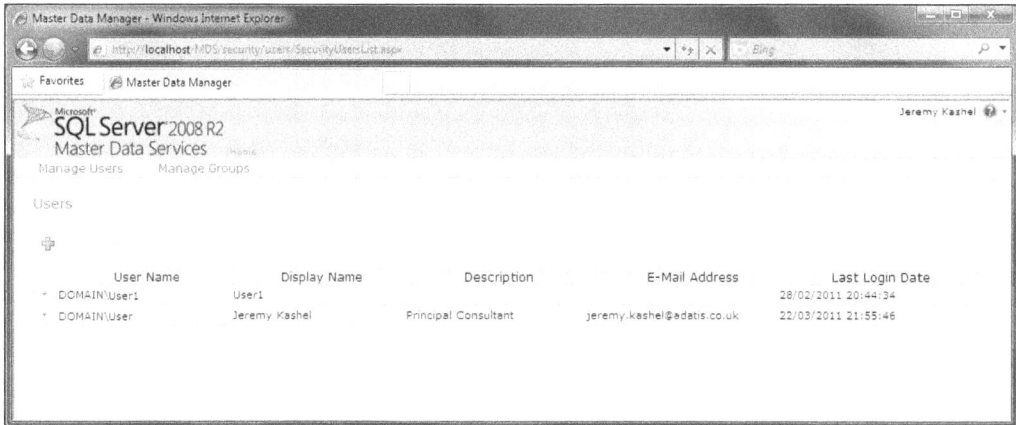

MDS allows a given Windows user access to Master Data Manager if the user has been added to the MDS list of users, which is done by adding the user in the form of DOMAIN\User or COMPUTER NAME\User. Alternatively, Windows groups can also be added to MDS, albeit on the adjacent menu option called **Manage Groups**.

Once the Windows user or group has been added to MDS, a variety of permissions can be applied. At a high level, access can be granted to one or more of the five Master Data Manager functions.

Detailed permissions can also be applied to a user or group, to the extent that read and write permissions can be altered for an entity, attribute, or even a single member. We will cover security in *Chapter 10, Master Data Services Security*.

Summary

In this chapter, we've gained an overview of Master Data Services and have learned the following key points:

- Master Data Services ships with the Enterprise and Data Center Editions of SQL Server, allowing organizations to carry out Master Data Management at a much lower cost.

- MDS assists with an MDM solution by providing generic entity modeling and maintenance capability.

- The underlying SQL Server database stores entity data as well as any required metadata.

- Master Data Manager is the main application that ships with MDS, providing the following features:

  - Data stewardship using the **Explorer** function

  - Versioning of entity data using the **Version Management** function

  - The ability to import data using the **Integration Management** function, as well as the ability to create objects to assist with data export

  - The creation and maintenance of entities and their related objects through the **System Administration** function

  - Management of security through the **User and Group Permissions** function

In the next chapter, we will learn how to install and configure Master Data Services.

3

Installing and Configuring
Master Data Services

Now comes the time for us to get Master Data Services installed. This chapter contains a step-by-step installation guide for MDS, as well as an explanation of the configuration settings. Finally, we will finish up by installing the samples that come with the product.

In this chapter, we will cover the following topics:

- Planning for a Master Data Services installation
- Installing Master Data Services
- Master Data Services Configuration Manager
- Installing sample models

Planning for a Master Data Services installation

Although some parts of the MDS installation process are thankfully just the standard **Next**, **Next**, **Next** as seen in a lot of Microsoft products, the configuration process, carried out using the Configuration Manager, requires some pre-installation planning.

The key areas to consider are:

- Server topology
- Database service account
- Administrator account

We will now examine each of these next.

Server topology

As we discovered in *Chapter 2*, *Master Data Services Overview*, Master Data Services requires SQL Server and also Internet Information Services (IIS) in order to function correctly. When planning for the installation, there are two basic server topologies to choose from, namely:

- Standalone Configuration — IIS and SQL Server installed on the same server
- Distributed Configuration — IIS and SQL Server installed on separate servers

A distributed configuration can offer the benefit of increased performance, as server resources can then be dedicated to a particular technology, for example, IIS. On the other hand, using more than one server for Master Data Services will require more licensing, as two servers are being used instead of one.

Depending on your infrastructure, you may also wish to consider creating an IIS Web Farm, to further increase IIS performance. That topic is out of the scope of this book, but the MDS Team Blog has a useful article on how to achieve this: `http://sqlblog.com/blogs/mds_team/archive/2010/02/05/configuring-a-mds-load-balanced-web-farm-using-iis-v7-arr.aspx`.

Database service account

The MDS database is created in the Configuration Manager, after the MDS installation has been completed. It is necessary to specify a service account for the database, which will be used by the Web Services to connect to the MDS database.

The service account will be added to the MDS database role called **mds_exec**, which has EXECUTE permission on all schemas, as well as a number of lower-level permissions.

> **Service account best practice**
>
> The best practice when setting up a service account is to follow the principle of least privilege. This means that the service account must only be able to access the resources that it needs for its purpose, and no more. In the case of MDS, the account should be a domain account (it can be a local account but this is not recommended by Microsoft), but the account does not actually need to grant any local or domain resources. Instead, the MDS setup process will add the service account to various database roles and user groups, in order that the service account has the permissions that it needs.

Administrator account

The Administrator account, specified by using the Configuration Manager, is the overall administrator for Master Data Services, and has access to all functional areas mentioned in *Chapter 2*.

There can only be one administrator account in a Master Data Services installation, so careful planning should be carried out to pick the most appropriate login to use. The user that has been set as the administrator account has automatic full permission to all MDS data and all functions that we covered in *Chapter 2*. As we will see when we cover security in *Chapter 10, Master Data Services Security*, it is possible to create a different type of administrative user that can effectively have the same permissions as the administrator account, with the exception that those permissions must be assigned manually.

Installing Master Data Services

Before installing MDS, it is worth noting that it is not merely an option on the main SQL Server 2008 R2 Setup, but is instead a completely separate install. The MSI file can be found on the installation media under the path: `\MasterDataServices\x64\1033_ENU\MasterDataServices.msi`.

> **Master Data Services updates**
>
> As with SQL Server itself, it is always recommended to check for Microsoft updates before installing MDS. At the time of writing, there are cumulative updates released that include some essential updates that didn't make it into the RTM version. The latest update is available at `http://support.microsoft.com/kb/2507770` and is a full installation package, meaning it can be used instead of the msi on the SQL Server installation media.

The following steps should be carried out in order to install MDS:

> **Administrative access**
>
> Note—the following installation steps assume that you have administrative access to the computer on which you are installing Master Data Services.

1. Double-click on the `MasterDataServices.msi` file (preferably using the downloaded cumulative update) to start the installation process. This will cause the following welcome screen to appear:

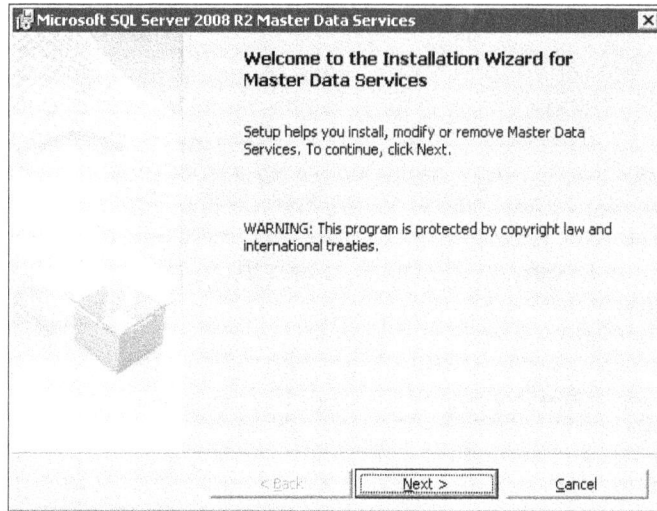

2. Click on **Next** to continue.

3. Accept the license agreement that will appear and then click on **Next** to continue.

4. Enter your name and your company in the registration window that will appear, then click on **Next** to continue.

5. Next, the **Feature Selection** window will appear, where you can change the installation path, as shown below:

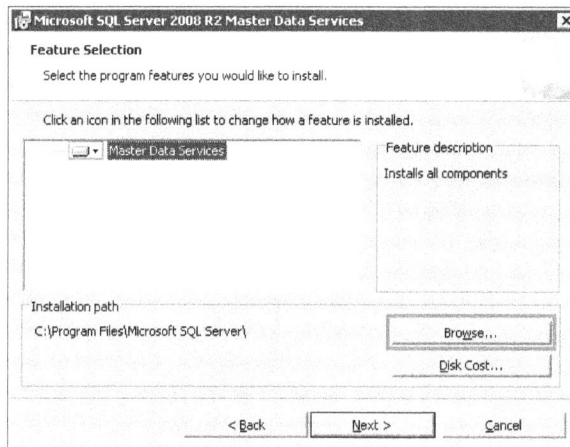

6. As shown, there is now the option to change the installation path. The default installation path of C:\Program Files\Microsoft SQL Server\ will suit most people, although it is possible to change the installation location according to company standards or personal preference. Click the **Browse** button if you wish to choose a different location. Once you have accepted to the default location or picked a new one, click on **Next** to continue.

7. This will cause an installation summary screen to appear. Once you are ready, click on **Next** to carry out the installation, which will take a few minutes.

8. If the installation completes successfully, you will see the following screen:

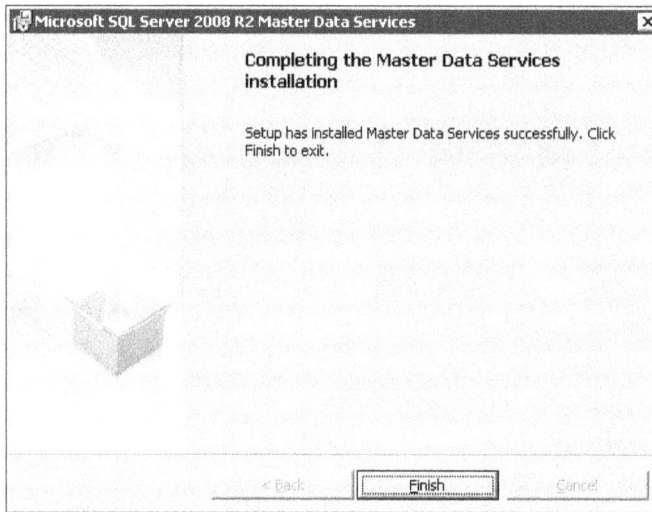

After carrying out these few steps, Master Data Services will now be installed. The more complex parts of the installation are carried out by the Master Data Services Configuration Manager, which will launch automatically once you click the **Finish** button, and is covered in detail next.

Master Data Services Configuration Manager

The Master Data Services Configuration Manager is a Windows-based application that can perform the following functions:

- Creation of the Master Data Services database
- Creation of an IIS Website and the Master Data Manager IIS Web Application
- Configuration of all Master Data Services settings

Although it will start automatically when installing MDS for the first time, it can be re-opened by navigating the Windows **Start** menu to SQL Server 2008 R2\Master Data Services and clicking on the Configuration Manager program.

Configuring Master Data Services for the first time

Once the Configuration Manager is started, a server configuration summary screen is displayed, which checks the Windows PowerShell and IIS versions, as shown in the following screenshot:

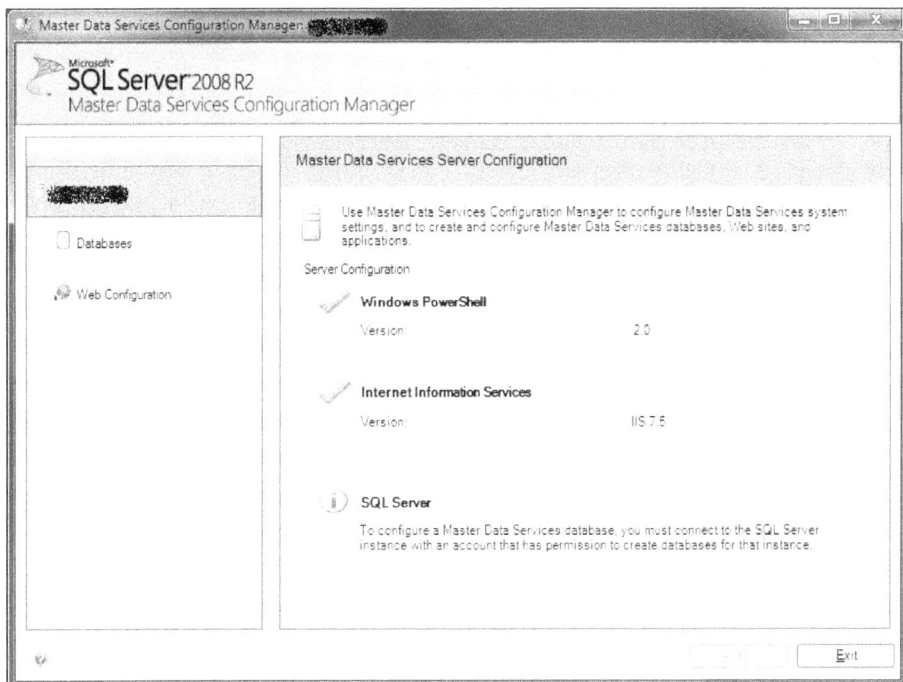

The Configuration Manger has a menu on the left-hand side, as shown in the previous screenshot, with just two options, namely **Databases** and **Web Configuration**.

In order to continue with the installation, choose the **Databases** option, which will display the following screen:

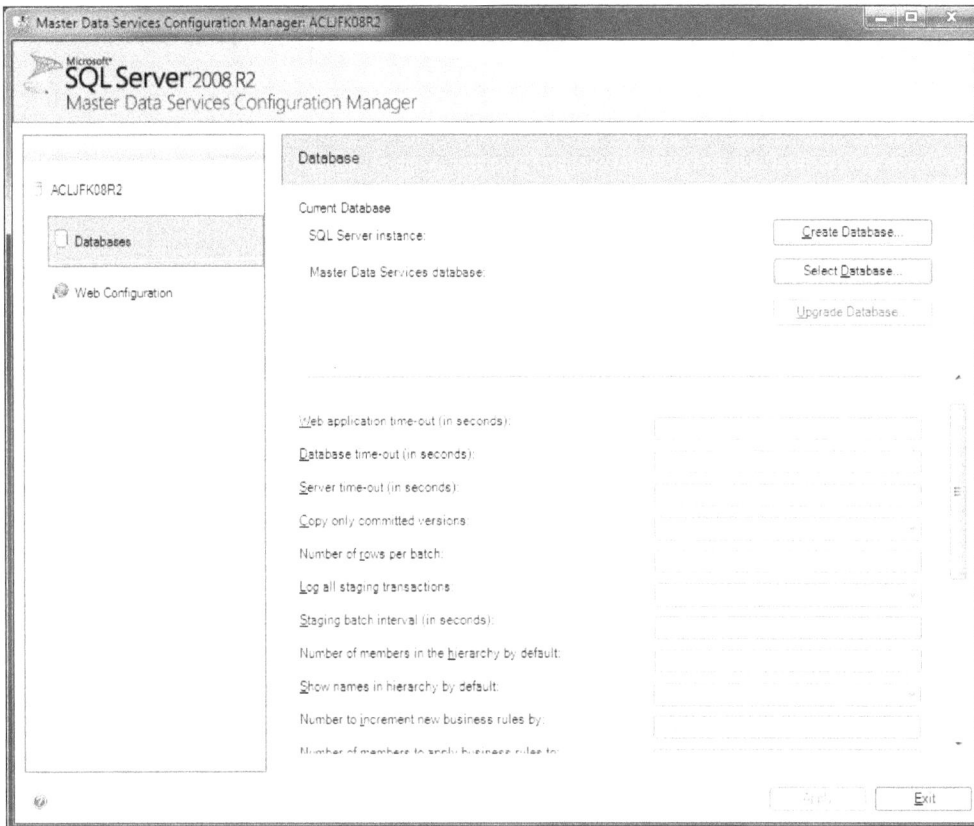

Database creation

The first task within the Configuration Manager is to create the Master Data Services database. This is done by clicking the **Create Database** button, which will launch the **Create Database Wizard**.

Once in the **Create Database Wizard**, carry out the following steps in order to create the Master Services Database:

1. The first window that is shown is a welcome window in the **Create Database Wizard**, so click on **Next** to continue. The **Database Server** window will appear:

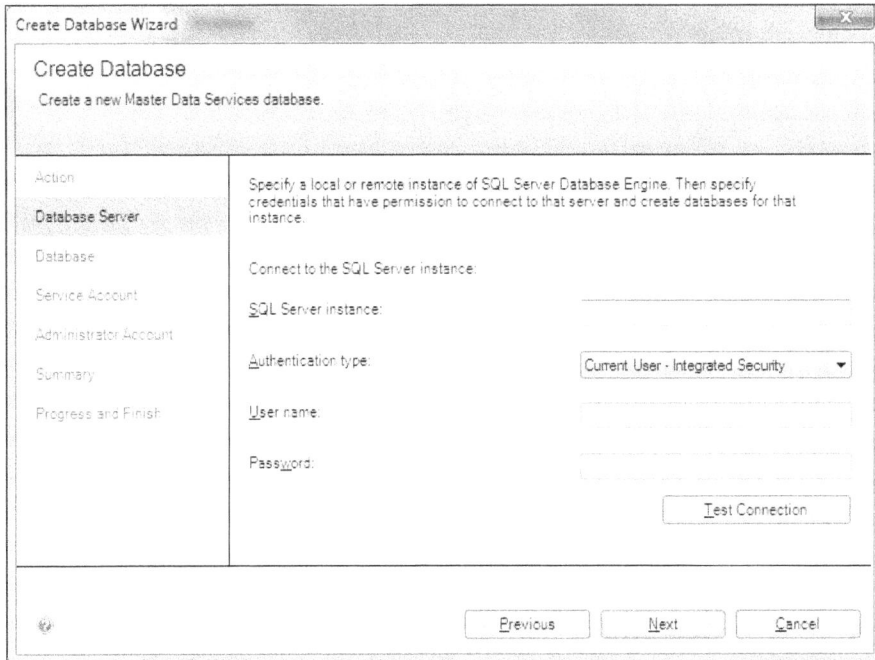

2. On the **Database Server** window, you must choose a SQL Server instance to store the Master Data Services database, and actually physically connect to it by providing an authentication type and related credentials. Enter the following information:

   ° **SQL Server instance** — Enter the name of the SQL Server instance, for example, "SERVERNAME" if you are using the default instance or "SERVERNAME\INSTANCE" if you are using a named instance.

   ° **Authentication type** — Select either "**Current User – Integrated Security**" to connect via Windows Integrated Security, or choose "**SQL Server Account**" to connect via a SQL login.

> **Login permissions**
>
> Note—the user that you connect with must be a member of the **sysadmin fixed server role** in order to create the MDS database.

- ° **User name**—If you are using the **Authentication type** of **SQL Server Account**, specify the user name.

- ° **Password**—If you are using the **Authentication type** of **SQL Server Account**, specify the password.

3. Click the **Test Connection** button in order to test the connection. If the test succeeds, click on **Next** in order to move to the next step, which will cause the **Database** window to appear.

4. The database name is entirely configurable, so enter your chosen database name.

5. You also need to pick a database collation. A collation in SQL Server controls the physical storage of character strings, providing rules to govern the appropriate use of characters for a language or alphabet, which can affect functionality such as sorting and case sensitivity. There are two choices when picking the collation:

   - ° **SQL Server Default Collation (checked)**—This will set the database to the default collation that will have been set at the instance level. Using the default collation will be suitable for most installations.

   - ° **SQL Server Default Collation (unchecked)**—Unchecking the checkbox will allow a Windows Collation to be chosen. If you feel that you may need to use a specific collation, review the following documentation for guidance: http://msdn.microsoft.com/en-us/library/ms143726.aspx.

6. Enter your chosen service account username, which must be a domain account, in the form of DOMAIN\Login. As mentioned in the "Planning" section of this chapter, this account will be used by the web services to connect to the database. Click on **Next** to continue, which will show the following **Administrator Account** window:

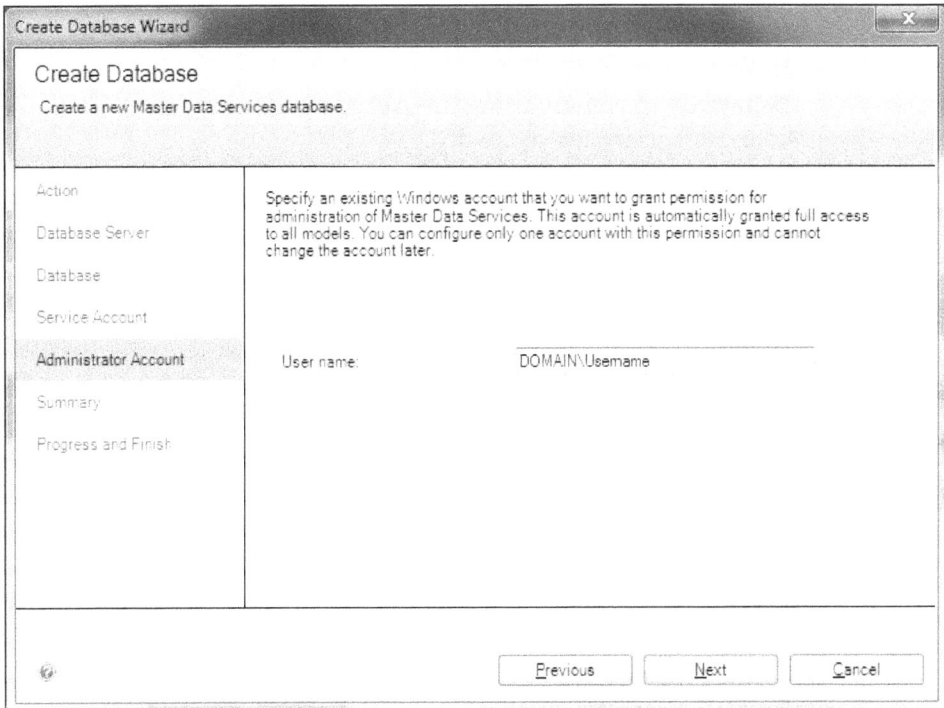

7. Enter the chosen **Administrator Account**, in the form of DOMAIN\Login. As mentioned in the "Planning" section of this chapter, this single account will be the overall administrator for the MDS installation. Click on **Next** to continue.

8. Review the settings that have been chosen in the **Summary** screen that will be displayed. Click on **Next** to start the database creation, which will display a progress window.

9. Once the **Create Database** window is complete, click on the **Finish** button in order to return back to the main screen, which will now be populated with the default database settings.

Database settings

There are several settings that can be changed in the Configuration Manager, each of which affects the behavior of Master Data Services in different ways. The settings are as follows:

Setting name	Alter in front-end?	Default value	Description
Web application time out	Y	900	The time, in seconds, before Master Data Manager will return a user to the home page after a period of inactivity.
Database time out	Y	3600	The time, in seconds, that Master Data Services allows for a database operation to complete.
Server time out	Y	120000	The time, in seconds, that IIS allows an MDS Asp.Net operation to complete.
Number of rows per batch	Y	50	The number of members that will be retrieved by the web service in a single batch, which impacts the number of members that will be displayed in the Explorer grid.
Copy only committed versions	Y	True	A Boolean setting that, if true, will only allow a version to be copied if it has been committed. If the setting is false, versions can be copied regardless of their state.
Log all staging transactions	Y	False	Controls whether or not the transactions that occur in the staging database are logged by MDS.
Staging batch interval	Y	60	The time, in seconds, after the **Process Unbatched Data** button has been clicked before the staged data will be loaded into the front-end
Number of members in the hierarchy by default	Y	50	The maximum number of members that can appear for a single hierarchy note before 'More...' is displayed.

Setting name	Alter in front-end?	Default value	Description
Show names in hierarchy by default	Y	Yes	A setting that controls whether entity hierarchies display a member's code or the code and the name. A value of 'Yes' will display the code and the name, whereas 'No' will display just the code.
Number to increment new business rules by	Y	10	The number to increment the current maximum business rule priority by when creating a new business rule.
Number of domain-based attributes in list	Y	500	Within Master Data Manager, the number of members that are displayed in an attribute drop-down list, when the attribute is based on another entity.
Number of members to apply business rules to	Y	500	The maximum number of members that business rules can be applied to within the Master Data Manager Explorer grid.
Master Data Manager URL for notifications	Y	None	The URL that is sent in the e-mail notifications.
Notification e-mail interval	Y	120	The time interval, in seconds, that MDS will send e-mails for notification purposes.
Notifications per e-mail	N	100	The number of notification issues that can be sent in a single e-mail.
Default e-mail format	Y	HTML	The format for e-mail notifications, which can be HTML or Text.
Regular expression for e-mail address	Y	<Long Regular Expression>	The regular expression that is used to check for a valid e-mail address when users are added to Master Data Services. This can, for example, be extended to only allow e-mail addresses from a specific domain.

Setting name	Alter in front-end?	Default value	Description
Database Mail account	N	mds_email_ user	The database mail account to use when sending the e-mail notifications.
Database Mail profile	Y	None	The name of the database mail profile user to use when sending the e-mail notifications.
Application Name	N	MDM	The name of the application when it is referenced in event logs.
Site Title	N	Master Data Manager	The title of the Master Data Manager site within the web browser.
Validation Issue HTML	N	<Long XSLT>	The HTML content of the e-mail that users get when a validation issue occurs.
Validation Issue Text	N	<Long XSLT>	The text content of the e-mail that users get when a validation issue occurs.
Version Status Change HTML	N	<Long XSLT>	The HTML content of the e-mail that users get when the status of a version changes.
Version Status Change Text	N	<Long XSLT>	The text content of the e-mail that users get when the status of a version changes.
Security Member Process Interval	N	3600	The time, in seconds, before user permissions are physically applied after they are set in the **User and Group Permissions** area of Master Data Manager.
Data Explorer Row Count Limit	N	10,000	The maximum number of rows that can be exported to Microsoft Excel from the Master Data Manager Explorer grid.
Grid Filter Default Fuzzy Similarity Level	N	0.3	The default level of similarity used when carrying out filtering in the Explorer grid.

As indicated, it is not possible to alter all of the settings within the Configuration Manager itself. Instead, it is necessary to alter those settings (if desired) within the MDS database, in a table called `mdm.tblSystemSetting`.

For the initial installation, most of the default settings will be suitable. There are two exceptions to this rule, namely:

- Master Data Manager URL for notifications
- Database Mail Profile

The Master Data Manager URL for notifications setting should be set to the root path of the Master Data Manager application. We haven't set up the Master Data Manager application yet, but the URL to enter will be `http://servername/MDS/`, if we accept the default settings.

Setting the Database Mail Profile requires us to click the **Create Profile** button, which launches the following **Create Database Mail Profile and Account** window:

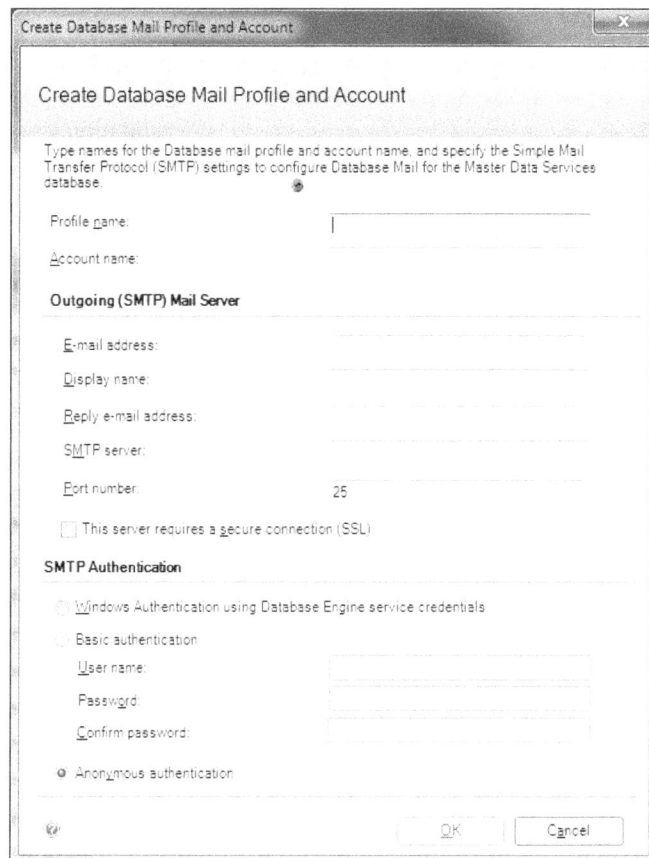

The following information should be entered in order to set up the Database Mail for MDS:

- **Profile name** — This is the name that will identify the Database Mail Profile within SQL Server.

- **Account name** — This is the name of the account that will be used in conjunction with the Database Mail Profile.

- **E-mail address** — This is the e-mail address that will be used to send MDS notifications.

- **Reply e-mail address** — This is the e-mail address that recipients may reply to when receiving MDS e-mail notifications.

- **SMTP server** — The name of the SMTP (Simple Mail Transfer Protocol) server that will send the MDS e-mails.

- **Port number** — The port number for the SMTP server.

- **This server requires a secure connection (SSL)** — A checkbox indicating whether or not mail data should be encrypted using SSL (Secure Sockets Layer).

- **SMTP authentication** — The method by which access to the SMTP server will be authenticated. There are three options, namely:

    ◦ **Windows Authentication using Database Engine service credentials** - The SQL Server Database Engine service account credentials will be used to connect to the SMTP server.

    ◦ **Basic authentication** — A specific **User name** and **Password** must be entered to connect to the SMTP server.

    ◦ **Anonymous authentication** — This option should be selected if the SMTP server requires no credentials for authentication.

Once the above Database Mail settings have been provided, click on **OK**, which will create the Database Mail profile and account within SQL Server, and return us to the Database page of the Configuration Manager. Click on **Apply** to conclude the database part of the configuration process.

Web configuration

Once the database has been created and configured, the next step is to set up the IIS Website and Web Application to host Master Data Manager.

In order to carry out the web configuration, perform the following steps:

1. Ensure that the Configuration Manager is open.

2. Choose the **Web Configuration** option from the menu on the left-hand side. This will open the following screen:

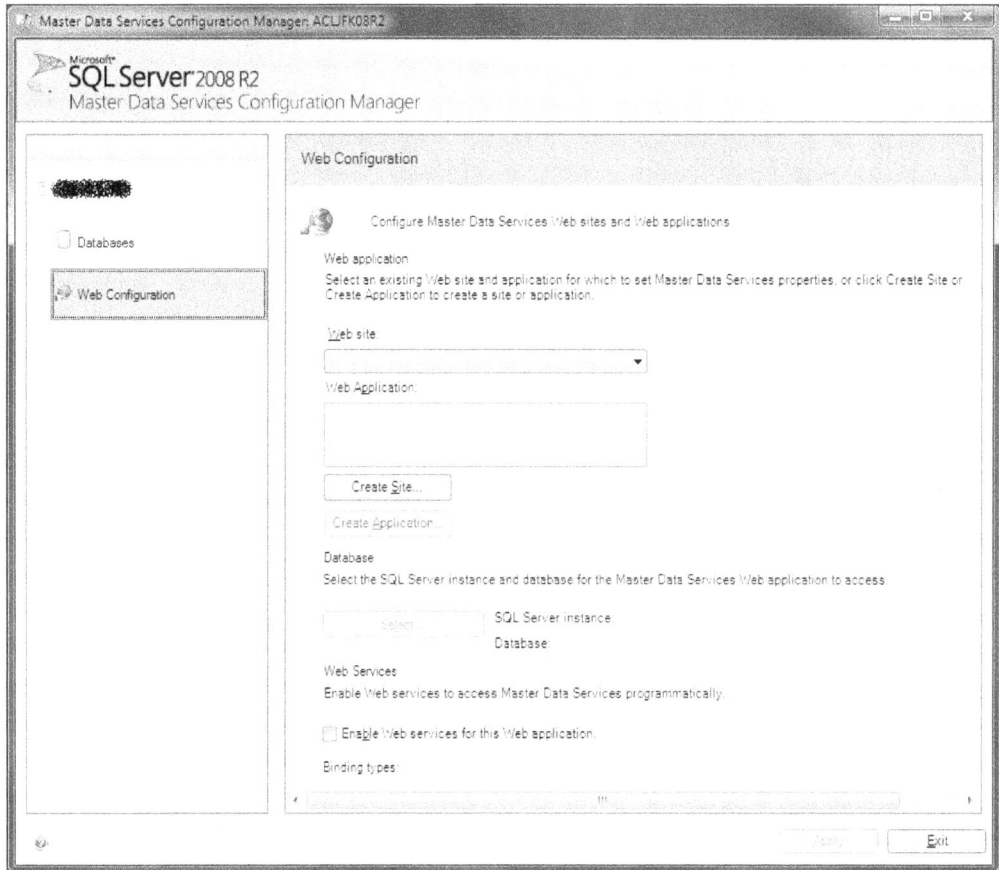

3. The first step for the web configuration is to create the MDS Web Application, which can be created in the **Default Web Site** or in a separate **Web Site**, which itself can be created within the Configuration Manager. If the IIS server will only host MDS, then using the Default Web Site is recommended. On the other hand, if the IIS server will also host other Web Sites and Applications, then setting up a separate Web Site for MDS may be required, depending on what applications are being used. If your IIS server will host multiple applications, then contact your IIS administrator for the appropriate configuration for your environment.

4. If you are planning to create the **Web Application** within the **Default Web Site**, then skip to step 8; otherwise, click the **Create Site** button, which will display the following window:

5. Within the previous window it is necessary to configure the most common properties of an IIS Website, namely:

   ° **Web site name** — Enter the chosen name of the new IIS Website, or accept the default of MDS.

   ° **IP address** — Choose an IP address from the drop-down.

   ° **Port** — Enter a port number for the new website.

   ° **Host header** — Enter a host header for the website.

6. Once the website properties have been entered, it is necessary to give the website an application pool. The following steps must be carried out in in order to configure the application pool:

   ° **Name** — Enter a name for the Application Pool or accept the default of MDS Application Pool

   ° **User name** — Enter the user name that will become the Identity account for the Application Pool. The account specified must be a domain account, and should be the same domain account that was specified when setting the database service account earlier in this chapter. As with the service account, we don't need to grant any additional permissions for the Identity account, as the appropriate permissions will be granted by MDS as part of the configuration process. The user name must be entered in the form "DOMAIN\User.

   ° **Password** — Enter a password for the Application Pool, which must match the actual password of the account that is being used. Repeat the password in the **Confirm Password** textbox.

7. Click **OK** to create the Website and its related Application Pool. Skip to step 11.

8. If you wish to create the MDS application within an existing website, then the next step is to pick that Website from the Website drop-down.

9. Once the Website has been selected, click the **Create Application** button, which will display the following **Create Web Application** window:

10. It is now necessary to configure the **Web Application** and its related
    Application Pool. To do this, enter the following information:

    ○ **Alias** — Enter an alias for the Web Application or accept the default of
      MDS.

    ○ **Name** — Enter a name for the Application Pool or accept the default of
      MDS Application Pool.

    ○ **User name** — Enter the username that will become the Identity
      account for the Application Pool. The username must be entered in
      the form "DOMAIN\Username".

    ○ **Password** — Enter a password for the Application Pool, which must
      match the actual password of the account that is being used. Repeat
      the password in the **Confirm Password** textbox.

11. Click on **OK** to create the **Web Application** and its related **Application Pool**, which will return you to the main **Web Configuration** window:

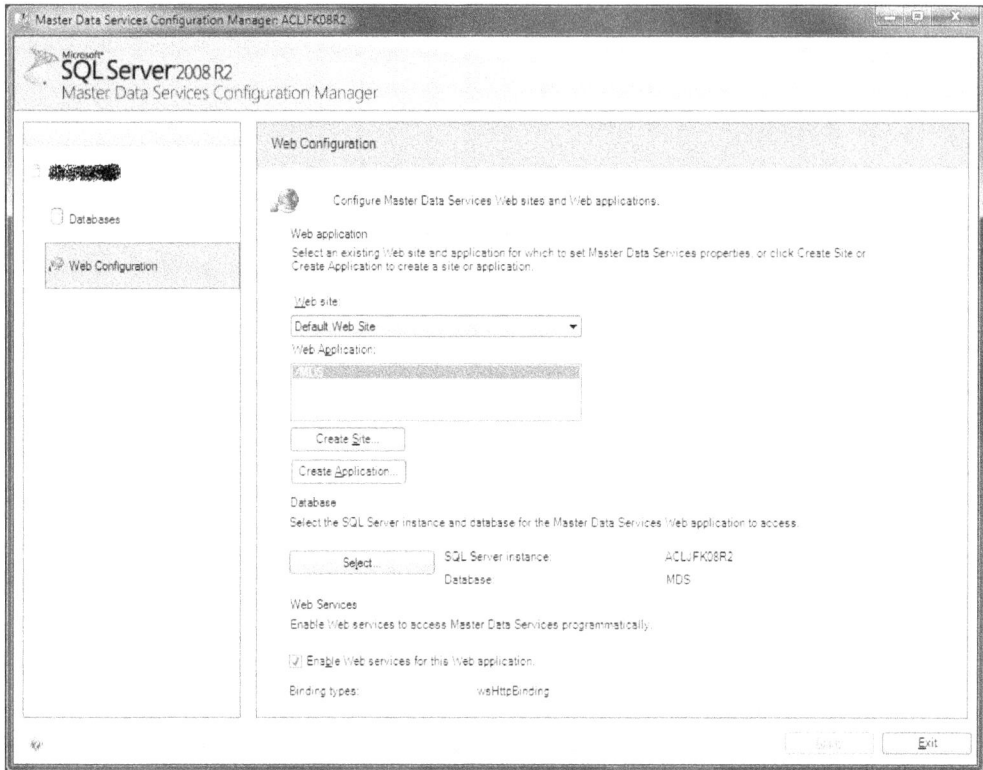

12. Whether you have created the MDS application in a new website, or in an existing website, there is now a common step to carry out, which is to associate the newly created Web Application with the newly created MDS database. To do this click on the **Select** button, which will display the following window:

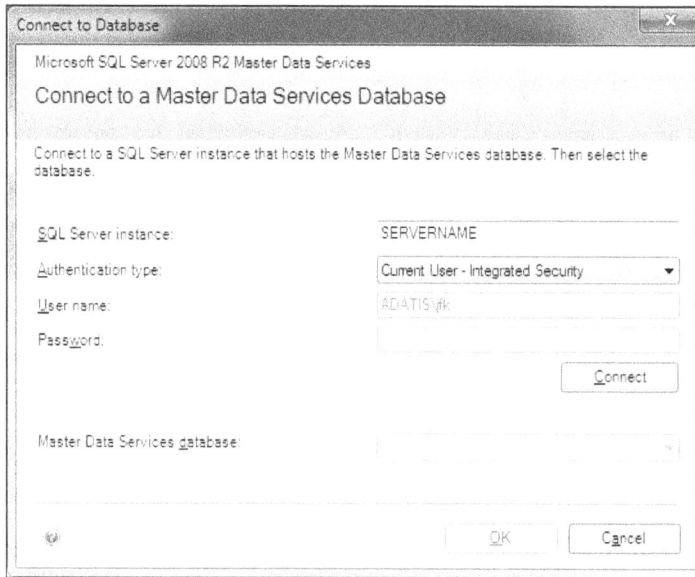

13. You may have noticed that the above window is very similar to the window that we encountered when creating the MDS database. Enter the **SQL Server instance**, the **Authentication type** and **also User name / Password** if connecting via a SQL Server account, then click **Connect**. As was the case when creating the MDS database, the user that is used to make the connection to the server must be a member of the SQL Server System Administrators (sysadmin) fixed server role.

14. Choose **the Master Data Services database** from the drop-down and click on **OK**.

15. The application will now return to the main **Web Configuration** screen. The final step is to choose whether or not to enable the MDS web services. Enabling the web services will mean that other applications will be able to programmatically access MDS data and carry out MDS functions by making the appropriate web service calls. If you want to enable the web services check the checkbox that is marked **Enable Web Services for This Web Application**.

16. The final step in the Web Configuration is to click the **Apply** button. If changes have been made, then a message box will prompt you to open the Web application in a web browser, as shown below:

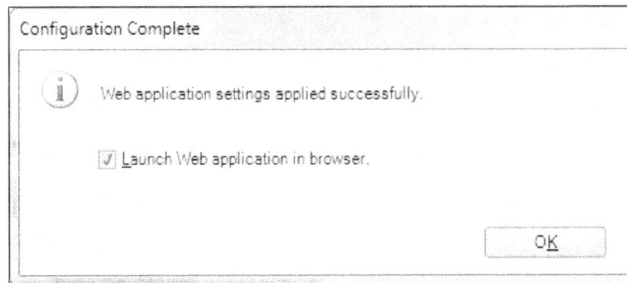

Configuration Complete

ⓘ   Web application settings applied successfully.

☑ Launch Web application in browser.

OK

17. Click on **OK** and verify that the Master Data Manager application opens successfully.

18. Return to the Configuration Manager and click on **Exit** to conclude the setup of Master Data Services.

Installing sample models

Although not required to work through the examples in the rest of this book, Master Data Services ships with three sample models, namely Customer, Product, and Chart of Accounts. These can be installed on your own server as a final, optional, step to this chapter.

The samples come in the form of `*.pkg` files, which can be found at `\Program Files\Microsoft SQL Server\Master Data Services\Samples\Packages`.

In order to install the sample models, carry out the following steps:

1. Open Master Data Manager through a web browser.

2. From the home page, click on **System Administration**.

3. Choose the **Deployment** option from the **System** menu at the top of the screen. This will display the following **Model Deployment Wizard**:

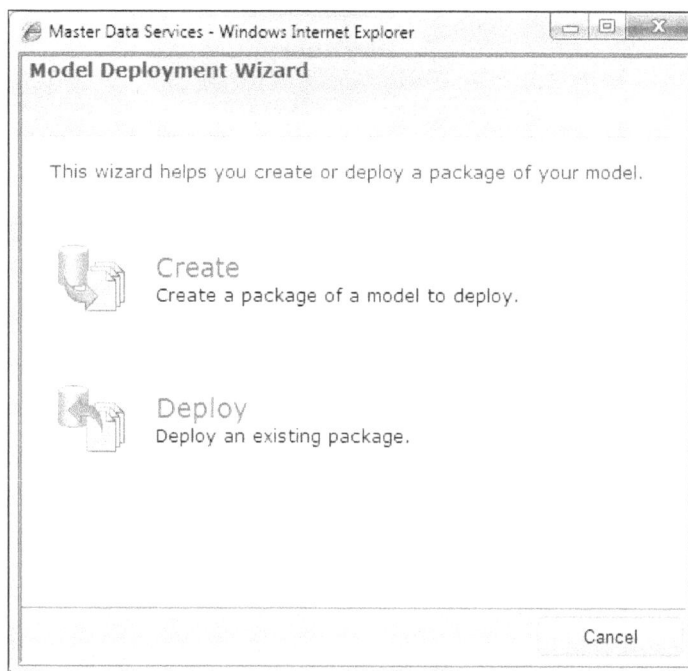

4. Click on the **Deploy** option.

5. The wizard will move on one step and prompt you to browse to a `*.pkg` file. Browse to the aforementioned path and choose `chartofaccounts_en.pkg`.

6. Click on **Next**, which will prepare the package for deployment.

7. In the screen that follows, click on **Next** again to actually deploy the package to Master Data Services. This process may take a few minutes to complete.

8. Click on **Finish** once the deployment completes.

9. Return to the Master Data Manager home page. We will now check that the model has been deployed successfully.

10. Choose the **ChartOfAccounts** model from the drop-down.

11. Choose **VERSION_1** from the version drop-down.

12. Click on the Explorer item, which will display the following screen:

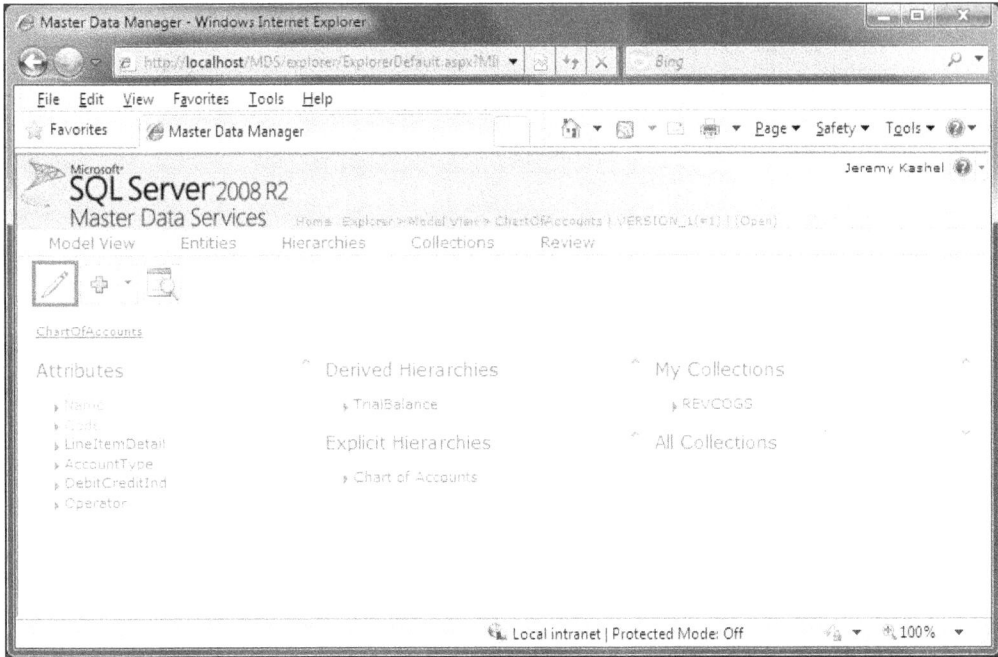

13. Click on the pencil icon, as highlighted in the above image. The Explorer grid will be displayed, which will contain a flat list of Chart Of Accounts.

14. Repeat the deployment process, if required, for the Customer and Product packages.

Summary

In this chapter, we have achieved the installation of a fresh copy of Master Data Services and have learned the following key points along the way:

- Installation planning is helpful in order to design how the various components of Master Data Services should interact with one another

- The actual installation of Master Data Services is relatively simple

- The configuration process is more complex and is carried out by the Master Data Services Configuration Tool, focusing on database settings and web configuration

- Sample models ship with the product in the form of *.pkg files and can be installed through Master Data Manager

In the next chapter, we will look in detail at Master Data Manager and start building and customizing our own models.

4
Creating and Using Models

In this chapter, we will start by creating a model within the Master Data Manager front-end, which will be the beginning of an example solution that will run for the rest of the book. Each of the different objects within the MDS object hierarchy will be covered, guiding you on how to build a model up step-by-step.

A sample script will be provided that will populate your newly created model, before we walk through the process of editing and creating members using the front-end.

In this chapter, we will cover the following topics:

- MDS object model overview
- Models
- Entities and attributes
- Members
- Attribute Groups
- Hierarchies
- Collections
- Master Data Services Metadata

MDS object model overview

We touched on the basics of the MDS object model in *Chapter 1, Master Data Management* and *Chapter 2, Master Data Services Overview*, when covering core concepts such as entities, attributes, members, and collections. The full MDS object model contains these objects, as well as a number of objects that we've not covered yet. The full MDS object model can be summarized by the following diagram:

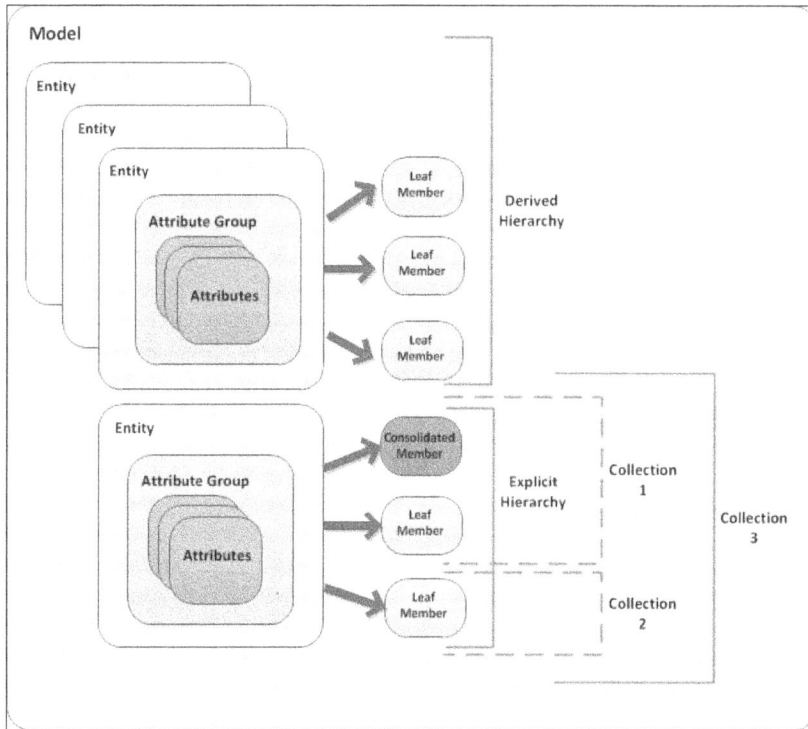

As indicated in the diagram, the *Model* object is the highest level object in the MDS object model. It represents an MDM subject area, such as Product or Customer. Therefore, it would be normal to have a model called Product, which would contain several different *Entities*, such as Color, Brand, Style, and an entity called Product itself.

As we know already from *Chapter 1*, entities have one or more *Attributes* and instances of entities are known as *Members*.

Instead of an entity just containing attributes, it is possible within MDS to categorize the attributes into groups, which are known as *Attribute Groups*.

There are two types of hierarchies within MDS, namely *Derived Hierarchies* and *Explicit Hierarchies.* Derived hierarchies are hierarchies that are created based upon the relationships that exist between entities. For example, the Customer entity may have an attribute called City that is based upon the City entity. In turn, the City entity itself may have a State attribute that is based upon the State entity. The State entity would then have a Country attribute, and so on. This is shown below:

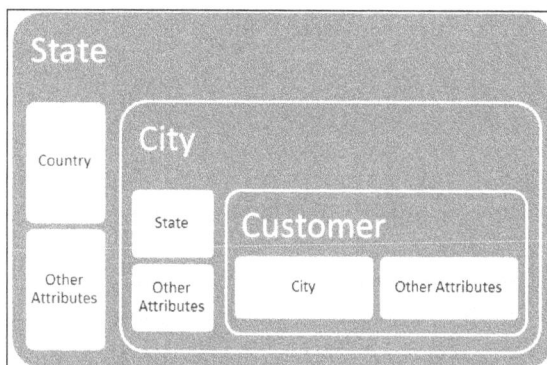

Using the relationships between the entities, a Derived Hierarchy called Customer Geography, for example, can be created that would break customers down by their geographic locations. A visual representation of this hierarchy is as follows:

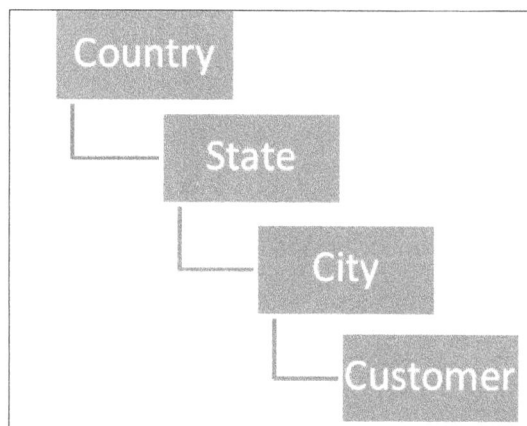

A Derived Hierarchy relies on separate entities that share relationships between one another. This is in contrast to an Explicit Hierarchy, whose hierarchy members must all come from a single entity. The point to note though is that the members in an Explicit Hierarchy can be both *Leaf Members* and also *Consolidated Members*.

The idea behind Explicit Hierarchies is that they can represent ragged data structures whereby the members cannot be easily categorized as being a member of any one given entity. For example, Profit and Loss accounts can exist at different levels. Both the accounts "Cash in Transit" and "Net Profit" are valid accounts, but one is low-level and one is a high-level account, plus there are many more accounts that sit in between the two. One solution is to create "Net Profit" as a consolidated member and "Cash In Transit" as a leaf member, all within the same entity. This way, a full ragged Chart of Accounts structure may be created within MDS.

Models

The first step to get started with Master Data Services is to create a model, as the model is the overall container object for all other objects.

We are going to start by creating a practice model called **Store**—meaning that it will be our single source of retail stores in our fictitious company.

Models are created in the Master Data Manager application, within the System Administration functional area. Carry out the following steps to create our Store model:

1. Ensure that the Master Data Manager application is open. To do this, type the URL into your web browser, which will typically be
   `http://servername/MDS/`.

2. Click on the **System Administration** option in the home page, which will take you to the following screen:

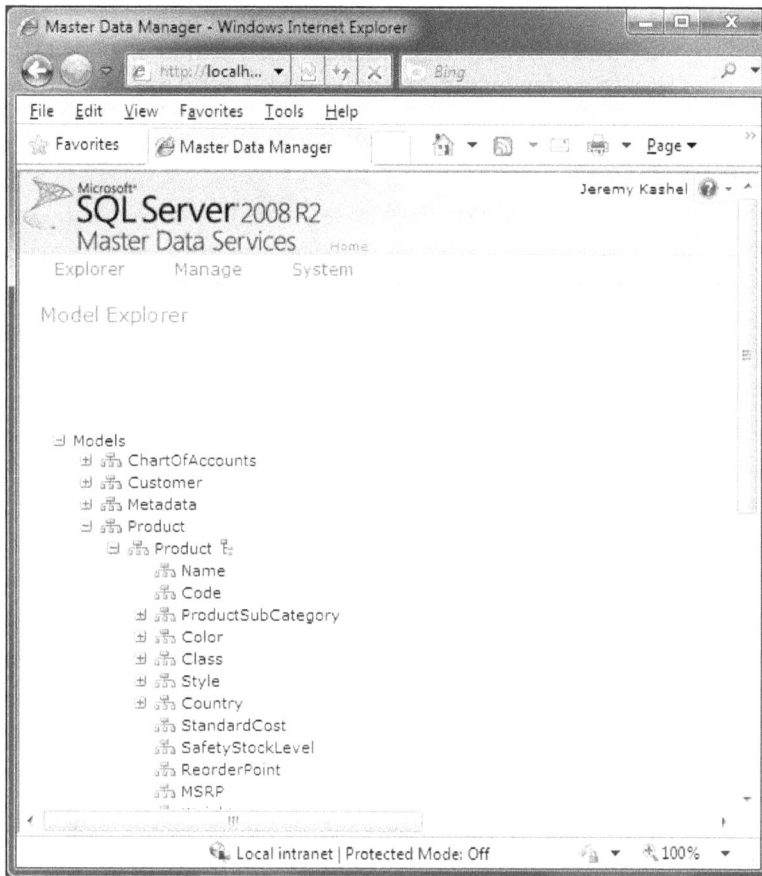

3. The tree view that is shown breaks down each of the models that are installed in the MDS environment, showing entities, attributes and other objects within the system. The tree view provides an alternate way to edit some of the MDS objects. Rather than using the tree view, we are going to create a model via the menu at the top of the screen. Hover over the **Manage** menu and choose the **Models** menu item.

4. The resulting screen will show a list of the current models within MDS, with the ability to add or edit a model. Click on the familiar Master Data Manager green plus icon in order to add our new model, which will produce the following screen:

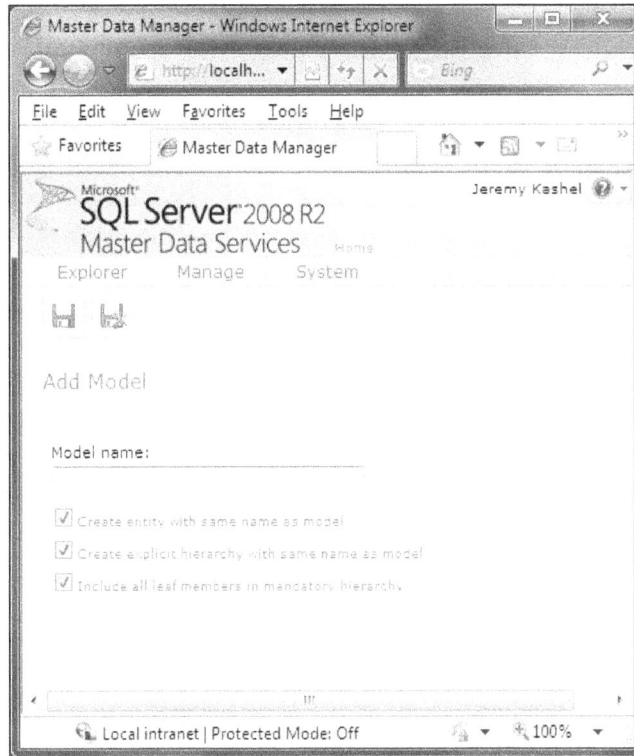

5. Enter **Store** as the **Model name**.

6. Next there are some settings to configure for the model, via three checkboxes. The settings are:

   ° **Create entity with same name as model** — This is essentially a shortcut to save creating an entity manually after creating the model. We want an entity called Store to be created, so leave this option checked.

   ° **Create explicit hierarchy with same name as model** — Another shortcut, this time to create an Explicit Hierarchy. We will manually create an Explicit Hierarchy later on, so uncheck this box.

○ **Include all leaf members in mandatory hierarchy** — This setting only applies if we are creating an Explicit Hierarchy. If checked, it will ensure that all leaf members must exist within an Explicit Hierarchy. By unchecking the previous option, this option will be unchecked.

7. Click the "Disk" icon to save and create the new model.

Entities and attributes

After creating the new model, we are now in a position to create all the entities and attributes that we need to manage our store data. However, before doing this, we need to plan what entities and attributes are needed. This can be summarized by the following table:

Entity name	Attribute name	Domain attribute	Description
Store	Name	N	The name of a store, for example, "Adventure Works Seattle"
	Code	N	The unique identifier for each Store member
	SquareFootage	N	The total floor space of a store
	StoreType	Y	The type of store, such as Retail or Outlet
	City	Y	The city where the store is located
	PostalCode	N	The zip code of the store
	TelephoneNumber	N	The store's central telephone number
	FaxNumber	N	The store's fax number
	EmailAddress	N	The store's general e-mail address.
StoreType	Name	N	The name of the store type, such as Mall or Outlet
	Code	N	The code (if any) of the store type
City	Name	N	The name of the city, such as Seattle
	Code	N	The unique identifier of the city
	State	Y	The state that the city belongs to, for example, Seattle would belong to Washington

Entity name	Attribute name	Domain attribute	Description
State	Name	N	The name of the state, for example, Washington
	Code	N	The unique identifier for the state
	Country	Y	The country that the state belongs to, for example, USA.
Country	Name	N	The country name, for example, USA
	Code	N	The unique identifier for the country

Attributes

Attributes are the building blocks of entities in MDS, and there are three different types, which we need to cover before we can start creating and altering entities. The different types are explained in the following table:

Attribute type	Description
Free form	An attribute of a given data type (for example, text or number) that has no restriction on its value other than the constraints of the data type.
Domain attribute	A domain attribute is an attribute of an entity that is based on another entity. The domain attribute can only contain a value if that value exists as a member within the entity that the domain attribute is based upon.
File	An attribute type that is designed to store files of a specific type. This could be a product photo, for example, if we had a Product model.

Domain attributes and relationships between entities

As we left the **Create entity with same name as model** option checked when creating the model, we will have an entity already created called Store. The task now is to edit the Store entity, in order to set up the attributes that we have defined previously. However, before we can complete the Store entity, we actually need to create several of the other entities. This is because we want some of the Store's attributes to be based on other entities, which is exactly why we need domain attributes.

Domain attributes are the method that allow us to create relationships between entities, which we need, for example, in order to create Derived Hierarchies. In addition, they also allow for some good data entity validation as, for example, it would not be possible for a user to enter a new attribute value of "New York" in the City attribute if the member "New York" did not exist in the City entity.

If we look at our table of entities and attributes again, there is a column to indicate where we need a domain attribute. If we were building an entity relationship diagram, we would say that a Store *has* a City and that a City *belongs to* a State.

Creating an entity

To focus on the Store entity first, before we can say that its structure is complete, we firstly need to create any entities that the Store entity wants to use as domain attributes. We can clearly see from the previous table that these are City and StoreType. The Country and State entities are also required as domain attributes by other entities. Therefore, carry out the following steps in order to create the remaining entities:

1. Ensure that you are in the **System Administration** function.
2. Hover over the **Manage** menu and click on the **Entities** menu item.
3. Ensure that the **Store** model is selected from the **Model** drop-down.
4. Click the green "plus" icon. This will open the **Add Entity** screen.
5. Enter the following information on the **Add Entity** screen, as shown below:

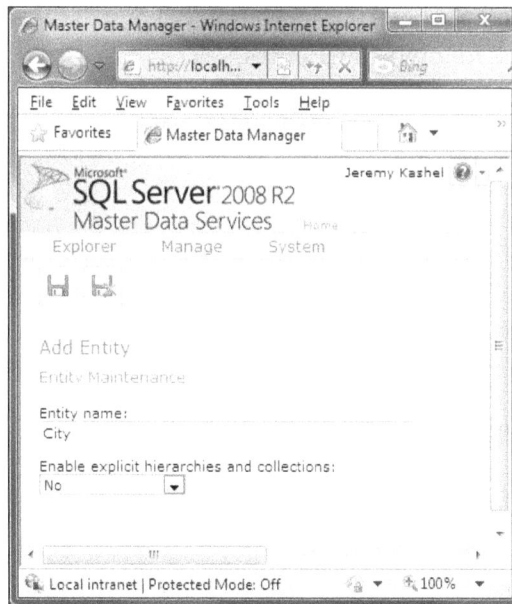

- Enter **City** as the **Entity Name**.
- Choose **No** to not **Enable explicit hierarchies and collections**.

6. Click the save icon to create the entity and return to the **Entity Maintenance** screen.

7. Repeat this process to create the **StoreType**, **Country**, and **State** entities.

Once you have finished the **Entity Maintenance** screen should look as follows:

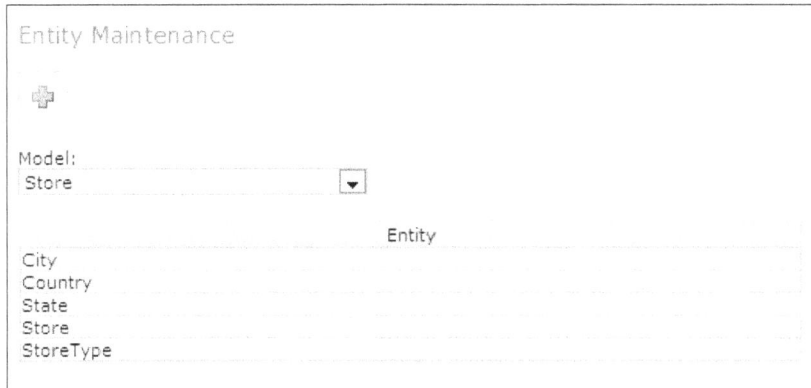

Editing an entity

Now that we have created all the required entities, we need to edit the Store entity, to add the attributes that it needs. If we recall the plan that we outlined earlier, the Store entity requires the following attributes:

- Name
- Code
- SquareFootage
- StoreType
- City
- PostalCode
- FaxNumber
- TelephoneNumber
- EmailAddress

All entities automatically get two default attributes called Name and Code, which saves us having to add them for each of the entities. The Code attribute within an entity uniquely identifies a given member, and therefore must be unique amongst the entity's members. It also cannot be left blank. The Name attribute can be left blank, and simply provides an attribute to enter a name for a member.

The first attribute for us to create is SquareFootage, which is an example of a free-form attribute. In order to do this, carry out the following:

1. Remaining in the **Entity Maintenance** screen, select the Store entity and then click on the pencil icon, as shown below:

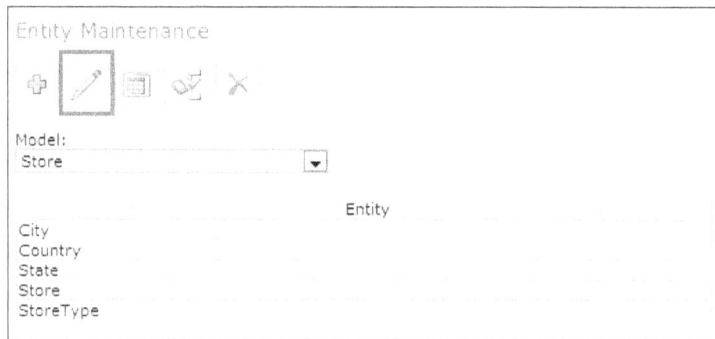

2. In the resulting **Edit Entity** screen, we now have the option to rename the entity if we wish, or to enable/disable explicit hierarchies and collections for the entity. We can also add, edit, or delete an attribute for the entity. This is exactly what we want to do on this occasion, so click the green plus icon to display the following **Add Attribute** screen:

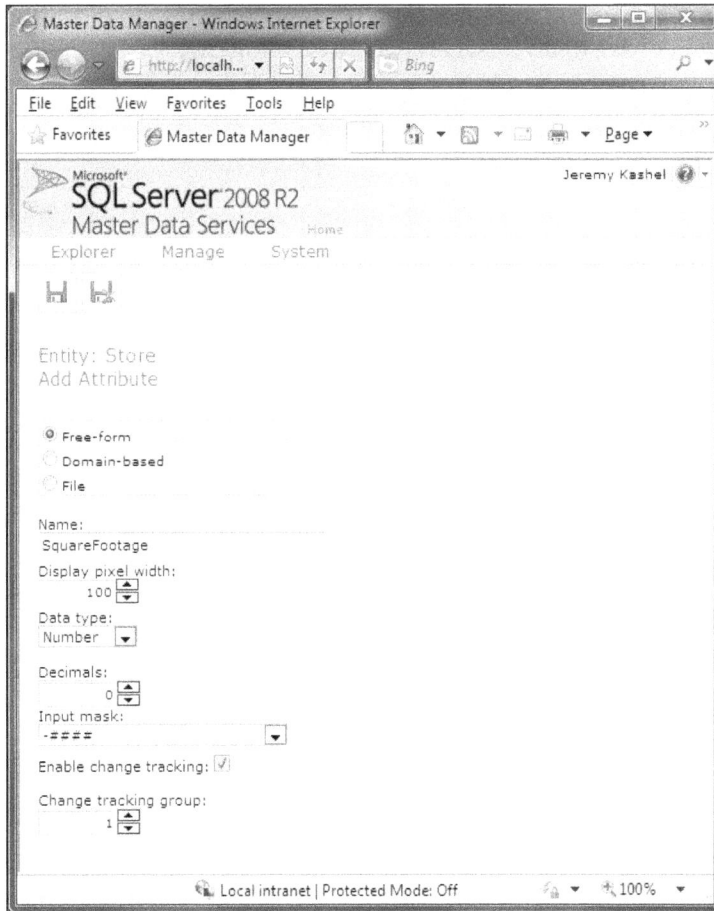

3. Enter the **Name** as **SquareFootage**, as shown.

4. Leave the default **Display pixel width** of **100**. This controls how wide the attribute column will be in the Master Data Manager grid.

5. Set the **Data type** as **Number**, as we want users to enter square feet of say 10,000 or 3,000 for a given store.

6. Alter the **Decimals**, by either typing or using the down arrows so that the **Decimals** for the attribute is **0**.

7. Pick the **Input mask** of **-####**, which will mean that negative numbers will be displayed with a minus sign rather than in brackets. This is not relevant for our **SquareFootage** attribute, but it is a mandatory setting.

8. Click the check box to **Enable change tracking**.

> **Enable change tracking and Change tracking group**
>
> The **Enable change tracking** option is used in conjunction with the MDS business rules. If change tracking is enabled on an attribute, then a business rule can be set up to fire whenever the attribute's value changes.
>
> A **Change tracking group** is a numerical indicator that groups attributes together. For example, it would be possible to have three attributes in the **Change tracking group** 1. The aforementioned business rules monitor a change in any attribute that is a member of a specific change tracking group, instead of being directly bound to the attribute itself. We will look at business rules in detail in *Chapter 7, Business Rules and Workflow*.

9. Leave the default **Change tracking group** of **1**.

10. Click on the save icon at the top of the screen to save the new attribute.

Saving will return us to the **Edit Entity** screen, where we will see that the Store entity will have a new attribute, namely SquareFootage. We now need to add the StoreType attribute to the Store entity, which will be the first of our domain attributes.

To do this carry out the following steps:

1. Click the green plus icon to display the following **Add Attribute** screen again:

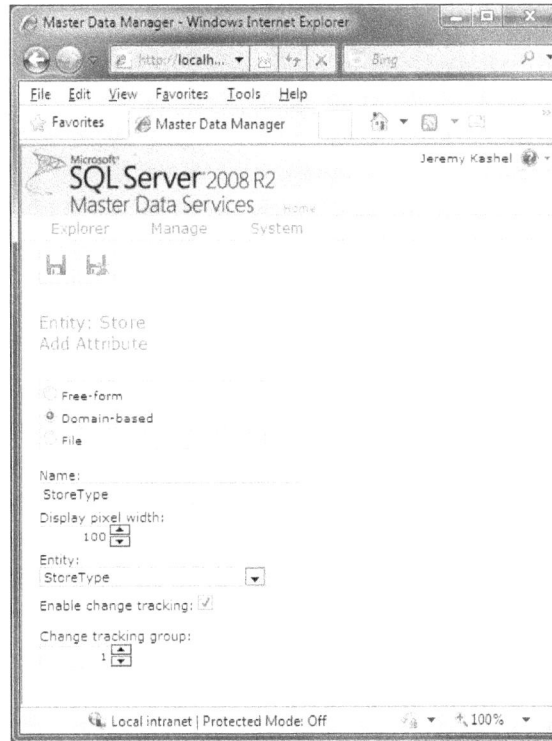

2. The most important setting to pick is to set the attribute to be a **Domain-based** attribute via the radio buttons at the top of the screen.

3. Enter the **Name** as **StoreType**, as shown above.

4. Leave the default **Display pixel width** of **100**.

5. As the domain-based setting has been chosen, we can now pick from the Entity drop-down, which is the entity to base the attribute upon. Pick the **StoreType** entity from this drop-down.

6. Click the check box to **Enable change tracking**.

7. Leave the default **Change tracking group** of **1**.

8. Click on the save icon at the top of the screen to save the new attribute.

Looking back at our table that we outlined previously, there are several attributes that still need to be created, in order to finish the structure of our model. Repeat the process that we have just gone through, using the settings shown in the following table:

Entity	Attribute name	Domain attribute	Domain attribute Entity	Data Type	Enable change tracking	Change tracking group
Store	City	Y	City	N/A	Y	1
Store	PostalCode	N	N/A	Text	Y	1
Store	TelephoneNumber	N	N/A	Text	Y	1
Store	FaxNumber	N	N/A	Text	Y	1
Store	EmailAddress	N	N/A	Text	Y	1
State	Country	Y	Country	N/A	N	N/A
City	State	Y	State	N/A	N	N/A

Once the structural changes are complete, we need to import some data into the model, in order that we have some data to work with in the forthcoming examples used in the book.

Our method to get data into the new model is to run a T-SQL script that will populate the MDS staging tables. We will then run a command that will move data from the staging tables into the actual MDS tables, before executing another T-SQL script that will validate our model.

Do not worry about how the script is constructed for the moment, as we will cover the data import process in detail in *Chapter 6, Importing Data into Master Data Services*.

In order to import the example data, carry out the following steps:

1. Ensure that you have downloaded the files `0509_04_PopulateModel1.sql` and `0509_04_PopulateModel2.sql` from the code bundle that is available with the book.

2. Open SQL Server Management Studio (SSMS).

3. Using **File**, then **Open**, open the file called `0509_04_PopulateModel1.sql`.

4. Ensure that you are connected to the server that hosts the MDS database and that you are also connected to the MDS database itself.

5. Execute the T-SQL script and verify that it completes successfully.

Downloading the example code for this book

You can download the example code files for all Packt books you have purchased from your account at http://www.PacktPub.com. If you purchased this book elsewhere, you can visit http://www.PacktPub.com/support and register to have the files e-mailed directly to you.

6. Now open the second `*.sql` file called `0509_04_PopulateModel2.sql`.

7. Ensure again that you are connected to the correct server and database.

8. Run the select statement at the top of the script and verify that a row is returned with a name called **STORE_unbatched** with no errors, as shown next. As the data is loaded asynchronously, it is also important to note the value of the **Status_ID** column, as shown below. If the **Status_ID** is 1 or 3, then the import is still running, so wait a minute or so and check again. Continue, only once the **Status_ID** is equal to **2**.

	ID	OriginalBatch_ID	MUID	Version_ID	ExternalSystem_ID	Name	Status_ID	TotalMemberCount	ErrorMemberCount	TotalMemberAttributeCount	ErrorMemberAttributeCount
1	1	NULL	FF1BE2C..	2	NULL	Product_VERSION_	2	1056	0	12421	0
2	2	NULL	BE9FA43..	14	NULL	STORE_Unbatched	2	1042	0	969	0

9. As instructed in the script, uncomment the lines below and execute the now uncommented statements, which will validate the data that we have just loaded and complete the import process.

We will now be in a position to use our new Store model structure to manage Store master data.

Members

The Explorer function in Master Data Manager is the place where we can perform the following functions on the members within an entity:

- **Add members**
- **Edit members**
- **Delete members**
- **Annotate members**
- **View member transactions**

Before we start on any of these activities, we need to define what types of members we can have. There are two types of members within Master Data Services, namely:

- Leaf members
- Consolidated members

Leaf members are entity members that cannot have any children, and therefore, typically exist at the bottom of a hierarchy of members. In contrast, consolidated members are entity members that are explicitly created for grouping other members.

The Master Data Manager Explorer

We took a quick look at the Explorer function of Master Data Manager back in *Chapter 2*. We now need to navigate there once again, in order to take a look at the Store members that have been imported. To do this, carry out the following steps:

1. Click the SQL Server 2008 R2 Master Data Services logo at the top of the current page. This will always return you to the MDS home page.

2. From the home page, choose the **Explorer** option. This will show the following **Model View** page, where we should see a full list of attributes for our **Store** entity, as shown below:

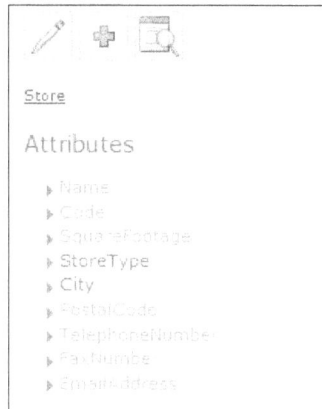

3. Click on the pencil icon, which will show the members that we have imported via the Explorer grid:

Store					
[All Attributes]					
X	Name		Code▲	SquareFootage	StoreType
☐ ▾ ✓	AW Duluth	001		2000	Mall{02}
☐ ▾ ✓	AW Nevada	002		2000	Mall{02}
☐ ▾ ✓	AW Memphis	003		2000	Mall{02}
☐ ▾ ✓	AW Detroit	004		2000	Mall{02}
☐ ▾ ✓	AW Cambridge	005		2000	Mall{02}
☐ ▾ ✓	AW Baltimore	006		2000	Mall{02}
☐ ▾ ✓	AW Minneapolis	007		2000	Mall{02}
☐ ▾ ✓	AW Clearwater 2	008		2000	Mall{02}

Adding a member

Depending on your MDM strategy, you may not actually ever need to physically add members to any of your entities within MDS, purely because the master data entity members may be added in the original source system, with MDS assigned to import, de-duplicate, and/or amend, before the members can be distributed to subscribing source systems. In some cases though, the original source of data will be an Excel spread sheet, meaning that creating members in MDS will be a far better option.

We will assume for the moment in our fictitious company that the requirement exists to add new Stores into MDS itself, and will now work through an example of adding a member:

1. Remaining on the current page, click the green plus icon to display the following **Add Store** page:

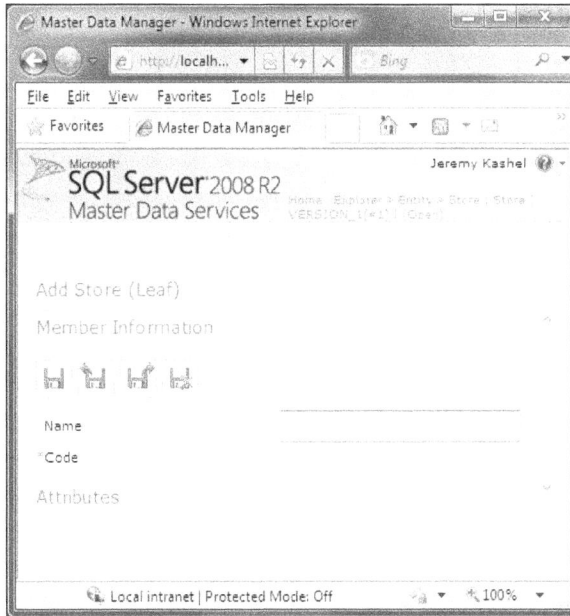

2. Enter the **Name** as **AW Houston**, as that is where the new store will be opened.

3. Enter the **Code** as 051. The code must be unique amongst the members in the current entity, and 051 is the next one in the sequence.

4. There are four buttons above the **Name** and **Code** labels, which carry out the following:

    ○ The first from left to right (**Save**) will save the new member, and then allow us to assign values to its attributes

- ◦ The second (**Save and Return**) will save the new member, but return us to the Explorer grid without specifying values for the attributes

- ◦ The third (**Save and Add Another**) will save the new member, without specifying the attributes, and then re-present the **Add Store** page, in order to allow us to add another member

- ◦ Finally the fourth (**Cancel**) will return us to the Explorer grid without adding anything

5. Choose the first button to save the member, which will cause the following **Edit Store** window to appear:

Edit Store (Leaf)

Member Information

Name   AW Houston
*Code   051

Attributes

[All Attributes]

Display:
  Code   Code {Name}   ◉ Name {Code}

  SquareFootage   StoreType

  City   PostalCode
                          {}
  TelephoneNumber   FaxNumber

  EmailAddress

  * Required

6. As shown in the image, all of the **Attributes** are now shown, along with a pencil edit icon that will allow us to provide values to the **Attributes**. Click on the pencil icon, which will enable editing of the **Attributes**.

7. Enter the following values for the attributes:

- ◦ **SquareFootage** – 3000

Explorer grid view

Depending on the view that is selected in the main Explorer grid (**Code**, **Code {Name}**, or **Name {Code}**) Domain attributes may not display the names that are set out next. Therefore, the domain attributes next are also shown with their code in order to avoid confusion.

        °   **StoreType** — Mall {02}

> **Number of Domain-Based attributes in List**
>
> The number of members displayed in a drop-down for a domain-based attribute is controlled by a setting called Number of Domain-based attributes in list. Depending on the value of this setting, you may have to search for the city called Houston, instead of picking it from a list.

        °   **City** — Houston {449}

        °   **PostalCode** — 77999

        °   **TelephoneNumber** — 713-999-9999

        °   **FaxNumber** — 713-999-9998

        °   **EmailAddress** — Houston@adventureworks.com

8. Click on the save icon.

9. Click the green back arrow at the top of the page to return to the Explorer grid.

Editing a member

As you might expect the Explorer grid also gives functionality to edit a member, as well as the ability to edit multiple members at once.

In our example model, we have some editing to do, as we do not have phone numbers for all of the stores, for example, the Duluth store. In order to edit the Duluth store, carry out the following steps:

1. If you are not already on the Explorer grid, for the Store entity, navigate back to the **Explorer** page, and choose the Store entity.

2. You will see that the Duluth store is missing a value for the **TelephoneNumber** attribute. Click the small drop-down arrow on the left-hand side of the member name **AW Duluth**, and choose **Edit Member** from the resulting sub menu. This is shown next:

3. Choosing **Edit Member** from the sub menu will cause the **Edit Store** window to appear, which is exactly the same window that appeared when we added a member earlier on.

4. Once in the **Edit Store** window, click the pencil icon, which will allow editing of the **Attributes**.

5. Enter a made up number for the **TelephoneNumber** attribute, as shown below:

6. Click on the save icon.

7. Click on the green arrow icon at the top of the screen to return to the Explorer grid.

Deleting members

Deleting members is also carried out from the Explorer grid. In our example scenario, we are closing the store in Nevada, so it must be deleted from our Store entity. In order to do this, carry out the following steps:

1. Using the check boxes on the far left-hand side of the grid, click to check the AW Nevada member.

2. Click the **Delete Selected Members** button, which is the button with a red cross above the Explorer grid.

3. Click **OK** to the message box that will appear, prompting for confirmation.

4. The member will now be deleted.

> **Alternative delete button**
>
> There is also a **Delete Member** option in the member pop-up menu that we used when editing a member.

Annotating members

Annotations can be added to a member, which may, for example, be useful to communicate to the others the changes that have been made to a particular member.

Annotations are also carried out using the member pop-up window. To create an annotation, carry out the following:

1. Using the Explorer grid, click the drop-down arrow next to a member of your choice and select **Annotate Member**.

2. The **Add Annotation** window will now open. Enter a comment of your choice and then click on the save icon.

3. The member will now have an annotation.

Annotations are created in the Explorer grid, but they are not actually visible on the grid. Instead, they are visible on the Transactions window, which we will cover next.

Transactions

The Transactions window is a feature within MDS that is used to view, and even reverse, any transaction that has occurred to a member. All types of transactions are shown, such as the update to an attribute, or a member annotation, and all transactions can be reversed by those with sufficient permissions, in order to rectify mistakes.

In our example scenario, we will now reverse the phone number that we entered earlier for the Duluth store. In order to do this, carry out the following steps:

1. Using the Explorer grid, click the drop-down arrow next to the **Duluth** member and choose **View Member Transactions** from the pop-up menu, which will cause the following **Transactions** grid to appear. Note that we get to see the attribute's **Prior Value**, its **New Value**, as well as who changed it and when:

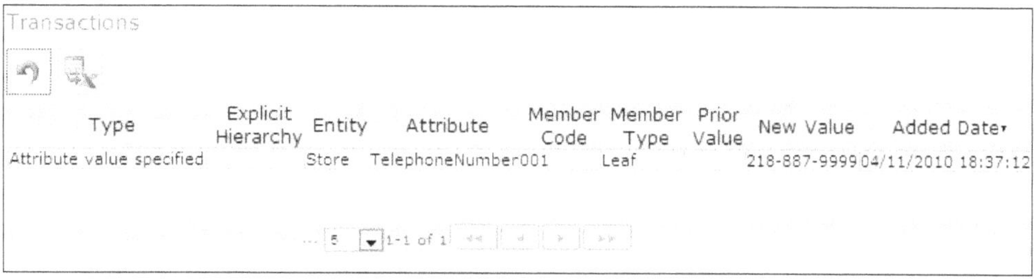

2. Click anywhere on the transaction in order to highlight it. As transactions, as well as members, can be annotated, it would be at this point that we would see any annotations another user had left for the transaction.

3. Now that the transaction is highlighted, click on the **Reverse Selected Transaction** icon at the top of the screen.

4. Click **OK** in response to the message box that will appear, in order to confirm that we do actually want to reverse the transaction.

5. Note that a new transaction has now appeared. The **Prior Value** will be the original **Telephone Number** that was entered, whereas the **New Value** will be blank.

6. Enter an annotation for the new transaction that we have just created and then click on the save icon. Note that the annotation is now displayed at the bottom of the screen, as it is associated with the new transaction, as shown below:

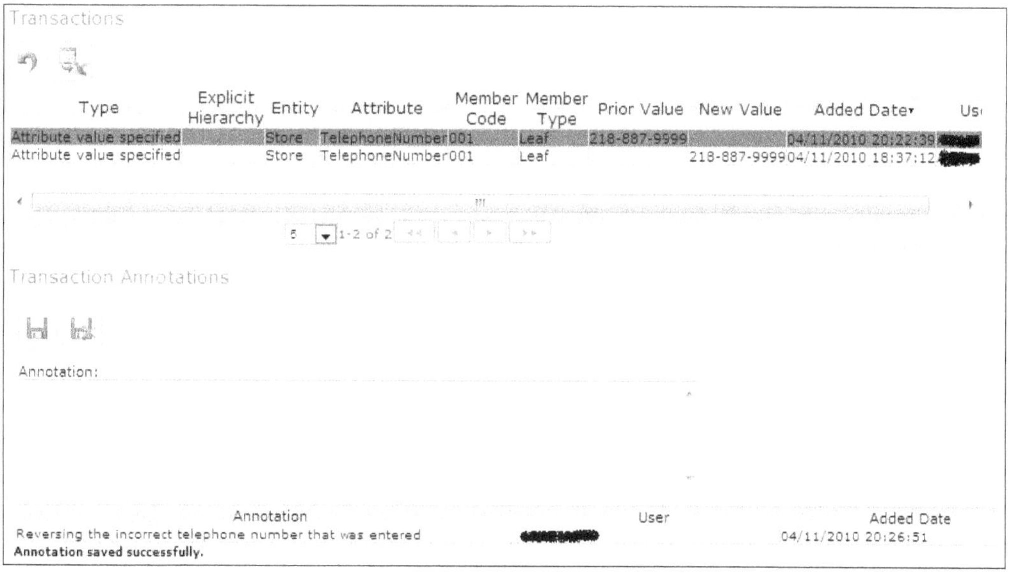

Browsing the Explorer grid again will show that the telephone number for the Duluth store is now blank, as we have reversed our original transaction.

Attribute Groups

We've now got to the point where we have built quite a comprehensive model to house our retail stores, but we've not gone to the nth degree in terms of all the attributes that we may need. In a production environment, especially for larger entities, we could require anything in the region of twenty attributes.

This situation is where Attribute Groups are able to help. As mentioned briefly at the start of this chapter, an Attribute Group is a container object that exists within an entity to group together one or more of the entity's attributes.

An entity can contain multiple Attribute Groups, and the reason for creating them is to make the data entry and browsing of an entity more usable. They are also able to act as a security object, meaning that you can grant users access rights to individual Attribute Groups, if certain Attribute Groups are applicable to a particular user. We will cover security in detail in *Chapter 10, Master Data Services Security*.

In our example scenario, we have the generic store attributes such as the PostalCode, SquareFootage, and StoreType, plus all the contact information for the store. We can therefore create two separate Attribute Groups, one called General and one called Contact Information.

Creating Attribute Groups

Carry out the following in order to create the two Attribute Groups that we need:

1. Navigate to the **System Administration** function, which can be accessed using the Master Data Manager home page.

2. Hover over the **Manage** menu and click on the **Attribute Groups** menu item.

3. In the **Attribute Group Maintenance** page that will have appeared, choose the **Store** Entity from the **Entity** drop-down.

4. Click on the **Leaf Groups** node that will have appeared. At this point, a plus icon and a pencil icon will appear, as we can add or edit an **Attribute Group** from this page. Click on the plus icon as we want to add an **Attribute Group**.

5. Enter the **Leaf Group Name** as **General**, as this will house our non-contact related attributes.

6. Click on the save icon.

7. There will now be an **Attribute Group** shown under the **Leaf Groups** node called **General**. Expand this node and click on the node called **Attributes**.

8. Another pencil icon will appear. Click on this icon to edit the **Attributes** in our new **Attribute Group**, which will cause the following screen to appear:

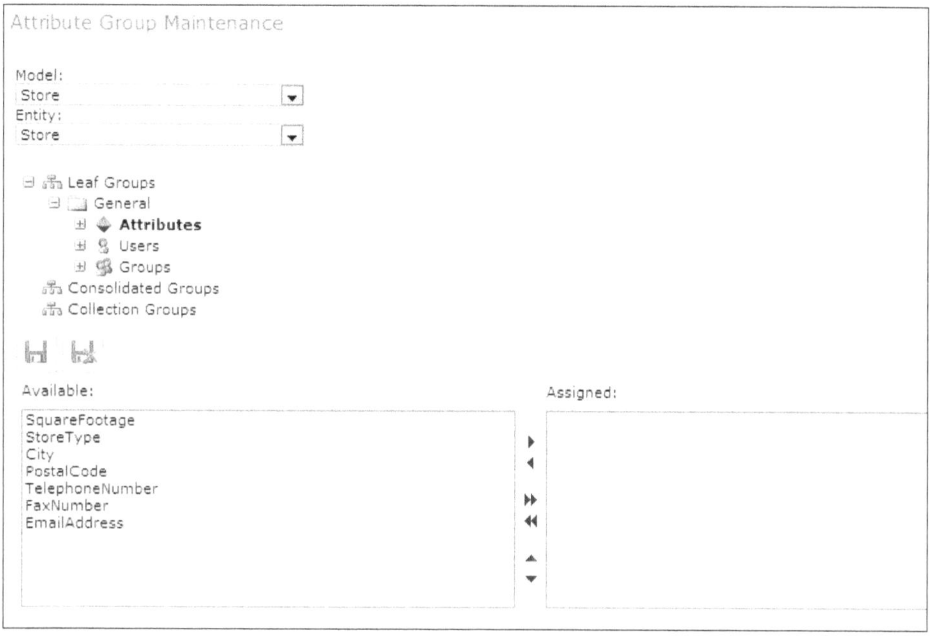

9. Highlight the **SquareFootage** attribute and then click the right pointing arrow, which will move the selected attribute from the **Available** list to the **Assigned** list.

10. Repeat the process for the attributes listed next. Note that the Name and Code **Attributes** are not included in the list, as they are always present in every **Attribute Group**.

     ° **StoreType**

     ° **City**

     ° **PostalCode**

11. Click on the save icon, which will create our **General Attribute Group**.

12. Repeat the entire process, but create an **Attribute Group** called **Contact Information**, with the following attributes assigned:

    ○ **TelephoneNumber**

    ○ **FaxNumber**

    ○ **EmailAddress**

13. Once completed, the fully expanded object hierarchy on the **Attribute Group Maintenance** page should be as follows:

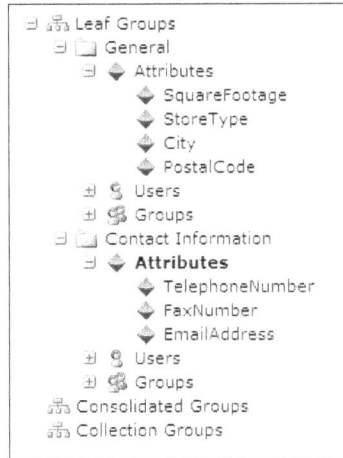

```
⊟ ⊞ Leaf Groups
   ⊟ ▢ General
      ⊟ ◆ Attributes
            ◆ SquareFootage
            ◆ StoreType
            ◆ City
            ◆ PostalCode
      ⊞ ⑧ Users
      ⊞ ⑧ Groups
   ⊟ ▢ Contact Information
      ⊟ ◆ Attributes
            ◆ TelephoneNumber
            ◆ FaxNumber
            ◆ EmailAddress
      ⊞ ⑧ Users
      ⊞ ⑧ Groups
   ⊞ Consolidated Groups
   ⊞ Collection Groups
```

This concludes the creation of our Attribute Groups, so now we will look at how we can use them.

Using Attribute Groups

Now that the Attribute Groups have been created, we will simply encounter them as part of the standard Explorer-based activities that we have already looked at. Carry out the following steps to get an example of where they are exposed to the user:

1. Navigate to the home page and select the **Explorer** function.

2. Edit the Store entity so that the standard Explorer grid opens. The grid will now be altered to show the following two new tabs at the top of the grid:

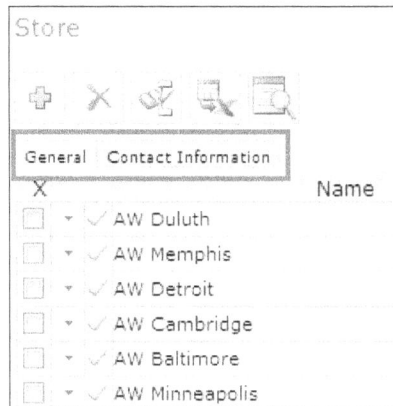

3. Click on the **Contact Information** tab to see the view of attributes change.

4. Click on the **General** tab to revert to the original view.

We will also encounter the attribute groups when adding or editing a member. Carry out the following steps to see an example of this:

1. Click on the **Contact Information** tab in the Explorer grid.

2. Notice that the **AW Cambridge** store is missing a Fax and TelephoneNumber. Click on the drop-down that is adjacent to the store name and choose **Edit Member**.

3. The **Attributes** section of the **Edit Store** page that will have appeared will now contain two tabs, one for each attribute group. The attributes in each group are edited independently. As we want to edit the **TelephoneNumber** attribute, click on the **Contact Information** tab, as shown below:

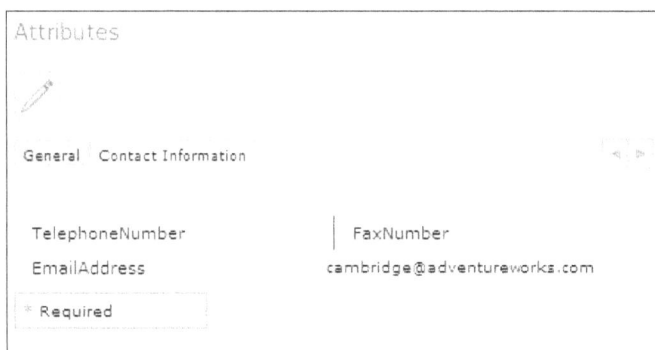

4. Click on the pencil icon to edit the attributes of the selected store.

5. Enter a made up value for the **TelephoneNumber** attribute.

6. Click on the save icon.

7. Click on the green back arrow to return to the Explorer grid.

We have now seen how Attribute Groups can help organize our attributes into meaningful groups.

Hierarchies

As mentioned in *Chapter 2*, Master Data Services includes a Hierarchy Management feature, where we can:

- Browse all levels of a hierarchy

- Move members within a hierarchy

- Access the Explorer grid and all its functionality for all members of a given hierarchy.

As we've seen already, there are two types of hierarchies in MDS—Derived Hierarchies and Explicit Hierarchies. We will look at how to create and use both types of hierarchies now.

Derived Hierarchies

In our example scenario, as we have stores in many different cities and states, we have a requirement to create a "Stores by Geography" hierarchy. In order to create the hierarchy, carry out the following steps:

1. Navigate to the **System Administration** function, which can be accessed using the Master Data Manager home page.

2. Hover over the **Manage** menu and click on the **Derived Hierarchies** menu item, which will open the **Derived Hierarchy Maintenance** page.

3. Click on the green plus icon to add a **Derived Hierarchy**, which will open the **Add Derived Hierarchy** page.

4. Enter **Stores By Geography** as the **Derived Hierarchy Name** and click on save.

5. The **Edit Derived Hierarchy** page will now be displayed, where we can build the hierarchy. On the left-hand side of the screen we can pick entities to be in our hierarchy, whereas the middle pane of the screen displays the hierarchy in its current state. A preview of the hierarchy with real data is also available on the right-hand side. Drag the **Store** entity from the left-hand side of the screen and drop it onto the red **Current Levels : Stores By Geography** node in the center of the screen:

Edit Derived Hierarchy: Stores By Geography

Available Entities and Hierarchies

Current Levels

Available levels: Stores By Geography
  StoreType
  City

Current levels: Stores By Geography
  Store

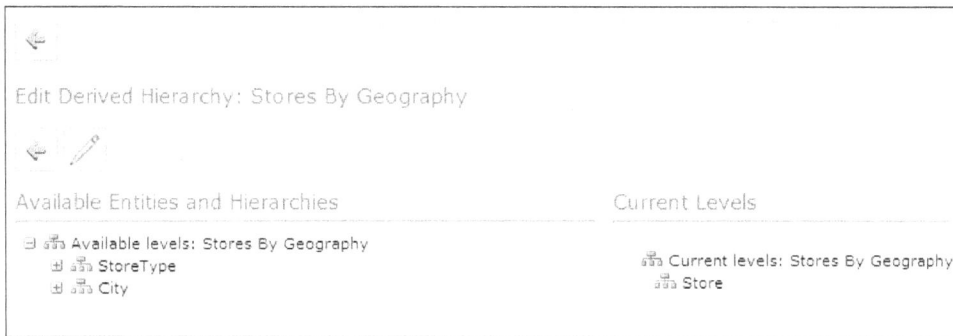

6. The choice of entities of on the left hand side will now change to the only two entities that are related to **Store**, namely **City** and **StoreType**. Repeat the drag-and-drop process, but this time drag the **City** entity onto the red **Current Levels** node so that the **Current Levels** hierarchy is as follows:

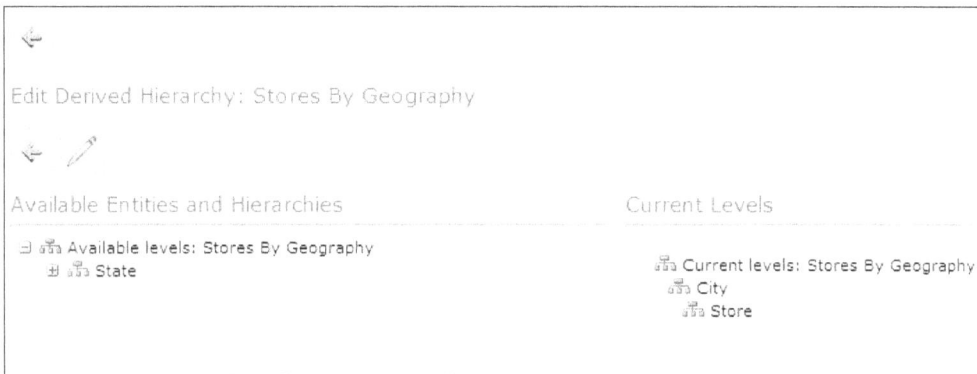

Edit Derived Hierarchy: Stores By Geography

Available Entities and Hierarchies

Current Levels

Available levels: Stores By Geography
  State

Current levels: Stores By Geography
  City
  Store

7. The **Available Entities and Hierarchies** pane will now be updated to show the **State** entity, as this is the only entity related to the **City** entity. Drag the **State** entity over to the red **Current levels** node, above the **City** entity.

8. The **Available Entities and Hierarchies** pane will now be updated to show the **Country**. Drag the **Country** entity over to the red **Current Levels** node, above the **State** entity. This is the last step in building our **Stores By Geography** hierarchy, which will now be complete.

We will now look at how we can browse and edit our new hierarchy.

Exploring Derived Hierarchies

Before we make any changes to the Derived Hierarchy, we will explore the user interface, so that we are comfortable with how it is used.

Carry out the following in order to browse the new hierarchy features:

1. Navigate to the home page and select the **Explorer** function.

2. Within the **Explorer** function, hover over the **Hierarchies** menu, where a menu item called **Derived: Stores By Geography** should appear. Click on this new item, which will display the Derived Hierarchy, as shown below:

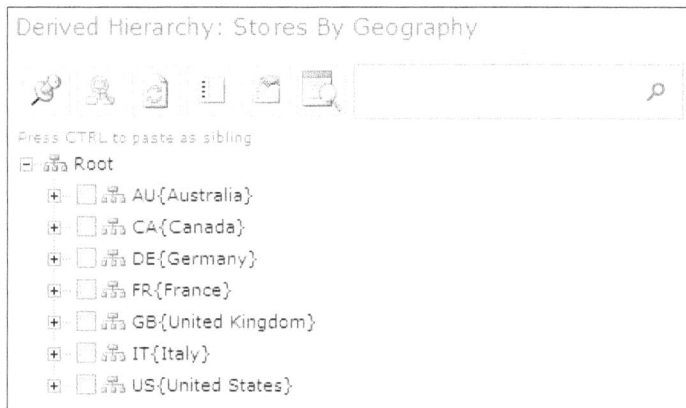

3. The buttons above the hierarchy tree structure are as follows (from left to right):

    ○ **Pin Selected Item**—Hides all members apart from the select item and all of its descendants. This option can be useful when browsing large hierarchies.

    ○ **Locate Parent of Selected Item**—The immediate parent of the selected member could be hidden, if someone has chosen to pin the item (as above). **Locate Parent of Selected Item** will locate and display the members parent, as well as any other children of the parent.

    ○ **Refresh Hierarchy**—Refreshes the hierarchy tree to display the latest version, as edits could occur outside the immediate tree structure.

    ○ **Show/Hide Names**—Toggles the hierarchy view to be either the member code and the name, or just the code. The default is to show the member name and code.

- ○ **Show/Hide Attributes**—On the right-hand side of the screen (not shown) the children of the selected item are shown in the Explorer grid, along with all their attributes. This button shows or hides the Explorer grid.

- ○ **View Metadata**—Displays a pop-up window that will display the metadata for the selected member. We will discuss metadata towards the end of this chapter.

4. Select the **DE {Germany}** member by clicking on it. Note: the checkboxes are not how members are selected; instead, clicking on the member name will select the member.

5. Use the **Pin Selected Item** button to pin the **DE {Germany}** member, which will hide the siblings of Germany as shown below:

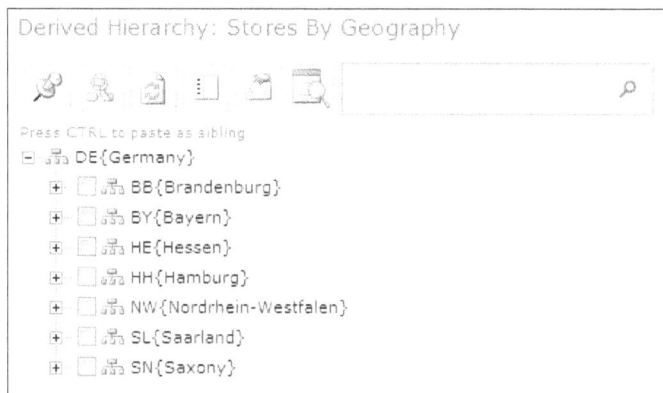

6. To now locate the parent of **DE {Germany}**, and display the parent's other children (for example, USA and United Kingdom), click on **DE {Germany}**, then click on the **Locate Parent of Selected Item** button. The hierarchy tree will revert back to the original structure that we encountered.

7. Now that we have returned to the original hierarchy structure, expand the US member until the member **CA {California}** is visible. Click on this member, which will display some of the cities, which we have loaded for the State of California:

City				
		Display: Code Code {Name} ● Name {Code}		
[All Attributes]				
X	Name	Code▲	State	
☐ ▾ ✓ Alhambra		040	California{CA}	
☐ ▾ ✓ Alpine		041	California{CA}	
☐ ▾ ✓ Altadena		042	California{CA}	
☐ ▾ ✓ Auburn		043	California{CA}	
☐ ▾ ✓ Baldwin Park		044	California{CA}	
☐ ▾ ✓ Barstow		045	California{CA}	
☐ ▾ ✓ Bell Gardens		046	California{CA}	

Editing multiple entities

The above point illustrates one of the useful features of the hierarchy editor. Although we can edit the individual entities using their respective Explorer grids, with a Derived Hierarchy, we can edit multiple entities on a single page.

8. We don't actually need to edit the cities for the moment, but we do want to look at showing and hiding the Explorer grid. Click on the **Show/Hide Attributes button** to hide the Explorer grid. Click on the button again to make the Explorer grid reappear.

9. Finally, we're able to look at the Metadata for the Derived Hierarchy. Click on the **View Metadata** button to open the Metadata Explorer, which is shown below. This is where we would look for any auxiliary information about the Derived Hierarchy, such as a description to explain what is in the hierarchy. We'll look at metadata in detail at the end of this chapter.

Attribute	Value
Name	Stores By Geography
Code	18_D_14
Description	

Filters

Metadata type: Hierarchy

Model: Store

Entity: Country

Hierarchy: Derived: Store: Stores By Geography

Metadata (Derived: Store: Stores By Geography Hierarchy)

Display: ● Code ○ Code {Name} ○ Name {Code}

General Hierarchy Information

We will now look at how we add a new member in a Derived Hierarchy.

Adding a member in a Derived Hierarchy

Adding a member in a Derived Hierarchy achieves exactly the same thing as adding a member in the entity itself. The difference is that the member addition process when carried out in a Derived Hierarchy is slightly simplified, as the domain attribute (for example, City in the case of the Store entity) gets automatically completed by MDS. This because in a Derived Hierarchy we choose to add a Store in a particular City, which negates the need to specify the City itself.

In our example scenario, we wish to open a new Store in Denver. Carry out the following steps to add the new Store:

1. Expand the **US {United States}** member of the **Stores By Geography** hierarchy, and then expand the **CO {Colorado}** member.

2. Click on the **136 {Denver}** member.

3. On the far right-hand side of the screen, the **Stores** for **Denver** (of which there are none) will be shown. Click on the green plus icon to begin the process of adding a **Store**.

4. Enter the **Name** as **AW Denver** and enter the **Code** as **052.**

5. Click on the save icon to create the member.

6. Click on the pencil icon to edit the attributes of the new member. Note that the **City** attribute is already completed for us.

7. Complete the remaining attributes with test data of your choice.

8. Click on the save icon to save the attribute values.

9. Click on the green back arrow button at the top of the screen in order to return to the Derived Hierarchy.

Notice that we now have a new Store that exists in the Derived Hierarchy, as well as a new row in the Explorer grid on the right-hand side of the screen.

We will now continue to explore the functionality in the hierarchy interface by using Explicit Hierarchies.

Explicit Hierarchies

Whereas Derived Hierarchies rely on the relationships between different entities in order to exist, all the members within Explicit Hierarchies come from a single entity. The hierarchy is made by making explicit relationships between leaf members and the consolidated members that are used to give the hierarchy more than one level.

Explicit Hierarchies are useful in order to represent a ragged hierarchy, which is a hierarchy where the leaf members exist at different levels across the hierarchy.

In our example scenario, we wish to create a hierarchy that shows the reporting structures for our stores. Most stores report to a regional center, with the regional centers reporting to Head Office. However, some stores that are deemed to be important report directly to Head Office, which is why we need the Explicit Hierarchy.

Creating an Explicit Hierarchy

As we saw when creating the original Store entity earlier in the chapter, an Explicit Hierarchy can get automatically created for us when we create an Entity.

While that is always an option, right now we will cover how to do this manually. In order to create the Explicit Hierarchy, carry out the following steps:

1. Navigate to the **System Administration** function.
2. Hover over the **Manage** menu and click on the **Entities** menu item.
3. Select the **Store** entity and then click on the pencil icon to edit the entity.
4. Select **Yes** from **Enable explicit hierarchies and collections** drop-down.
5. Enter **Store Reporting** as the **Explicit hierarchy name**.
6. Uncheck the checkbox called **Include all leaf members in mandatory hierarchy**. If the checkbox is unchecked, a special hierarchy node called **Unused** will be created, where leaf members that are not required in the hierarchy will reside. If the checkbox is checked, then all leaf members will be included in the Explicit Hierarchy. This is shown next:

Edit Entity: Store

Entity Maintenance

Entity name:
Store

Enable explicit hierarchies and collections:
Yes ▼

Explicit hierarchy name:
Store Reporting

☐ Include all leaf members in mandatory hierarchy

7. Click on the save icon to make the changes to the entity, which will return us to the **Entity Maintenance** screen, and conclude the creation of the hierarchy.

Consolidated members

Before we can properly use our new Explicit Hierarchy, we need to create some consolidated members to group the Stores into a reporting structure.

Like leaf members, consolidated members belong to an entity and have a number of attributes. The difference is that consolidated members can only exist in Explicit Hierarchies, whereas leaf members can exist in any type of hierarchy.

We can create consolidated members in the standard Explorer grid, or in the hierarchy editor, but on this occasion, we will choose the hierarchy editor. Carry out the following steps to browse to the Explicit Hierarchy and add some consolidated members:

1. Navigate to the **Explorer** function.

2. Hover over the **Hierarchies** menu and choose the **Explicit: Store Reporting** menu item. This will cause the same hierarchy editor to appear as the one that we encountered with the Derived Hierarchy. One immediate difference to note is that we have an extra node in the hierarchy tree, which is called **Unused**.

3 Expand the **Unused** node to see all the leaf members that are present.

4. In order to create the consolidated members, change the member type selection of the Explorer grid to be **Consolidated**, by using the radio buttons, as shown below:

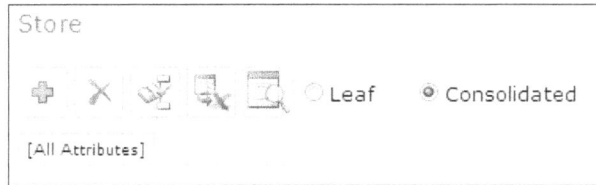

5. As the member type of **Consolidated** is selected, clicking the green plus icon will add a **Consolidated**, rather than a **Leaf**, member. Click on the icon now to add a new consolidated member.

6. In the standard **Add Store** page that we have seen before, enter the **Name** as **North** and the **Code** as **N**, to represent the Northern reporting region.

7. We actually want to add several consolidated members, so instead of just clicking on the regular save button, click on the **Save and Add Another** button to save the consolidated member.

8. Repeat the process to create the following consolidated members, which are shown in the Code {Name} format:

    ○ **S {South}**

    ○ **E {East}**

    ○ **W {West}**

    ○ **HO {Head Office}**

9. Return to the hierarchy editor, which should show the following view:

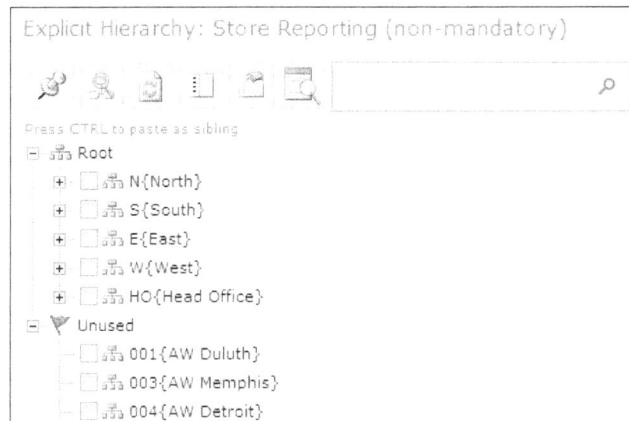

We will now look at creating the ragged hierarchy structures by moving members to a parent.

Moving hierarchy members

There are two ways in which we can move a member to a parent in an Explicit or a Derived Hierarchy, namely:

- Drag-and-drop
- The MDS clipboard

Our desired goal is for all regions to report to Head Office, but for some of the stores to report to Head Office directly. We will start off by dragging and dropping the regions to Head Office. To do this:

1. Click on the **North** member and without releasing the mouse button, hover over the **Head Office** member and then release the mouse button.

2. Repeat the process for the **East, South**, and **West** members. The final hierarchy structure should be as follows:

Dragging and dropping may not be so useful when moving a large amount of members, which is what we need to do in order to move the stores to their regions. This is where the clipboard can help, as we shall see by carrying out the following steps:

3. Expand the **Unused** node to expose the leaf members.

4. We will start by moving the Northern stores to the **North** member. Check the checkboxes for the following members:

    ○   **001 - AW Duluth**
    ○   **007 - AW Minneapolis**
    ○   **010 - AW Woodburn**
    ○   **020 - AW Kirkland**
    ○   **023 - AW Chicago 3**
    ○   **024 - AW Spokane**
    ○   **025 - AW Lake Oswego**
    ○   **030 - AW Oregon City**
    ○   **035 - AW Casper**
    ○   **038 - AW Chicago 2**
    ○   **046 - AW Branch**
    ○   **048 - AW Billings**
    ○   **049 - AW Chicago**

5. We will now use the MDS **Clipboard** to move the checked members to a new parent. The **Clipboard** is located at the bottom of the page, and has the following buttons, which are explained next from left to right:

    ○   **Copy to Clipboard** (first on the left)—Stores any members that are checked on the clipboard
    ○   **Paste as Child**—Pastes any members on the clipboard as children of the selected member
    ○   **Paste as Sibling**—Pastes any members on the clipboard as siblings of the selected member
    ○   **Clear Clipboard**—Clears the clipboard temporary storage area
    ○   The textbox on the far right displays the current contents of the clipboard

6. Click the **Copy to Clipboard** button. Notice that the textbox at the bottom of the page will change to indicate that the clipboard has some members.

7. Expand the **Head Office** member and then select the **North** member by clicking on it, so that it is highlighted bold, as shown below:

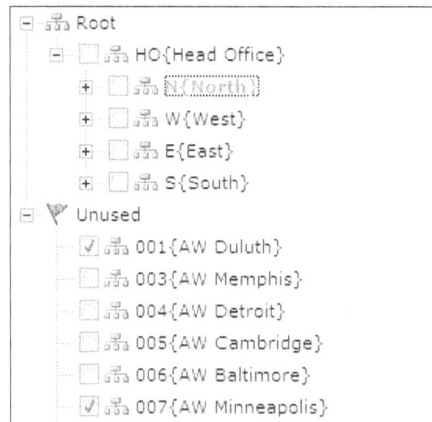

8. Click on the **Paste as Child** button at the bottom of the screen to paste the members on the clipboard as children of the **North** member.

9. Expand the **North** member to verify that it now contains a number of children.

10. Repeat the process, for the following members, noting that some of the members map directly to **Head Office**:

Member code	Member name	Parent name
004	AW Detroit	East
005	AW Cambridge	East
006	AW Baltimore	East
015	AW Braintree	East
021	AW Charlotte	East
022	AW Columbus	East
026	AW Clay	East
027	AW Cheektowaga	East
039	AW Chantilly	East
012	AW Cincinnati 2	Head Office
014	AW Branson	Head Office

Member code	Member name	Parent name
032	AW Campbellsville	Head Office
033	AW Cincinnati	Head Office
041	AW Central Valley	Head Office
045	AW Cheyenne	Head Office
050	AW Bellevue	Head Office
052	AW Denver	Head Office
003	AW Memphis	South
008	AW Clearwater 2	South
009	AW Clarkston	South
011	AW Baytown	South
018	AW Cedar Park	South
019	AW Bluffton	South
029	AW Birmingham	South
031	AW College Station	South
034	AW Clearwater	South
036	AW Byron	South
037	AW Biloxi	South
044	AW Bradenton	South
051	AW Houston	South
013	AW Burbank	West
016	AW Burbank 2	West
017	AW Bountiful	West
028	AW Redwood City	West
040	AW Cedar City	West
042	AW Downey	West
043	AW Chandler 2	West
047	AW Chandler	West

After the aforementioned steps have been completed, we will have now completed the creation of our Explicit Hierarchy. The final version should look as follows, noting, for example, that **AW Cincinnati 2** and **AW Branson** now report directly to **Head Office**:

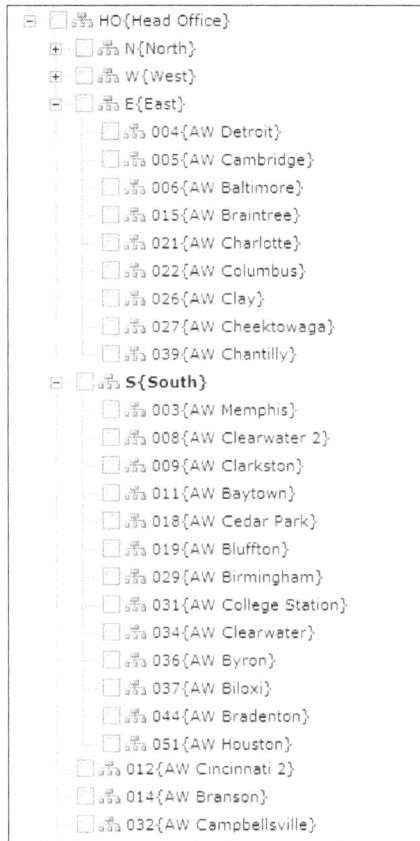

Collections

When we altered the Store entity to enable Explicit Hierarchies, we did so by changing an option called **Enable explicit hierarchies and collections**. As the name of the option suggests, this action also enabled collections for our entity.

Collections are customized lists and hierarchies of members that are created by manually specifying the members that can be in the collection. A collection can contain a mix of members from different instances of the following MDS objects:

- Explicit Hierarchies (both consolidated and leaf members)
- Other collections

Therefore, it would be possible to make a collection that contained 10 members from a Collection, 10 from an Explicit Hierarchy, and 10 from another Explicit Hierarchy.

Collections are useful when we have the requirement to isolate a subset of an entity or hierarchy, for example, to carry a marketing campaign to a select list of customers, or to list a number of products that may be on promotion.

Creating a collection

In our example scenario, Head Office wishes to run a marketing campaign for a select number of stores that run a particular product line. Carry out the following steps in order to create the collection:

1. Navigate to the home page and select the **Explorer** function.

2. Hover over the **Collections** menu, where a menu item called **Store** is now visible, as **Store** has been enabled for **explicit hierarchies and collections**. Click on the **Store** menu item, which takes us to the **Collection** editor page.

3. Click on the green plus icon to add a collection. Enter the following values in the **Add Store (Collection)** page:

    ◦ **Name — Store Marketing November 2010**

    ◦ **Code — STC001**

4. Click on the save icon to create the collection.

5. This will cause the **Attributes** area to appear, as they would if we were creating a member. Collections default to having an attribute called **Description**, which defaults to blank, and an **Owner_ID** attribute, which defaults to the logged in user. On this occasion, accept the defaults and click the green arrow to return.

6. One collection will now appear in the Explorer grid, in a similar fashion to if we had just created a single member in an entity. Click on the drop-down arrow that is adjacent to the collection name, which will make the following pop-up menu appear:

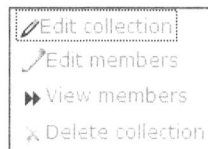

7. Click on the **Edit members** menu item, which will allow us to specify what members we want in the collection, by loading the following page:

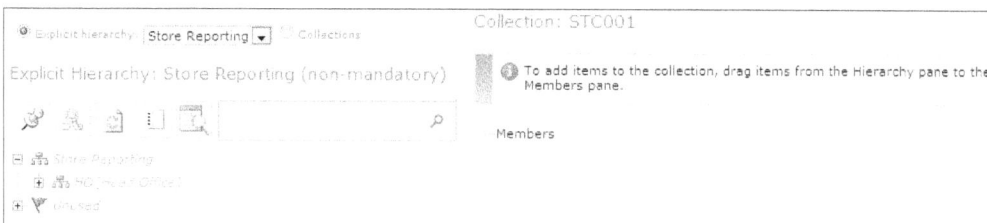

8. From the **Edit members** page, we can use the radio buttons at the top of the screen to switch between choosing members from an **Explicit Hierarchy** or a **Collection**. The default **Explicit Hierarchy** of **Store Reporting** will suit us for this task.

9. It is possible to add a whole hierarchy to a collection, but this is not necessary for us, as we need to cherry pick individual stores to be members of our collection. Navigate down the **Explicit Hierarchy** and click on the **AW Kirkland** member.

10. Drag the selected member from the **Explicit Hierarchy** to be on top of the **Members** node that appears in the right-hand side pane.

11. Repeat the process with the following members:
     ○ **049 — AW Chicago**
     ○ **006 — AW Baltimore**
     ○ **021 — AW Charlotte**
     ○ **033 — AW Cincinnati**
     ○ **041 — AW Central Valley**
     ○ **050 — AW Bellevue**

12. Click the green Back arrow when the above has been carried out, which will return us to the Collection grid. Notice that on the right-hand side of the screen, the contents of the collection are displayed. The contents should be as follows:

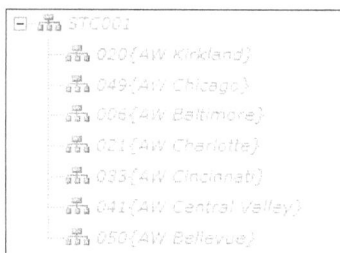

> **Model View for Collections**
>
> The Model View, which is displayed by default when clicking on the Explorer function provides a shortcut to access Collections. The Collections are listed on the right-hand side of the Model View page. When the Collection code name is clicked on, MDS takes you directly to the **Edit Members** part of the collection process.

As with entities, and Derived/Explicit Hierarchies, collections may be exported from MDS to allow the users who need them to consume the data. Exporting data from MDS is something that we will cover in *Chapter 8, Extracting Data From Master Data Services*.

Master Data Services Metadata

Metadata can be defined as any data that we capture for Master Data Management that is not the master data itself. It is often described in a generic way, applying to many industries, as "data about the data". The case of MDM, the "data about the data" is anything that helps to describe the master data. A few examples of metadata that we may want to capture as part of an MDM initiative are:

- The business owner of an entity
- Business definitions and meanings for objects such as entities and attributes
- The source system(s) for entities and/or members

Metadata can be created in MDS without resorting to code. A system model called Metadata gets created when MDS is installed, and can be edited by users so that the MDS metadata can be tailored to suit your business.

Altering the default MDS Metadata

By default MDS includes three different types of Metadata that apply to a number of objects. The Metadata types are:

- Name
- Code
- Description

The Name and Code are automatically completed for each entity. The Name is the name that the user gives for the object in the MDS front-end, such as "Store" for the Store Entity. The Code is auto-generated, meaning that the Store entity also has a code, although it's not that obvious unless you look at the metadata. The Description, however, is not populated for any of the system objects by default.

We have created a total of five entities as part of this chapter. Therefore, adding descriptions for these entities would be a good place to start. To do this, carry out the following instructions:

1. From the MDS home page, choose **Metadata** from the **Model** drop-down, and choose **Version 1** from the **Version** drop-down.

2. Click on the **Explorer** function. The **Model View** for the Metadata model will display five entities, which represent the objects that Metadata can be created for. They are:

    ° **Attribute Group Metadata Definition**

    ° **Attribute Group Definition**

    ° **Entity Metadata Definition**

    ° **Hierarchy Metadata Definition**

    ° **Model Metadata Definition**

3. Click on the **Entity Metadata Definition** entity.

4. Click on the familiar pencil icon in the next screen. The Explorer grid will be displayed, but it will contain the Metadata for all the entities that exist within the MDS system:

Entity Metadata Definition

General Entity Information

X	Name	Code▲	Description
	AccountType	13_50	
	ChartOfAccounts	13_51	
	Class	13_52	
	DebitCredit	13_53	
	Group	13_54	
	LineItem	13_55	
	LineItemDetail	13_56	
	Operator	13_57	
	SubClass	13_58	
	Store	18_63	
	City	18_66	
	StoreType	18_67	
	State	18_68	
	Country	18_69	

5. Edit the **Store** member and enter "Adventure Works full or partly owned Retail Stores" in the **Description** column.

6. Save the member.

7. Repeat the process, supplying the following descriptions for the following entities:

    ° **City** — Cities where Adventure Works retail stores are located

    ° **StoreType** — A classification of Adventure Works retail stores

    ° **State** — States where Adventure Works retail stores are located

    ° **Country** — Countries where Adventure Works retail stores are located

We will now be able to view the metadata that we have entered for our entities.

Viewing Metadata

As we touched on when looking at hierarchies, metadata in the Master Data Manager application is viewed by using the Metadata Explorer throughout the various different pages of the **Explorer** function.

To view the Metadata that we have just created, carry out the following steps:

1. Navigate to the MDS home page.

2. Select **Store** from the **Model** drop-down, and choose **VERSION_1** from the **Version** drop-down.

3. Click on the **Explorer** function.

4. Click on the **View Metadata** button, which is located to the right of the green plus button. The **Metadata** window will open.

5. Expand the **Filters** section, which will display the following full view of the **Metadata Explorer**:

Filters	
Metadata type:	Model ▼
Model:	Store ▼
Entity:	▼
Attribute:	▼

Metadata (Store Model)

Display: ○ Code   ○ Code {Name}   ○ Name {Code}

General Model Information   ◂ ▸

Attribute	Value
Name	Store
Code	18
Description	

6. Change the **Metadata type** to be **Entity**, which will display Metadata for entities in the Store model. Notice in doing this that the **Entity** drop-down changes to **City**, which is the first alphabetical entity in the model, meaning we get our **Description** returned successfully.

7. Change the selected **Entity** in the **Entity** drop-down to each of the other entities that we created, just to verify that the **Description** is returned successfully.

By changing the **Metadata type**, we can choose between the different types of MDS objects that support metadata, and view the metadata of these objects across any model (even though we are currently in the Store model) in the MDS system.

User-defined Metadata

While the built-in metadata is useful, as we have already highlighted, an MDM program may facilitate the need to capture more metadata than just an object's description.

Thankfully in MDS it's possible to create customized metadata for the objects that exist within the system Metadata model.

As part of our example scenario, we need to record the Owner of our entities, so that users understand who has ultimate responsibility for the entities. In order to do this, carry out the following steps:

1. Navigate to the home page and select the **System Administration** function.

2. Hover over the **Manage** menu and click on the **Entities** menu item.

3. Choose the **Metadata** model from the **Model** drop-down.

4. Click on **Entity Metadata Definition** in the grid, and then click on the pencil icon.

5. The view will now show the current attributes that can be captured when altering the Metadata of an entity. Click on the green plus icon, as we want to add an attribute.

6. In the **Add Attribute** page, enter the following:
   - **Attribute Type – Free Form**
   - **Name – Owner**
   - **Data Type – Text**
   - **Enable Change Tracking – Unchecked**

7. Save the new attribute.

8. Save the entity.

Now that we have added the attribute, we have a further administrative task to carry out in order to be able to use the attribute. The attributes that are displayed for entities in the Metadata model are governed by an attribute group. We need to add our new attribute to this Attribute Group. Carry out the following tasks in order to do this:

1. Remaining in the **System Administration** section, hover over the **Manage** menu, and click on the **Attribute Groups** menu item.

2. Choose the **Metadata** Model from the **Model** drop-down.

3. Choose **Entity Metadata Definition** from the **Entity** drop-down.

4. Expand the **General Entity Information** Attribute Group, and then click on the node.

5. Click on the pencil icon to edit the Attribute Group.

6. Move the **Owner** from the **Available** list to the **Assigned** list. Ensure that **Owner** appears above **Description** in the list, which will ensure the order of the attributes in the Explorer grid. The selection should be as follows:

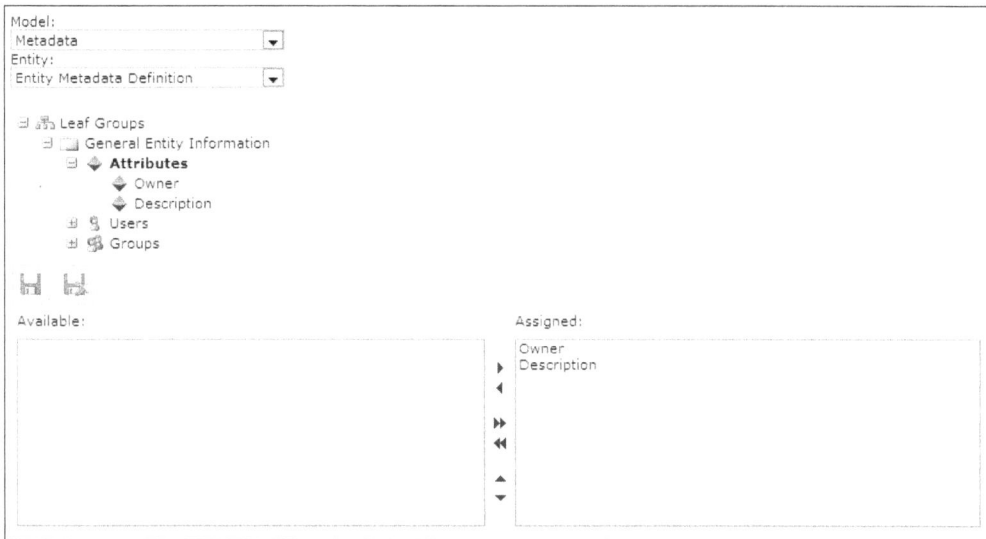

7. Finally click on the save icon to save the Attribute Group.

We now have the new attribute that we needed, and it's now assigned to the correct Attribute Group. Now our final task is to populate and view the attribute. Carry out the following steps in order to do this:

1. From the MDS home page, choose **Metadata** from the **Model** drop-down and choose **Version 1** from the **Version** drop-down.

2. Click on the **Explorer** function.

3. Click on the **Entity Metadata Definition** entity.

4. Click on the pencil icon, which will display the metadata for all entities in the system once more.

5. Edit the entity members in the grid that belong to our Store model. Set the owner attribute to yourself for the Store entity and to Joe Bloggs for the other four entities.

6 Return to the MDS home page and choose **Store** from the **Model** drop-down, and choose **VERSION_1** from the **Version** drop-down.

7. Click on the Explorer function, which will take us to the Model View screen.

8. Click on the **View Metadata** button, which will display the Metadata Explorer.

9. Expand the **Filters** section.

10. Alter the **Metadata type** to **Entity**. As shown below, we can already see that we have our **Owner** attribute added correctly:

Filters	
Metadata type:	Entity ▾
Model:	Store ▾
Entity:	City ▾
Attribute:	

Metadata (City Entity)

Display: ● Code   ○ Code {Name}   ○ Name {Code}

General Entity Information

Attribute	Value
Name	City
Code	18_66
Owner	Joe Bloggs
Description	Cities where Adventure Works retail stores are located

11. Change the **Entity** drop-down to each of the entities that are in our model and verify that the owner is populated.

We have now seen how it is possible to extend the Metadata Model within MDS for entities, and the same concept can be applied to attributes, attribute groups, hierarchies, and models.

Summary

We've covered a great deal in this chapter, as we've essentially looked at how to create and populate an MDS model from start to finish. Specifically we've learnt the following points:

- The model is the overall container object with MDS. The models, and all the objects that they contain, are created within the **System Administration** section of Master Data Manager.

- Entities are contained within models, and themselves contain attributes and Attribute Groups.

- We can view and also reverse transactions that have been made against entities.

- We can make annotations against members and against transactions.

- A Derived Hierarchy is a hierarchy that is built from the relationships that exist between entities in a model.

- An Explicit Hierarchy's members must all come from one entity, although Explicit Hierarchies can contain consolidated members.

- Collections allow us to create subsets of entities by taking specific members from Explicit Hierarchies and other collections.

- The system-created Metadata model allows us to record metadata about MDS objects, as well as creating our own metadata attributes.

5
Version Management

Version Management is the second function on the home page of the MDS Master Data Manager, where we can create different versions of our master data, which can be useful for archiving, testing, what-if, and auditing purposes.

In this chapter, we will walk through the MDS versioning features, applying changes to our example Store model.

The remainder of the chapter will cover the following topics:

- Introduction to versions
- Creating and managing versions
- Validating versions
- Locking, unlocking, and committing
- Flags
- Transactions

Introduction to versions

Versions are an integral part of working with models in Master Data Services. Each and every change that occurs to a model is carried out against a given version. So when, for example, you want to add a Member to an Entity, you must pick a version to make the change against. We've brushed over this until now, simply accepting the default version called VERSION_1 that always gets created when you create a model.

The changes that are made to one version (for example, member addition, updates or deletes, hierarchy changes) are not made to the other versions, meaning we can maintain independent copies of master data if we want to. This can help us with a variety of business scenarios, which we will now explore.

The need for versions

There are a number of reasons why keeping and maintaining separate copies of your master data can be useful:

- Business entity restructuring — Although business users will make minor changes to Master Data Entities from time to time, there will be occasions when corporate events will demand significant changes to an entity or model. For example, in the case of an Employee model that groups employees by management layers, the organization could introduce a new management layer, causing the model to change. In such an example, it would be prudent to be able to keep a copy of the old reporting structure to aid the full transition to the new structure.

- What-if analysis — In order to help make better business decisions, it may be useful to contrast different versions of a given master data entity against one another. For example, changing the structure of the Chart of Accounts will have a significant impact on the way that financial data is reported. If there are several options to consider, then creating several versions of the Chart of Accounts is an option. The different versions can then be combined with the financial data using the reporting systems, in order to pick which structural change is the best.

- Testing — Depending on the data governance process that surrounds your MDM implementation, it may be desirable to prevent users from accessing the "live" version of your master data, while changes are being made. Versions support this kind of control, as you can create a test version to carry out the changes, and then only allow users access to the live version while the changes are in progress.

The version interface

As we touched on briefly in *Chapter 2, Master Data Services Overview*, the Version Management function is accessed by clicking on the **Version Management** item on the MDS home page. Carrying out this action will take us to the following **Manage Versions** page:

We can see from the screenshot that there are three menus for us to choose from:

- **Manage** — This allows us to get to the **Manage Versions** screen (shown previously) and also the **Manage Flags** screen
- **Validate Version** — This allows us to manually attempt to validate the whole version
- **Review** — This allows us to review any issues that have arisen from validation, as well as to look at any transactions that have occurred

Version status

Looking at the screenshot again, there is also a grid that shows all the versions that exist within the currently selected model. One of the columns in the model is **Status**, which can have one of three values, namely:

- **Open**
- **Locked**
- **Committed**

When a version is open, changes can be made to the model by any users who have permissions to the relevant objects that exist within the model.

In contrast, when a version is locked, regular users cannot change the data within the model. Although regular users cannot change the model data, users with administrative access to the model can still make changes.

Finally, when a version is committed, no-one can make changes to the data within the model. It is also worth noting that a committed version cannot be reverted back to a locked or open status, meaning that it is permanently locked. A committed version can, however, be copied, so it is possible to create a version from a committed version. When this process occurs, the new version that gets created will have a status of open.

Creating and managing versions

There is no button to create a version in MDS. Instead, a version may only be created by copying another version.

> **Version configuration settings**
>
> By default it is only possible to copy a version once it has been committed. This may be fine for some implementations, but prevents you from running two open versions side-by-side. Thankfully, there is a configuration setting that overrides this behavior. The setting is called **Copy Only Committed Versions** and can be accessed via the MDS Configuration Manager.

Copying a version

The process of copying a version quite simply takes all the members that exist within the source version and copies them into the new version. The supporting structures that the copied members require, such as entities, attributes, attribute groups, derived hierarchies, and collections are all made available to the new version.

Regardless of the status of the source version, the new version that gets created will have a status of open.

In our example scenario, we have the situation whereby management wish to introduce some changes to the way in which our Stores are managed, by introducing a new level in our reporting hierarchy.

Carry out the following steps in order to copy the existing version:

1. If you haven't done so already, change the default **Copy Only Committed Versions** setting to **No** by using the Configuration Manager. We covered the Configuration Manager back in *Chapter 3, Installing and Configuring Master Data Services*.

2. After verifying the configuration setting, ensure that you are on the **Manage Versions** page, which you can reach by clicking on **Version Management** from the MDS home page.

3. By default, the single version that exists is not selected in the versions grid. Click on the only row that is shown in the grid, which will select the version, causing the row to be highlighted and several buttons to appear above the grid.

4. Click on the leftmost button, which is the **Copy Selected Version** button, as indicated in the following screenshot:

Manage Versions

Model:
Store

To edit a version, click a cell in the corresponding row. To edit a cell, double-click it.

Version #	Name	Description
1	VERSION_1	Version 1 for Model: Store

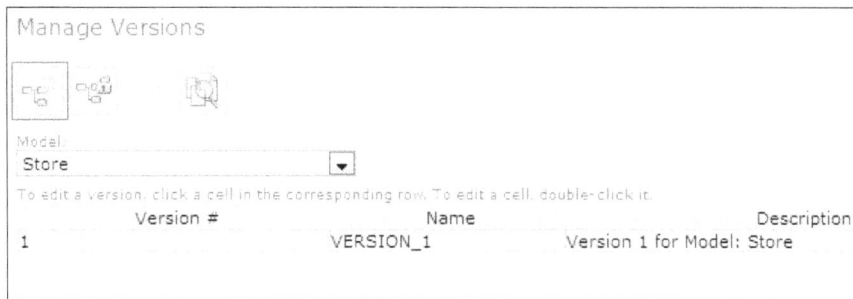

5. Click on **OK** to confirm copying of the version when the message box appears. There will now be two versions in the grid, as shown below:

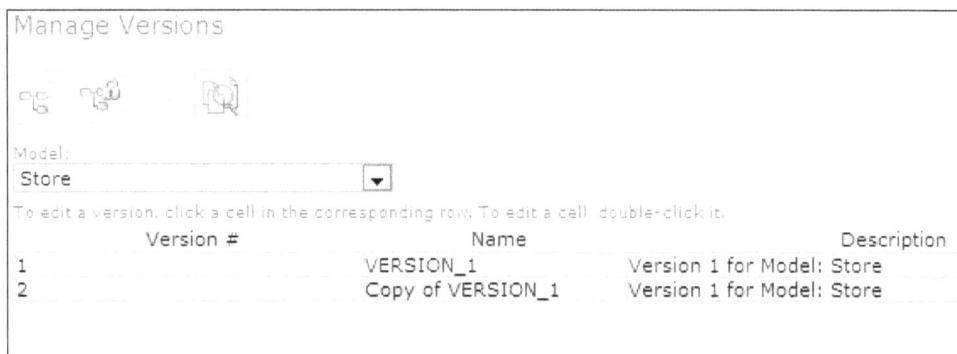

Manage Versions

Model:
Store

To edit a version, click a cell in the corresponding row. To edit a cell, double-click it.

Version #	Name	Description
1	VERSION_1	Version 1 for Model: Store
2	Copy of VERSION_1	Version 1 for Model: Store

Managing versions

Now that we have successfully created a new version, we will carry out some house-keeping tasks on our versions, before we look at how we actually use them.

Much like the Explorer grid that we've seen in earlier chapters for members, the version grid can be edited, albeit only two properties of the version, namely:

- **Version Name**
- **Version Description**

We will alter these two properties now, in order to give a more accurate description of our versions:

1. Remaining on the **Manage Versions** page, double-click on the first row in the grid, on the **Name** of **VERSION_1**.

2. Change the **Name** from **VERSION_1** to **2010_Stores**, as we want to give a more accurate description of what the version contains.

3. Double-click on the **Description** column and alter the description to be **2010 Store Structure**.

4. Repeat the process on the second row of the grid, entering the following values:

   ◦ **Name — 2011_Stores**

   ◦ **Description — 2011 Store Structure**

The version grid should now look as follows:

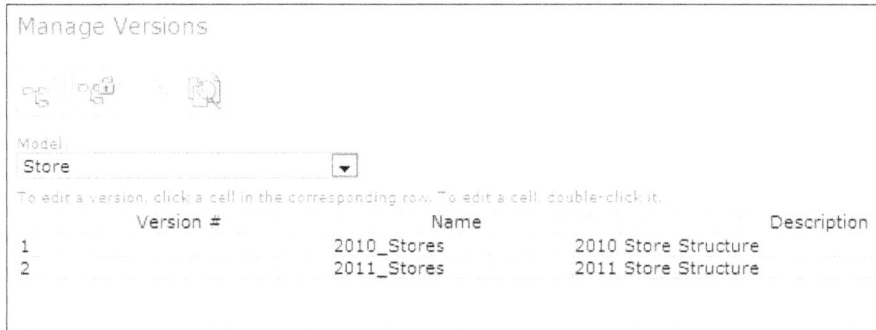

Manage Versions

Model
Store ▾

To edit a version, click a cell in the corresponding row. To edit a cell, double-click it.

Version #	Name	Description
1	2010_Stores	2010 Store Structure
2	2011_Stores	2011 Store Structure

Using versions

Having created and renamed our versions, we will now make some changes to a single version only, in order to demonstrate maintaining two separate versions of a model.

In our example scenario, we need to introduce a new reporting level for our Store Reporting hierarchy that we created in *Chapter 4, Creating and Using Models*. The new reporting level must only apply from 2011 onwards, so we will only make this change in the 2011_Stores version.

As a starting point, we need to ensure that we pick the correct version. To do this, carry out the following steps:

1. Return to the MDS home page.

2. At the top of the screen, pick the **2011_Stores** version from the **Version** drop-down, as shown next:

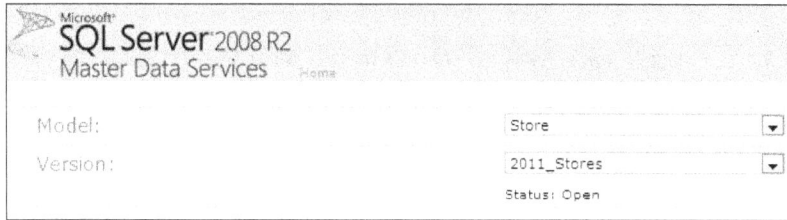

By selecting the 2011_Stores version, we will ensure that our changes only happen in that version alone.

Now that the correct version is selected, carry out the following steps in order to add the new reporting level:

1. Select the **Explorer** function from the MDS home page.

2. Within the **Explorer** function, click on the pencil icon to take us into the Explorer grid for the **Store** entity.

3. Click on the **Consolidated** radio button, which will display the following Consolidated Members that we added in *Chapter 4*:

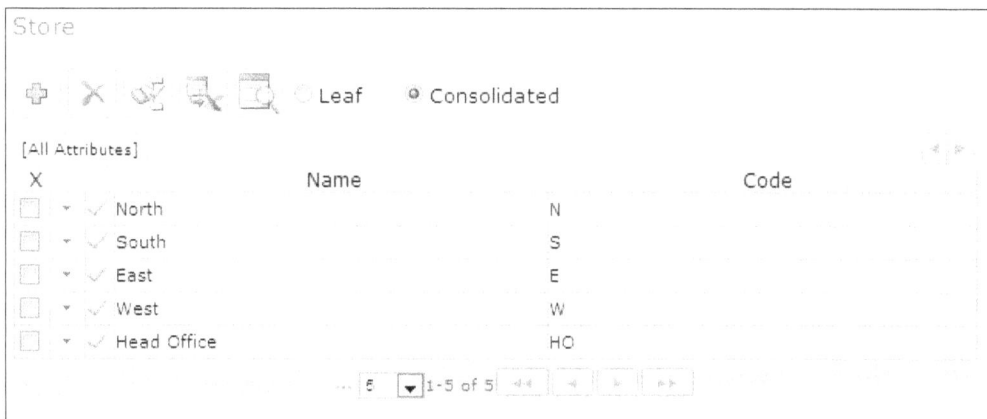

4. In our example scenario, there is a need to introduce an additional regional reporting center. Click on the green plus icon to start this process.

5. Enter the following values for the new member:
   - **Name — Central**
   - **Code — C**
   - **Parent — Head Office**

6. Click the save icon to create the new member.

7. Click the green back arrow to return to the member grid.

8. Change the **Member type** to **Consolidated**, which should now show the following members:

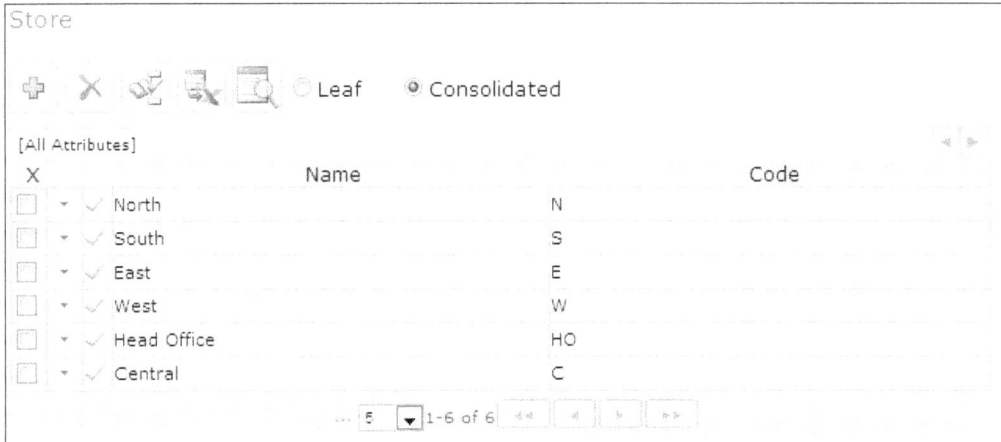

Now that we have a new consolidated member to use in our store reporting structure, we need to go and edit our Store Reporting Explicit Hierarchy to make use of the new member.

Carry out the following steps to alter the Store Reporting Hierarchy for the 2011_ Stores version:

1. Remaining on the same page, hover over the **Hierarchies** menu and choose the **Explicit Stores Reporting** menu item.

2. Expand the **Head Office** member.

3. Check the following three members:
    ◦ **AW Branson**
    ◦ **AW Cheyenne**
    ◦ **AW Denver**

4. Click on the copy button at the bottom of the screen, so that the **Clipboard** contains the following contents:

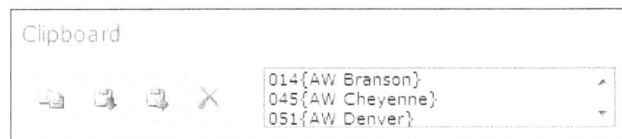

5. Click on the new **Central** member, so that its font changes to bold.

6. Click on the **Paste As Child** button, at the bottom of the screen.

7. Expand the **Central** member and verify that the contents are as follows:

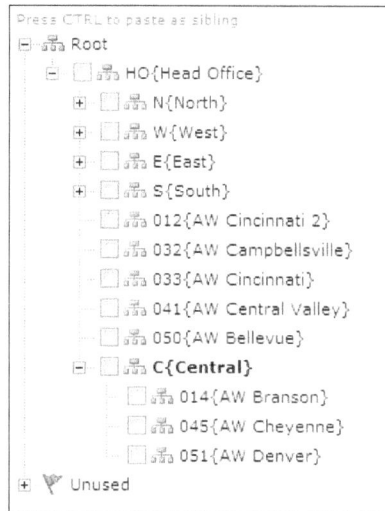

```
Press CTRL to paste as sibling
□ ‍ Root
    □ □ ‍ HO {Head Office}
        ⊞ □ ‍ N {North}
        ⊞ □ ‍ W {West}
        ⊞ □ ‍ E {East}
        ⊞ □ ‍ S {South}
            □ ‍ 012 {AW Cincinnati 2}
            □ ‍ 032 {AW Campbellsville}
            □ ‍ 033 {AW Cincinnati}
            □ ‍ 041 {AW Central Valley}
            □ ‍ 050 {AW Bellevue}
        □ □ ‍ C {Central}
            □ ‍ 014 {AW Branson}
            □ ‍ 045 {AW Cheyenne}
            □ ‍ 051 {AW Denver}
⊞ ⚐ Unused
```

Now that we have modified our new 2011_Stores version, we need to return to our 2010_Stores version to note the changes there. In order to do this, carry out the following steps:

1. Return to the MDS home page.

2. Ensure that the **2010_Stores** version is selected from the **Version** drop-down.

3. Click on the **Explorer** function.

4. Hover over the hierarchies menu and choose the **Explicit Stores Reporting** menu item.

5. Expand the **Head Office** member.

6. Notice that the hierarchy structure is as follows:

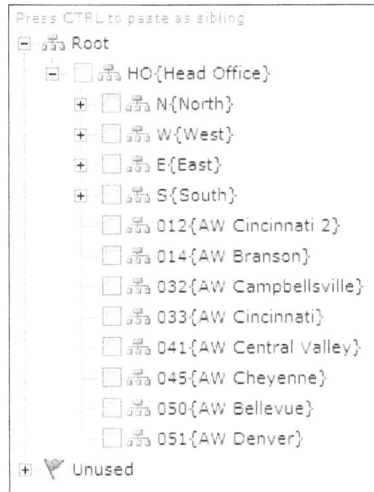

As shown in the above screenshot, the three members that we moved (**Branson**, **Cheyenne**, and **Denver**) are all in their original position, reporting to **Head Office**. In addition, the new member that we created, **Central**, is not present in the hierarchy. Furthermore, if you look at the basic Explorer grid for the Store Entity, you will see that the **Central** member does not appear whatsoever in the **2010_Stores** version.

The above means that MDS does not propagate member changes (inserts/updates/ deletes) from one version to other historical versions — they are independent. With object changes (for example, a new attribute or entity), the new objects are shown in the historical versions but they will not be populated.

In addition to just using the different versions in the front-end, MDS also supplies the ability to extract different versions, which is a process that we will examine in detail in *Chapter 8*, *Extracting Data From Master Data Services*.

Validating versions

MDS has a core concept known as validation, which is the process of running pre-defined MDS Business Rules against each member within an entity. We will cover the Business Rules that run as part of validation in detail in *Chapter 7*, *Business Rules and Workflow*.

Validation happens for a single member when a member is added or edited, and for all members in all entities of a model when the version is validated from the Version Management function that we are currently focused on.

Validation does not happen when changes to members are made directly in the Explorer grid. In this case, members are marked as awaiting validation, which is explained next.

Member validation status

The validation status of a member can be one of five states, namely:

- **Validation Succeeded**
- **Awaiting Validation**
- **Awaiting Dependant Member Validation**
- **Awaiting Re-Validation**
- **Validation Failed**

From within the Master Data Manger front-end, the Explorer grid is the place where it is possible to find out the status of an individual member. An icon is rendered in the third column of the Explorer grid for each member. In the example shown below, there is one member that has succeeded validation, one that is awaiting validation, and one member that has failed validation, as indicated by the "tick", "question mark", and "exclamation mark" icons respectively:

The changes that caused a member to fail validation (for example, perhaps a missing field) are still saved to MDS, but the member is clearly marked as invalid, as shown in the above screenshot.

It is only possible to commit a version when the entire version (that is, all entities within the model) has been validated completely. Therefore, in the above example, as there is only one member out of three that has been validated, it would not be possible to commit the version.

The validation status of a member is also useful when extracting data from Master Data Services. When extracting data from MDS, it is possible to determine a member's validation status, meaning it is possible to feed only the valid members to subscribing downstream systems. We will cover extracting data from MDS in *Chapter 8*.

Validating a version

Validating an entire version is necessary when:

- Data has been imported into MDS from a source system
- Business Rules have been added or changed
- Edits to members have occurred directly in the Explorer grid

We now need to validate our 2011_Stores version. However, before we do so, we need to ensure that some members in our version have a status of awaiting validation. To do this, carry out the following steps:

1. Return to the MDS home page.
2. Ensure that the **2011_Stores** version is selected from the **Version** drop-down.
3. Click on the Explorer function.
4. Once in the **Model View** section of the Explorer function, click on the pencil icon to display the Explorer grid.
5. Alter the **SquareFootage** attribute of the first three members to be **2500**, by editing the members in the gird directly. As the editing process has been carried out in the grid, this will cause the three members to have a validation status of **Awaiting Validation**, as indicated by the following orange icons:

As one of the Entities (namely Store) in the Store model now contains one member that is not validated, the version as a whole is considered not to be validated. We can now validate the whole version from the Version Management function, by carrying out the following steps:

1. Return to the MDS home page.
2. Click on the **Version Management** function.
3. Note that the **Version** column in the grid displays as **Not Validated**.
4. Click on the **Validate Version** menu, which will show counts of members that require validation, have succeeded validation, or have failed validation.
5. Verify that the **Model** is **Store** and the **Version** is **2011_Stores**.

6. Click on the **Validate Version** button, which is highlighted below:

```
Versions: Validate Version

 ⌐┐
 ⌐┘
 ✓

Model:
Store                          ▼
Version:
2011_Stores                    ▼


Validation Summary
To validate awaiting items, click the Validate Versions button.
              Status                    Member Count
Awaiting validation                  0
Awaiting revalidation                3
Validation succeeded                 282
Validation failed                    0
Awaiting dependent member revalidation 0
```

7. Click on **OK** for the confirmation message box that will appear. Validation will now occur asynchronously in the background and should take around 20 seconds, depending on the specifications of your environment.

8. Once the validation has completed, verify that the **Member Count** column only has values for the **Validation Succeeded** row of the grid.

9. Return to the **Manage Versions** page by clicking on the **Manage** menu item and verify that the **2011_Stores** version is now **Validated** in the **Validation** column.

As we will see when we cover Business Rules in *Chapter 7*, any validation issues that occur during validation are returned on the **Validate Version** page. In addition, we can view validation issues across different versions by looking at the **Validation Issues** page, which is found on the **Review** menu.

Locking, unlocking, and committing versions

We covered the different statuses that versions can have in the introduction of this chapter. We will now look at how the different statuses affect the versions.

Notifications

When any version changes status, an e-mail notification will be sent to any users that are Model Administrators, informing them of the change. This can be useful in order to keep administrators up-to-date with developments in the model.

Before we change the status of any version, we will make the necessary configuration changes for the notifications to work. In order to do this:

1. Ensure that the **Database Mail Profile** has been setup, as specified in *Chapter 3*.

2. Using Master Data Manager, click on the **User and Group Permissions** function.

3. If the e-mail address is missing or incorrect for your own user, carry out the following changes:

4. Click on the row in the grid that represents your user.

5. Click on the pencil edit icon.

6. In the tabbed interface, click on the edit icon again.

7. Alter the **Email** address to match your own e-mail address.

8. Click on the save icon to save your changes.

The setup of additional users, as well as their permissions will be covered in detail in *Chapter 10, Master Data Services Security*. For now, we have made the necessary changes to see the e-mail notifications working.

Locking versions

Locking a version will prevent users from making any changes to the version, but will continue to allow administrative users to make changes.

To lock our 2010_Stores version, carry out the following steps:

1. Return to the MDS home page and select the **Version Management** function. This will default to the **Manage Versions** page again.

2. Click on the first version in the grid.

3. Click on the **Lock Selected Version** button, which is highlighted next:

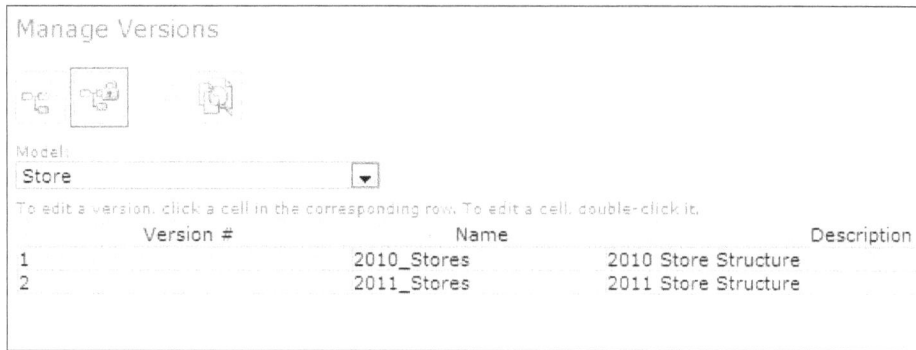

The status of the version will now be locked, meaning that non-Administrative users cannot make changes to the version.

As the status of the version has changed, we should receive a notification. This may not happen immediately, as the notifications are sent on a cycle. The frequency of the cycle is determined by a system setting called Notification Email Setting, which is an interval in seconds. Instructions on how to change the interval are provided in *Chapter 3*.

Once the interval has passed, we should receive the following notification:

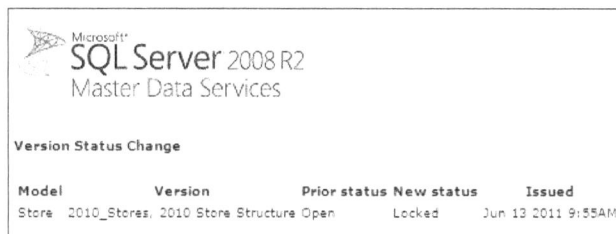

Unlocking versions

Unlocking a version will perform the reverse of the lock operation, changing the status of the version from **Locked** back to **Open**.

To unlock our 2010_Stores version, carry out the following steps:

1.   Ensure that you remain on the **Manage Versions** page.

2.   Click on the first version in the grid.

3. Click on the **Unlock Selected Version** button, which is now enabled (as the version is Locked) and is shown below:

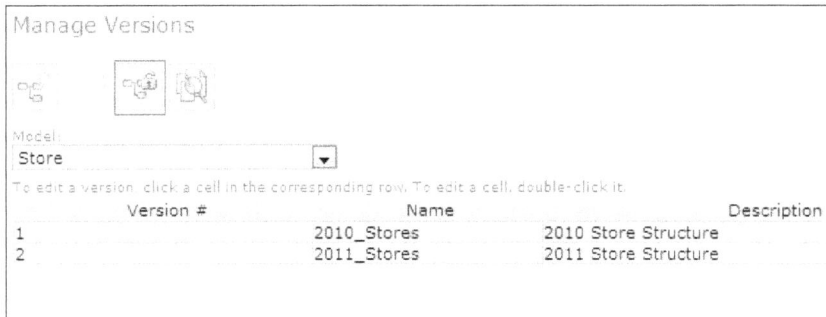

The status of the version will now be restored to **Open**, meaning that non-Administrative users can make changes to the version, as before. A notification should also be received, as we saw when locking the version.

Committing versions

To recap, committing a version makes the version read-only for all user types, including Administrative users. Furthermore, the committing process cannot be reversed, meaning that the selected version will always have a status of committed. Thankfully, a copy of a committed version can be taken, if changes need to be made to the data inside the version.

In our example scenario, we are 100% happy with our 2010_Stores version, so we therefore wish to commit it by carrying out the following steps:

1. Remaining on the **Manage Versions** page, lock the **2010_Stores** version again.

2. Click on the **Validate Version** menu.

3. From the **Version** drop-down, alter the version to be **2010_Stores**. Notice that the **Validate Version** button is disabled, whereas the **Commit Version** button is enabled.

4. Click on the **Commit Version** button, as shown next:

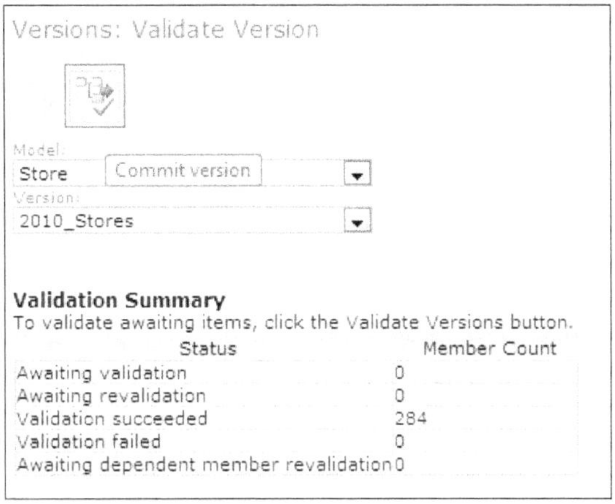

A message should be returned, stating that the version has been validated successfully, meaning that the entire version is now locked, without the ability to unlock it. In addition, an e-mail notification should be received stating that the version status has changed.

We can now see the effect that this will have had on the members in the 2010_Stores version by carrying out the following steps:

1. Return to the MDS home page.

2. Ensure that **2010_Stores** is selected from the **Version** drop-down.

3. Click on the Explorer function.

4. Click on the pencil icon to open the Explorer grid.

Notice that the entire grid is grayed out, as it is now not possible to edit any of the members, as shown below:

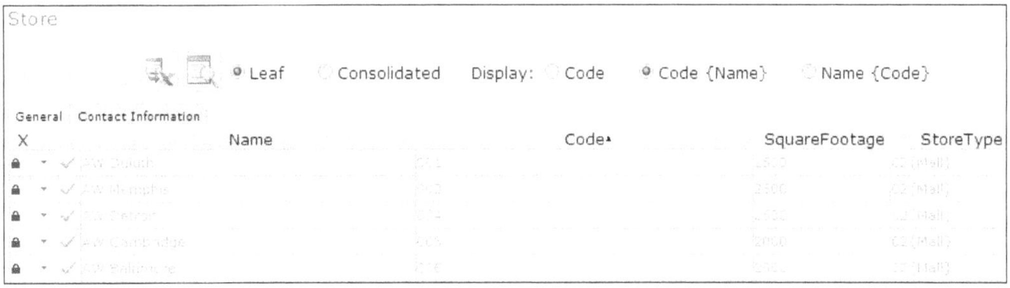

Managing Flags

Flags are indicators that can be associated with versions to provide an indication of what is contained inside the version. For example, a flag of "Current" could be associated with the latest version, to indicate to downstream application(s) which is the latest version, in a consistent manner.

Carry out the following to create a new flag and associate it with our latest version:

1. Return to the MDS home page.

2. Click on the **Version Management** function.

3. Hover over the **Manage** menu and choose the **Manage Flags** menu item.

4. Ensure that the Store **Model** is selected and click on the plus icon.

5. Enter the following values for the new flag:

    ○ **Name — Current**

    ○ **Description — The current Store Version**

    ○ **Committed Versions Only — False**

6. Click the save icon, which should result in the following single **Flag** being created:

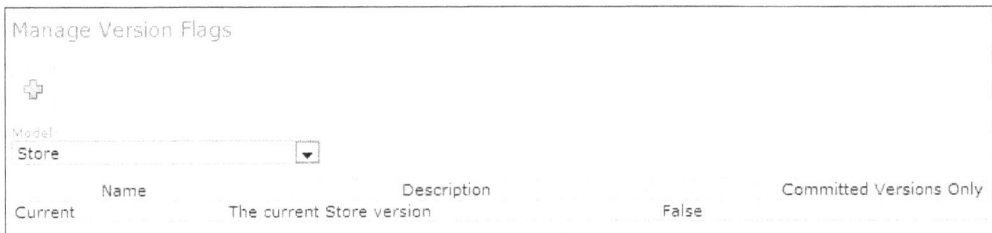

Now that the flag has been created, we need to associate it with one of our versions. To do this, carry out the following steps:

1. Hover over the **Manage** menu and choose the **Manage Versions** menu item.

2. Double-click on the **Flag** column of the **2011_Stores** Version, so that a drop-down appears.

3. Choose the **Current Flag**, as shown next:

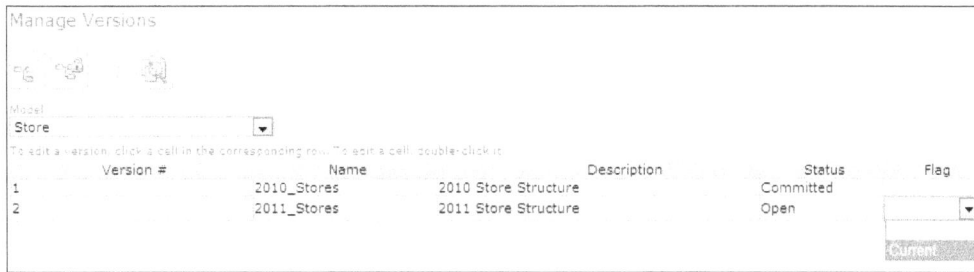

This process will now have associated 2011_Stores version with the Current flag, meaning that we know whenever we need to find the current Store version, we simply need to look for the Current flag.

We will see this process in action in *Chapter 8*, when we will extract members from a model by using the Current flag.

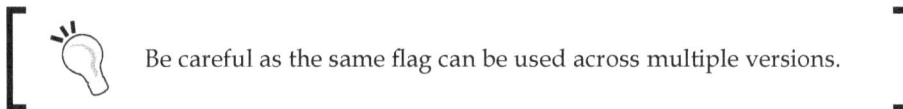

> Be careful as the same flag can be used across multiple versions.

Transactions

We covered transactions back in the previous chapter when we looked at the Explorer function, as the Explorer provides the ability to look at and even reverse the transactions that have occurred against an Entity.

This ability is present also within the Version Management function, but it takes transactions one step further, by providing the ability to choose a transaction within a specific version.

We will now use the Transactions page to view the differences in transactions across our two versions:

1. Remaining in the **Version Management** function, hover over the **Review** menu, and choose the **Transactions** menu item.
2. Choose the **2010_Stores** version from the **Version** drop-down. Verify that several pages of transactions are returned.
3. Change the **Version** to **2011_Stores** and note that only a handful of transactions are displayed, as we've only made a few edits in this chapter.

The same ability to annotate and undo transactions is present in the version's Transactions page, but the major difference is that it's possible to pick transactions across separate versions.

Summary

Now that we have finished the chapter, a summary of what we have covered is as follows:

- Versions are an integral part of MDS and are useful for maintaining separate copies of master data, for archiving, what-if, or testing purposes.

- A version can have one of the following statuses:

    - **Open** — Users can edit members within the version according to their Security permissions.

    - **Locked** — Only Administrative users can edit data within the version. A version can be unlocked, in which case it will return to a status of **Open**.

    - **Committed** — The version data will be permanently read-only for all users and cannot be reversed.

- We can create a new version by copying an old version.

- Validation causes the MDS Business Rules to fire, which will result in the members of a version being marked as valid or invalid, which will impact how external applications interact with the master data.

- Flags can be useful to provide an indicator to versions, which can help provide information to systems that get fed from MDS.

- As in the Explorer function, it is possible to view the transactions that have occurred to a version, and reverse them if needed.

6
Importing Data into Master Data Services

In *Chapter 4, Creating and Using Models*, we looked at the different objects that make up the Master Data system as well as how to add, edit, and delete single members using the web-based user interface. In this chapter, we will look at how to populate the MDS repository using the SQL Server Staging tables and how to automate this process using SQL Server Integration Services (SSIS).

We will extend the example carried out in previous chapters to include a walk-through of loading, updating, and deleting members.

In this chapter, we will cover the following topics:

- The staging load process
- Populating the staging tables
    - Creating new members
    - Creating new collections
    - Adding members to collections
    - Updating member attributes
    - Deleting members
- Invoking the staging process
- Invoking the validation process
- Clearing the staging tables
- Errors in the staging process
- Automating the MDS load process with SSIS

> All the example T-SQL scripts and SSIS package are available in the code bundle that accompanies this book

The staging load process

As we saw in *Chapter 4*, a key component of MDS is the web interface that allows you to add, edit, and delete members, attributes, and collections. While this interface is useful, it can be overly time-consuming when you are working with any more than a handful of members. Automating the loading of new and updating of existing records is an essential part of a system that incorporates any form of master data.

Master Data Services supports this automation in two ways:

- Inserting data into SQL Server staging tables
- Calling the MDS Web Service/API

This chapter will focus on the former method demonstrating how to use T-SQL and the stored procedures built in to MDS to populate the repository. MDS and the API are covered in detail in *Chapter 9, Application Programming Interface*.

Introduction

Populating the MDS repository with data from your source systems is carried out by loading data into one or more of the MDS staging tables, invoking the staging process, and then optionally validating the model. The following diagram shows a high-level overview:

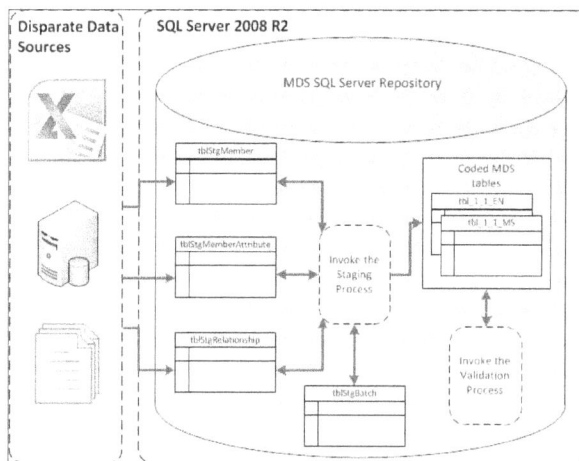

Once the process completes, the staged records will be either loaded into the appropriate model and entity, or marked as failed in the staging tables with a specific error code. Invoking the staging and validation processes can be carried out by either using the user interface or by calling T-SQL stored procedures. We will look at both the options in this chapter.

Staging tables

MDS provides three different tables for use in the staging process. Each table is used for a number of functions as listed next:

Table name	Function
tblStgMember	Create leaf member
	Create consolidated members
	Create collections
tblStgMemberAttribute	Update attributes values of existing members
	Update attributes values of existing collections
	Delete and "undelete" members
	Delete and "undelete" collections
tblStgRelationship	Add members to a collection
	Move members in an explicit hierarchy

A fourth table, tblStgBatch, is used to manage the current status of each batch of data.

Data import security

To be able to carry out the loading of data into the MDS staging tables, the user carrying out the process (or service if you are automating) needs the following MDS permissions:

- Model Administrator of the model you are importing into
- The integration management MDS function
- Permissions to insert data into the relevant staging tables

Populating MDS step 1—populating the staging tables

Populating the staging tables with your source data in the correct format is the core part of getting data loaded into MDS. Once this is done correctly, MDS (almost) takes care of the rest. The process is very similar for each of the staging tables and in fact each of the stage tables is used for more than one process. To understand how to populate the tables, it is important to look at the definition for each of the staging tables, and the uses of each field:

tblStgMember

Field name	Data type	Description
ID	bigint	Identity column used as internal key.
Batch_ID	int	Updated with the id of the batch once the staging process is invoked.
UserName	nvarchar(100)	The name of the user running the staging process batch in format 'domain\username' – *optional*.
ModelName	nvarchar(50)	The name of the model into which the row is to be loaded.
HierarchyName	nvarchar(50)	The name of the hierarchy into which the row is to be loaded – *optional depending on* MemberType_ID.
EntityName	nvarchar(50)	The name of the entity into which the row is to be loaded.
MemberType_ID	tinyint	The type of member you wish to load this row as: 1 – Leaf member 2 – Consolidated member 3 – Collection
MemberName	nvarchar(250)	The name for the member or collection you wish to create.
MemberCode	nvarchar(250)	The code (natural key) for the member or collection you wish to create.
Status_ID	tinyint	Current status of the row in the staging process: 0 – Ready to be processed (default value on load) 1 – Succeeded 2 – Failed
ErrorCode	nvarchar(10)	A code indicating the reason for failure (or success) of the row in the staging process.

The fields shaded in grey are for use by the staging process and should not be amended by the user.

tblStgMemberAttribute

Field name	Data type	Description
ID	bigint	Identity column used as internal key.
Batch_ID	int	Updated with the id of the batch once the staging process is invoked.
UserName	nvarchar(100)	The name of the user running the staging process batch in format 'domain\username'.
ModelName	nvarchar(250)	The name of the model in which the member to be updated is stored.
EntityName	nvarchar(250)	The name of the entity into which the row is to be loaded.
MemberType_ID	tinyint	The type of member you want to update the attributes for: 1 – Leaf member 2 – Consolidated member 3 – Collection
MemberCode	nvarchar(250)	The code (natural key) for the member for which you want to update the attributes.
AttributeName	nvarchar(250)	The name of the attribute you want to update.
AttributeValue	nvarchar(2000)	The value of the update you want to update. Note if this is a domain attribute this must be the member code of the corresponding domain attribute.
Status_ID	tinyint	Current status of the row in the staging process: 0 – Ready to be processed (default value on load) 1 – Succeeded 2 – Failed
ErrorCode	nvarchar(10)	A code indicating the reason for failure (or success) of the row in the staging process.

The fields shaded in grey are for use by the staging process and should not be amended by the user

tblStgRelationship

Field name	Data type	Description
ID	bigint	Identity column used as internal key.
Batch_ID	int	Updated with the id of the batch once the staging process is invoked.
VersionName	nvarchar(250)	
UserName	nvarchar(100)	The name of the user running the staging process batch in format 'domain\username'.
ModelName	nvarchar(250)	The name of the model in which the member to be updated is stored.
EntityName	nvarchar(250)	The name of the entity into which the row is to be loaded.
HierarchyName	nvarchar(250)	The name of the explicit hierarchy you are amending. Leave blank for collections
MemberType_ID	tinyint	Whether you are adding the member to an explicit hierarchy or to a collection: 4 – explicit hierarchy 5 – collection
MemberCode	nvarchar(250)	The code of the member you are updating.
TargetCode	nvarchar(250)	For collections, the code of the collection you are adding the member to. For explicit hierarchies, the sibling or parent you want to put your member against.
TargetType_ID	int	For collections this value should always be 1. For explicit hierarchies, use 1 to add the specified member as a child of the target member, and 2 to add as sibling.
SortOrder	int	Only used for explicit hierarchies. A unique number that indicates the position of a member under its parent.
Status_ID	tinyint	Current status of the row in the staging process. 0 – Ready to be processed (default value on load) 1 – Succeeded 2 – Failed
ErrorCode	nvarchar(10)	A code indicating the reason for failure (or success) of the row in the staging process.

The fields shaded in grey are for use by the staging process and should not be amended by the user

In our examples, we will use the 2008 R2 version of the AdventureWorks OLTP sample database. Our scenario sees our sample company having acquired a UK-based adventure store chain. We will load the newly acquired stores into our MDS repository, update attributes about those stores, create collections within the hierarchies, and delete members no longer required.

Creating new members

Creating new members in an MDS model is likely to be one of the more common processes you will carry out. New members are created by loading data into the mdm.tblStgMember table. As noted in the table definition in the previous section, a MemberType_ID of 1 will create a leaf member and a MemberType_ID of 2 will create a consolidated member. The differences between these two member types are discussed in *Chapter 4*.

In the following example, we will insert records as new leaf members from a view in the AdventureWorks database containing UK store details into the **Store** entity of our **Store** model. Note the MemberType_ID of 1 indicating we are loading new leaf members.

> In a production environment, to avoid duplication you may need to join your source data to a MDS Subscription View to ensure that you don't reload existing members, only new ones. Subscription Views are covered in detail in *Chapter 8, Extracting Data from Master Data Services*

```
/* Load new leaf members into the staging tables */
USE MDS -- replace with the name of your master data repository
GO

/* Declare the variables for use in the insert statement */
DECLARE @ModelName nvarchar(50)
DECLARE @EntityName nvarchar(50)

/* Set the variables appropriately */
SET     @ModelName  = 'Store'
SET     @EntityName = 'Store'

/* Insert records into the staging table */
INSERT INTO mdm.tblStgMember
(
        ModelName
        ,EntityName
```

```
            ,MemberType_ID
            ,MemberName
            ,MemberCode
    )
    SELECT  @ModelName       /* Load into the specified model    */
            ,@EntityName      /* Load into the specified entity   */
            , 1               /* create a new leaf member         */
            ,SA.[Name]        /* the member name                  */
            ,SA.BusinessEntityID /* the member code               */
    FROM        AdventureWorks2008R2.Sales.vStoreWithAddresses AS SA
    WHERE       SA.CountryRegionName = 'United Kingdom' /* only UK    */
```

After running your `Insert` statement, query the `mdm.tblStgMember` table to see your results:

```
    /* query the staging table to validate it's loaded correctly*/
    SELECT  *
    FROM        mdm.tblStgMember
    WHERE       Batch_ID IS NULL
    AND         EntityName = @EntityName
```

You will see that the `Batch_ID` field is set to `NULL` and the `Status_ID` is set to `0`. This indicates the records are now ready for staging:

	ID	Batch_ID	UserName	ModelName	HierarchyName	EntityName	MemberType_ID	MemberName	MemberCode	Status_ID	ErrorCode
1	11708	NULL	NULL	Store	NULL	Store	1	Bulk Discount Store	432	0	
2	11709	NULL	NULL	Store	NULL	Store	1	Prosperous Tours	534	0	
3	11710	NULL	NULL	Store	NULL	Store	1	Channel Outlet	588	0	
4	11711	NULL	NULL	Store	NULL	Store	1	Metro Metals Co.	596	0	
5	11712	NULL	NULL	Store	NULL	Store	1	Uttermost Bike Shop	602	0	
6	11713	NULL	NULL	Store	NULL	Store	1	Vigorous Sports Store	658	0	
7	11714	NULL	NULL	Store	NULL	Store	1	Rampart Amusement Company	810	0	
8	11715	NULL	NULL	Store	NULL	Store	1	Action Bicycle Specialists	856	0	
9	11716	NULL	NULL	Store	NULL	Store	1	Central Bicycle Specialists	868	0	
10	11717	NULL	NULL	Store	NULL	Store	1	Cycles Wholesaler & Mfg.	940	0	
11	11718	NULL	NULL	Store	NULL	Store	1	Number One Bike Co.	944	0	
12	11719	NULL	NULL	Store	NULL	Store	1	Riding Cycles	984	0	
13	11720	NULL	NULL	Store	NULL	Store	1	Leisure Cleaning House	1192	0	

To create a consolidated member instead of a leaf member, set the `MemberType_ID` to `2` and populate the `HierarchyName` with the name of the hierarchy you want to add the member to.

Creating new collections

As we saw in *Chapter 4*, a collection is a grouping of members that isn't defined by one of the existing attributes. Creating collections is very similar to the process for creating new members. The syntax is exactly the same, other than setting the MemberType_ID to 3, populating the MemberName column with the name of the collection, and populating the MemberCode column with a unique code for the collection. The syntax for this can be seen shortly.

In this example, we are creating a new collection for stores where we want to include a marketing campaign named "2011 Campaign Targets":

```
/* Create a new collection in the staging tables */
USE MDS -- replace with the name of your master data repository
GO

/* Declare the variables for use in the insert statement */
DECLARE @ModelName nvarchar(50)
DECLARE @EntityName nvarchar(50)

/* Set the variables appropriately */
SET     @ModelName  = 'Store'
SET     @EntityName = 'Store'

/* Insert records into the staging table. */
INSERT INTO mdm.tblStgMember
(
        ModelName
        ,EntityName
        ,MemberType_ID
        ,MemberName
        ,MemberCode
)
VALUES
(
        @ModelName      /* Create collection into the specified model*/
        ,@EntityName    /* Create collection into the specified enitity*/
        ,3              /* create a new collection                */
        ,'2011 Campaign Targets'   /* the collection name         */
        ,'2011CT'                  /* the collection code         */
)
```

Once again we can review the results of our `Insert` script by querying the staging table `mdm.tblStgMember`:

```
/* query the staging table to validate it's loaded correctly*/
SELECT    *
FROM      mdm.tblStgMember
WHERE     Batch_ID IS NULL
AND       EntityName = @EntityName
```

Adding members to collections

Once we have created a collection, the obvious next step is to add members to it. This is achieved by adding records to the staging table `mdm.tblStgRelationship`.

In the following example, we will add records to the staging table that will add two of our new stores ("Number One Bike Co" and "Metropolitan Bicycle Supply") to the "2011 Campaign Targets" collection:

```
/* Insert records into the staging table that
will add members to a collection          */
USE MDS -- replace with the name of your master data repository
GO

/* Declare the variables for use in the insert statement */
DECLARE @ModelName nvarchar(50)
DECLARE @EntityName nvarchar(50)

/* Set the variables appropriately */
SET    @ModelName  = 'Store'
SET    @EntityName = 'Store'

/* Insert records into the relationship staging table   */
INSERT INTO mdm.tblStgRelationship
(
        ModelName
        ,EntityName
        ,MemberType_ID
        ,MemberCode
        ,TargetCode
        ,TargetType_ID
)
VALUES
(
       @ModelName     /* Update collection in the specified model   */
       ,@EntityName   /* Update collection in the specified entity*/
```

```
      ,5               /* update a collection                  */
      ,'1844'          /* Code for Metropolitan Bicycle Supply    */
      ,'2011CT'        /* target collection code              */
      ,1               /* target type (1 for collections)         */
   ),
   (

      @ModelName       /* Update collection in the specified model   */
      ,@EntityName     /* Update collection in the specified entity*/
      ,5               /* update a collection                  */
      ,'944'           /* Code for Number One Bike Co          */
      ,'2011CT'        /* target collection code               */
      ,1               /* target type (1 for collections)          */

   )
```

As before, we can check our logic, this time by querying `mdm.tblStgRelationship`:

```
/* query the staging table to validate it's loaded correctly*/
SELECT      *
FROM        mdm.tblStgRelationship
WHERE       Batch_ID IS NULL
AND         EntityName = @EntityName
```

> The `mdm.tblStgRelationship` table is also used for adding and moving members in an explicit hierarchy.

Updating member attributes

As well as creating new members, the other more common use of the staging process will be to update attributes for existing members (or indeed new members that you have created in the same batch). This is carried out by loading records into the staging table `mdm.tblStgMemberAttribute`.

As we saw in *Chapter 4*, there are two main types of attribute: **domain** and **free-form**. When loading domain attributes, we obviously need to ensure that the values we are trying to set already exist in the entity that the domain attribute is based on. In our example, we will update the following attributes for our newly-loaded UK stores:

- City (domain attribute based on the City entity)
- Postcode (free-form)

In the following example, we first load records to `mdm.tblStgMember`, which will add new members for the Cities for any UK stores to the City entity to ensure the attribute update is successful. We then load records to `mdm.tblStgMemberAttribute` that will update the City domain attribute and finally load records to the same table that will update the Postalcode attribute:

```
/* Update attributes for the UK stores we have already loaded */
USE MDS -- replace with the name of your master data repository
GO

/* Declare the variables for use in the insert statement */
DECLARE @ModelName nvarchar(50)
DECLARE @EntityName nvarchar(50)

SET    @ModelName  = 'Store'
SET    @EntityName = 'City'

/* First we need to insert any cities we don't yet have as these will
be
required for the domain attribute   */
INSERT INTO mdm.tblStgMember
(
        ModelName
        ,EntityName
        ,MemberType_ID
        ,MemberName
        ,MemberCode
)
SELECT DISTINCT @ModelName    /* Load into the specified model   */
            ,@EntityName    /* Load into the specified enitity  */
            , 1             /* create a new leaf member          */
            ,MAX(SA.City)    /* the member name                  */
            ,LEFT(SA.City, 2) /* the member code - slightly crude
              generation of code but will work for his example   */
FROM        AdventureWorks2008R2.Sales.vStoreWithAddresses      SA
WHERE       SA.CountryRegionName = 'United Kingdom'
GROUP BY    LEFT(SA.City, 2)

/* Set the entity name back to store */
SET   @EntityName  = 'Store'

/* Now we Insert records into the attribute staging table to
update the city attribute of the store members */
INSERT INTO mdm.tblStgMemberAttribute
```

```
(
        ModelName
        ,EntityName
        ,MemberType_ID
        ,MemberCode
        ,AttributeName
        ,AttributeValue
)
SELECT DISTINCT @ModelName/*Update Attribute in the specified model*/
            ,@EntityName   /*Update Attribute in specified entity */
            , 1            /*update a leaf member attribute        */
            ,SA.BusinessEntityID/* code of the member to update    */
            ,'City'              /* the attribute name              */
            ,LEFT(SA.City, 2)    /* the attribute value             */
FROM        AdventureWorks2008R2.Sales.vStoreWithAddresses    SA
WHERE       SA.CountryRegionName = 'United Kingdom'

/* Then we Insert records into the attribute staging table to
update the city attribute of the store members */
INSERT INTO mdm.tblStgMemberAttribute
(
        ModelName
        ,EntityName
        ,MemberType_ID
        ,MemberCode
        ,AttributeName
        ,AttributeValue
)
SELECT DISTINCT @ModelName /* Update Attribute in specified model  */
            ,@EntityName   /* Update Attribute in specified entity */
            , 1            /* update a leaf member attribute       */
            ,SA.BusinessEntityID/* code of the member to update    */
            ,'PostalCode'        /* the attribute name             */
            ,SA.PostalCode   /* the attribute value                */
FROM        AdventureWorks2008R2.Sales.vStoreWithAddresses    SA
WHERE       SA.CountryRegionName = 'United Kingdom'
```

As we did when creating new members, we can query the staging table to check that the required records have loaded, this time querying the mdm. tblStgMemberAttribute table:

```
/* Retrieve the data from the staging table to validate it is loaded
correctly*/
SELECT      *
FROM        mdm.tblStgMemberAttribute
WHERE       Batch_ID IS NULL
AND         EntityName = @EntityName
```

We should see our newly added attribute rows in the table:

	iD	Batch_ID	UserName	ModelName	EntityName	MemberType_ID	MemberCode	Attribute Name	Attribute Value	Status_ID	ErrorCode
1	33616	NULL	NULL	Store	Store	1	432	City	Lo	0	
2	33617	NULL	NULL	Store	Store	1	534	City	Lo	0	
3	33618	NULL	NULL	Store	Store	1	588	City	Hi	0	
4	33619	NULL	NULL	Store	Store	1	596	City	Lo	0	
5	33620	NULL	NULL	Store	Store	1	602	City	Br	0	
6	33621	NULL	NULL	Store	Store	1	658	City	Ox	0	

Deleting a member (or collection)

Deleting a member or collection follows a very similar pattern to updating a member attribute and indeed uses the same staging table (mdm.tblStgMemberAttribute) to do so. MDS follows the good practice of never permanently (or "hard") deleting any data and instead the record in the table is marked as "De-Activated".

The process to de-activate a member is to update a system attribute of the member named MDMMemberStatus. This will prevent it from appearing in the MDS user interface. The example that follows sets the value of MDMMemberStatus to "De-Activated" for the store:

```
/* Insert a record into the staging table that will mark a member as
deactivated */
USE MDS -- replace with the name of your master data repository
GO

/* Declare the variables for use in the insert statement */
DECLARE @ModelName nvarchar(50)
DECLARE @EntityName nvarchar(50)

/* Set the variables appropriately */
SET     @ModelName  = 'Store'
SET     @EntityName  = 'Store'
```

```
/* Insert records into the staging attribute table. */
INSERT INTO mdm.tblStgMemberAttribute
(
        ModelName
        ,EntityName
        ,MemberType_ID
        ,MemberCode
        ,AttributeName
        ,AttributeValue
)
VALUES
(
      @ModelName     /* Update Attribute in the specified model   */
      ,@EntityName   /* Update Attribute in the specified entity  */
      ,1             /* update a leaf member attribute            */
      ,'013'         /* update the attribute with code '013'      */
      ,'MDMMemberStatus'           /* the attribute name          */
      ,'De-Activated'              /* the attribute value         */
)
```

As with previous examples you can query the staging tables to check your results.

It's important to note that deactivating a member changes its MemberCode to a random GUID. If you wish to re-activate it, you will need to query the MDS database tables to retrieve the GUID. The Master Data Services online documentation discusses in detail how you can re-activate the record at: http://msdn.microsoft. com/en-us/library/ff487056.aspx.

You can add as many records as you like to the staging tables before invoking the staging process but keeping your batches to reasonable sizes will be easier to manage.

Populating MDS step 2—invoking the staging process

Once you have loaded one or more of the staging tables with data, the majority of the practical work has been done. You can invoke the staging process using either the user interface or the T-SQL stored procedure. To understand what happens when the staging process runs, it is worth exploring exactly what happens in the MDS database when the process is invoked:

1. Data is inserted into one or more of the staging tables. The Batch_ID for each record will be Null and the Status_ID will be 0.

2. The `mdm.udpStagingSweep` stored procedure is called (either using the user interface or using T-SQL). This does the following:

   ° Calls the `mdm.udpStagingBatchSave` stored procedure that does a simple insert into the `mdm.tblStgBatch` table. This returns a `Batch_ID`.

   ° Updates any new records in the `mdm.tblStgMember` with the `Batch_ID`.

   ° Updates any new records in `mdm.tblStgMemberAttribute` with the `Batch_ID`.

   ° Updates any new records in `mdm.tblStgRelationship` with the `Batch_ID`.

   ° Updates `mdm.tblStgBatch` with the count of new records in each stage table.

   ° Starts a Service Broker conversation on the `microsoft/mdm/service/stagingbatch` queue.

3. The stored procedure `mdm.udpStagingBatchQueueActivate` associated with the queue `microsoft/mdm/queue/stagingbatch` is called. When this runs it does the following:

   ° Updates the entry in `mdm.tblStgBatch` with a status of 1 (running).

   ° Calls the stored procedure `mdm.udpStagingProcessAllReadyToRun` that:

       i. Updates `mdm.tblStgBatch` with a status of 3 (running).

       ii. Calls `mdm.udpStagingProcess`. This in turn:

           1. Calls `mdm.udpStagingMemberSave` that writes to the coded MDM table.

           2. Calls `mdm.udpStagingMemberAttributeSave` that writes to the coded MDM table.

           3. Calls `mdm.udpStagingRelationshipSave` that writes to the coded MDM table.

4. Sets the status to 2 (complete) in `mdm.tblStgBatch`.

The staging process is invoked for a particular model and version. Any records in any of the three staging tables that have a `null Batch_ID` and a `Status_ID` of 0 will be included in the staging process. You can begin the staging process using the user interface as follows:

1. Select the **Integration Management** function from the MDS home page.

2. Select the **Model** and **Version** you want the process to run for:

```
Unbatched Staging Records

Model:
StoreCh5                        ▾
Version:
VERSION_1                       ▾

Total member records:        0
Total attribute records:     0
Total relationship records: 0
```

3. The process icon is used to start the process. However, for the purposes of this exercise do not click this now as we will invoke the process using T-SQL in the following example.

While it is useful to be able to call the staging process from the user interface, it is much more likely that, as well as automating the load of the stage tables, you will want to automate the invocation of the staging process. Once again this is a case of calling a T-SQL stored procedure with the correct parameters. The stored procedure is named mdm.udpStagingSweep and its definition is as follows:

mdm.udpStagingSweep

Parameter name	Data type	Description
@UserID	int	MDS user id of the user running the process
@VersionID	int	Version of the model that you are loading
@Process	tinyint	Indicates whether to process the batch immediately or not

> Hint: The interval for the batch process queue can be set using the MDS Configuration Manager. This is discussed in detail in *Chapter 3, Installing and Configuring Master Data Services*.

Before calling the main stored procedure, we need to query the mdm.tblUser table to get the User ID of the user running the process and the mdm.viw_SYSTEM_SCHEMA_VERSION table to bring back the correct Version ID for the current version of our model we are working with. The staging process is then invoked using the following syntax:

```
/* Invoke the MDS Staging process */
USE MDS -- replace with the name of your master data repository
GO
```

```
/* Declare the variables to pass to the stored procedure */
DECLARE @RC INT
DECLARE @UserID INT
DECLARE @VersionID INT
DECLARE @Process TINYINT
DECLARE @ModelName nvarchar(250)

/* set the variables as required */
SET @ModelName =    'Store'
/* retrieve the correct user id for the user running the process */
SET @UserID =     (
                SELECT  ID
                FROM    mdm.tblUser u
                WHERE   u.UserName = 'domain\user'
                )
/* retrieve the id for the latest version of the specified model */
SET @VersionID =  (
                SELECT  MAX(ID)
                FROM    mdm.viw_SYSTEM_SCHEMA_VERSION
                WHERE   Model_Name = @ModelName
                )
/* set the process parameter to specify if we want the batch to be
processed immediately or added to the queue and process at the
next configured interval 0 = queue, 1 = immediate         */
SET @Process = 1

/* Execute the staging stored procedure passing your parameters */
EXECUTE @RC = mdm.udpStagingSweep
    @UserID
  ,@VersionID
  ,@Process
GO
```

As this is an asynchronous process (using Service Broker), the command should complete straight away but you may not see the results in MDS immediately. We can monitor progress of the batch by querying the batch table `mdm.tblStgBatch`:

```
/*Query the batch table to see the results*/
SELECT    *
FROM      mdm.tblStgBatch
ORDER BY  ID desc
```

We can see in the following results that the batch process for our batch has begun as the **TotalMemberCount** columns have been populated, but the batch is yet to complete as the **Status_ID** value is still set to **1**:

	ID	OriginalBatch_ID	MUID	Version_ID	ExternalSystem_ID	Name	Status_ID	TotalMemberCount	ErrorMemberCount
1	84	NULL	62A93A34-DA06-4E56-944D-81862752A2ED	10	NULL	StoreCh5_Unbatched	1	285	NULL
2	83	NULL	90168107-861A-43B4-85E2-E0B991C23156	8	NULL	FORMAT_Unbatched	2	4	0
3	82	NULL	82BCC4FF-E44C-4B2F-8B18-AE7765A09B7C	2	NULL	ORGANISATION_Unbatched	2	0	0
4	81	NULL	89B3CEAC-3BF6-49B0-8EC0-B756DEDC6468	2	NULL	ORGANISATION_Unbatched	2	19	1
5	80	NULL	822DDDDF-52E5-496E-8063-92B3A30739A4	2	NULL	ORGANISATION_Unbatched	2	0	0
6	79	NULL	C675AF9C-1802-4A95-9BE2-DE757899E2E2	8	NULL	FORMAT_Unbatched	2	25	4
7	78	NULL	D2CC3DBC-5A92-450D-B8C5-3C40F602D69E	8	NULL	FORMAT_Unbatched	2	263	0
8	77	NULL	E6EAE424-357C-41E3-8697-9B2FD5543B33	3	NULL	CUSTOMER_Unbatched	2	0	0
9	76	NULL	1D73E5FB-4FBF-46EA-8279-5DD33D3D7212	3	NULL	CUSTOMER_Unbatched	2	0	0

Hint: If your batch is taking longer than expected to complete (or indeed never completes) check that the Service Broker is enabled for your MDS database.

Once the batch completes (**Status_ID = 2**) we should check the **ErrorMemberCount** columns for our batch. Should these columns be set to zero, then our entire batch has completed successfully and we can review the changes using the MDS user interface. We should see that:

- The UK store members we loaded are shown in the **Store** list:

- The collection we created is shown in the **Collections** list of the Store entity:

- The stores we added to the new collection are shown correctly:

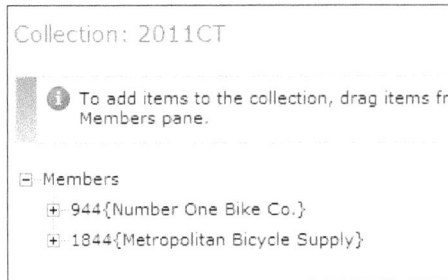

  Collection: 2011CT

  (i) To add items to the collection, drag items fro
  Members pane.

  ⊟ Members
  ⊞ 944{Number One Bike Co.}
  ⊞ 1844{Metropolitan Bicycle Supply}

- The city and postcode attributes for the new UK stores have been updated correctly:

  Store

  ⊕ ✕ ☑ ☑ ☑ ⦿ Leaf ○ Consolidated Display: ○ Code ○ Code {Name} ⦿ Name {Code}

  General Contact Information

X		Name		Code▲		SquareFootage	StoreType	City	PostalCode
☐	⋅	Leisure Cleanng House	1102			{}		Birmingham{Bi}	B29 6SL
☐	⋅	Area Sheet Metal Supply	1116			{}		London{Lo}	EC1R 0DU
☐	⋅	Tubeless Tire Company	1122			{}		Oxon{Ox}	OX14 4SE
☐	⋅	Express Bike Services	1140			{}		London{Lo}	SW6 5BY
☐	⋅	Exceptional Cycle Services	1152			{}		Basingstoke Hants{Ba}	RG24 8PL
☐	⋅	Little Sports Center	1208			{}		York{Yo}	YO3 4TN
☐	⋅	Commerce Bicycle Specialists	1220			{}		Berkshire{Be}	RG11 5TP
☐	⋅	Mail Market	1232			{}		York{Yo}	YO24 1GF

- And the store we deleted (**013 — Aw Burbank**) is no longer shown in the **Store** list:

  Store

  ⊕ ✕ ☑ ☑ ☑ ⦿ Leaf ○ Consolidated Display: ⦿ Code ○ Code {Name} ○ Nai

  General Contact Information

X		Name	Code▲	SquareFo
☐	⋅ ✓	AW Woodburn	010	2000
☐	⋅ ✓	AW Baytown	011	2000
☐	⋅ ✓	AW Cincinnati 2	012	2000
☐	⋅ ✓	AW Branson	014	2000
☐	⋅ ✓	AW Braintree	015	2000

Populating MDS step 3—validating the model

Once the staging process is complete, you can optionally validate your model to ensure that any business rules you have set up are applied, any members breaking these rules are marked as invalid, and notifications can be sent to MDS users if required.

As with all our previous steps, this can be achieved either using the MDS user interface or by calling a T-SQL stored procedure. Using the user interface to validate your model is covered in detail in *Chapter 5*, so we won't go over this again here.

> Important— If you call the validation process before the staging process is complete, some or all of your members may not be validated.

As with the staging process, the validation process is run for a particular model and version. The stored procedure for validating a model is called `mdm.udpValidateModel` and its definition is shown below:

mdm.udpValidateModel

Parameter name	Data type	Description
@User_ID	Int	MDS user id of the user running the validation process
@Model_ID	Int	ID of the model that you are validating
@Version_ID	Int	ID for the version of the model that you are validating
@Status_ID	Int	Whether or not to commit the changes

The syntax for calling the validation process is shown. This example will validate the latest version of our `Store` model:

```
/* Invoke the MDS Validation process */
USE MDS -- replace with the name of your master data repository
GO
/* Declare the variables to pass to the stored procedure */
DECLARE @RC INT
DECLARE @UserID INT
DECLARE @VersionID INT
DECLARE @ModelID INT
DECLARE @ModelName nvarchar(250)
```

```
/* set the variables appropriately  */
SET @ModelName =    'Store'
/* retrieve the correct user id for the user running the process */
SET @UserID =       (
            SELECT  ID
            FROM  mdm.tblUser u
            WHERE  u.UserName = 'domain\user'
            )
/* retrieve the id for  model */
SET @ModelID =      (
            SELECT  Model_ID
            FROM  mdm.viw_SYSTEM_SCHEMA_VERSION
            WHERE  Model_Name = @ModelName
            )
/* retrieve the id for the latest version of the specified model */
SET @VersionID =    (
            SELECT  MAX(ID)
            FROM  mdm.viw_SYSTEM_SCHEMA_VERSION
            WHERE  Model_Name = @ModelName
            )

/* Execute the validation stored procedure passing your parameters */
EXECUTE @RC = mdm.udpValidateModel
    @UserID
    ,@ModelID
    ,@VersionID
    ,1
GO
```

We can check the results of this process using the user interface:

1. Select the **Version Management** function from the MDS home page.

2. Select **Validate Version** from the top menu

3. Review the results on the validation screen as shown:

Once again, we can use T-SQL to carry out the process by calling a stored procedure named mdm.udpValidationStatusSummaryGet passing in the Version_ID of the model we validated. The syntax is as follows:

```
DECLARE @Version_ID int
DECLARE @ModelName nvarchar(50)

SET     @ModelName  = 'Store'

/* retrieve the id for the latest version of the specified model */
SET @Version_ID =     (
          SELECT  MAX(ID)
          FROM  mdm.viw_SYSTEM_SCHEMA_VERSION
          WHERE  Model_Name = @ModelName
          )

/* return the validation status */
EXECUTE [mdm].[udpValidationStatusSummaryGet]
    @Version_ID
GO
```

This will return the contents of the validation summary grid seen on the validation screen of the user interface:

	ValidationID	Count
1	0	0
2	4	0
3	3	324
4	2	0
5	5	0

However, as we can see from the results, we need to translate the **ValidationID** into a validation status type. These are as follows:

- 0 – New, Awaiting Validation
- 4 – Awaiting Revalidation
- 3 – Validation Succeeded
- 2 – Validation Failed
- 5 – Awaiting Dependent Member Revalidation

Clearing the staging tables

If you regularly load large amounts of data into your staging tables, you will want to clear them out on a regular basis as part of your SQL Server maintenance plans. You can do this easily for individual batches using the MDS UI as follows:

1. Select the **Integration Management** function from the MDS home page.
2. Highlight an individual batch entry in the grid on the staging batches screen.
3. Click the delete icon (circled in the following screenshot):

ID		Model	Version	Status	Started	Completed	Records	Errors
30	CUSTOMER unbatched	Customer	VERSION_1	Not Running	19/08/2010 11:42:42	19/08/2010 11:42:49	3	0
31	CUSTOMER unbatched	Customer	VERSION_1	Not Running	19/08/2010 12:10:42	19/08/2010 12:10:43	36	0
32	CUSTOMER unbatched	Customer	VERSION_1	Not Running	19/08/2010 12:24:43	19/08/2010 12:24:43	13	0
33	CUSTOMER unbatched	Customer	VERSION_1	Not Running	19/08/2010 12:29:43	19/08/2010 12:29:48	60	30
34	CUSTOMER unbatched	Customer	VERSION_1	Not Running	19/08/2010 13:16:43	19/08/2010 13:16:43	13	0
35	CUSTOMER unbatched	Customer	VERSION_1	Not Running	19/08/2010 13:23:43	19/08/2010 13:23:43	30	0
36	CUSTOMER unbatched	Customer	VERSION_1	Not Running	19/08/2010 13:35:43	19/08/2010 13:35:43	1	0
37	CUSTOMER unbatched	Customer	VERSION_1	Not Running	19/08/2010 14:46:43	19/08/2010 14:46:48	626	1
38	CUSTOMER unbatched	Customer	VERSION_1	Not Running	19/08/2010 15:35:44	19/08/2010 15:35:50	3039	0
39	ORGANISATION unbatched	Organisation	VERSION_1	Not Running	07/09/2010 13:32:32	07/09/2010 13:32:45	42	0
40	ORGANISATION unbatched	Organisation	VERSION_1	Not Running	07/09/2010 13:35:47	07/09/2010 13:35:48	42	0
41	ORGANISATION unbatched	Organisation	VERSION_1	Not Running	07/09/2010 13:43:14	07/09/2010 13:43:15	160	47
42	ORGANISATION unbatched	Organisation	VERSION_1	Not Running	07/09/2010 15:11:19	07/09/2010 15:11:26	1025	0
43	PRICECATEGORY unbatched	PriceCategory	VERSION_1	Not Running	07/09/2010 17:44:26	07/09/2010 17:44:37	56	20
44	PRICECATEGORY unbatched	PriceCategory	VERSION_1	Not Running	07/09/2010 17:46:50	07/09/2010 17:46:50	20	20
45	PRICECATEGORY unbatched	PriceCategory	VERSION_1	Not Running	07/09/2010 17:49:36	07/09/2010 17:49:40	20	20
46	PRICECATEGORY unbatched	PriceCategory	VERSION_1	Not Running	07/09/2010 17:52:24	07/09/2010 17:52:24	24	0
47	SEGMENT unbatched	Segment	VERSION_1	Not Running	07/09/2010 21:42:15	07/09/2010 21:42:28	28	14
48	SEGMENT unbatched	Segment	VERSION_1	Not Running	07/09/2010 21:45:16	07/09/2010 21:45:17	14	0
49	SEGMENT unbatched	Segment	VERSION_1	Not Running	07/09/2010 21:50:35	07/09/2010 21:50:35	30	0
50	SEGMENT unbatched	Segment	VERSION_1	Not Running	08/09/2010 13:42:09	08/09/2010 13:42:19	17	0
51	SEGMENT unbatched	Segment	VERSION_1	Not Running	08/09/2010 13:44:34	08/09/2010 13:44:35	15	1
52	SEGMENT unbatched	Segment	VERSION_1	Not Running	08/09/2010 13:45:30	08/09/2010 13:45:31	8	0
53	SEGMENT unbatched	Segment	VERSION_1	Not Running	08/09/2010 13:49:10	08/09/2010 13:49:11	52	0

Of course, this could be time consuming if you have many batches you need to clear. As with most MDS functions you can alternatively clear the staging tables by calling a SQL stored procedure—mdm.udpStagingClear. This can be run with a number of different parameters as described next:

mdm.udpStagingClear

Parameter name	Data type	Description
@User_ID	Int	MDS user id — when specified with relevant @DeleteType_ID only data loaded by the specified user will be cleared. Pass NULL for all user data to be cleared.
@StagingType_ID	Int	Indicates which staging table to clear: 1 — mdm.tblStgMember 2 — mdm.tblStgMemberAttribute 3 — mdm.tblStgRelationship 4 — All staging tables Note that this parameter is only valid with @DeleteType_ID of 0 and 1
@DeleteType_ID	Int	Indicates which records to clear: 0 — All records loaded by the specified user into the specified model 1 — Successful records (**Status_ID** = 1) loaded by the specified user into the specified model 2 — All records loaded by the specified user 3 — All records loaded in the specified batch (including the batch record in mdm.tblStgBatch) 4 — All records for the specified user
@ModelName	nvarchar(250)	The model for which stage records will be cleared. NULL by default. Note that this parameter is only valid with @DeleteType_ID of 0 and 1.
@Batch_ID	int	The batch for which stage records will be cleared. NULL by default. Note that this parameter is only valid with @DeleteType_ID of 3.

In our following code example, we declare and set the parameters and call the stored procedure to clear the required rows from the stage tables. By setting the @StagingType_ID parameter to 1, we will only clear records from mdm.tblStgMember. We are also setting the @DeleteType_ID parameter to 1 that in combination with setting the @ModelName and @User_ID parameters will ensure we only clear records that were loaded into the Store model by the specified user and were marked as successfully loaded:

```
/*Clear the MDS staging tables  */
USE MDS -- replace with the name of your master data repository

DECLARE @RC int
DECLARE @User_ID int
DECLARE @StagingType_ID INT
DECLARE @DeleteType_ID INT
DECLARE @ModelName nvarchar(250)

SET @User_Id =      (
          SELECT  ID
          FROM  mdm.tblUser u
          WHERE  u.UserName = 'domain\user'
          )
SET @StagingType_ID =  1 /* only clear tblStgMember */
SET @DeleteType_ID =  1 /* only clear records successfully loaded into
the Store Model by 'domain\user'*/
SET @ModelName =    'Store'

EXECUTE @RC = [mdm].[udpStagingClear]
   @User_ID
  ,@StagingType_ID
  ,@DeleteType_ID
  ,@ModelName
  ,DEFAULT -- Pass the default value (NULL) for batch id
GO
```

We can query `mdm.tblStgMember` once again to check that the records have been successfully cleared:

```
SELECT     *
FROM       mdm.tblStgMember
ORDER BY   Batch_ID desc
```

The results of this query can be seen in the following screenshot:

	ID	Batch_ID	UserName	ModelName	HierarchyName	EntityName	MemberType_ID	MemberName	MemberCode	Status_ID	ErrorCode
1	11423	84	NULL	StoreCh5	NULL	City	1	Birmingham	003	0	
2	11424	84	NULL	StoreCh5	NULL	City	1	Calgary	001	0	
3	11425	84	NULL	StoreCh5	NULL	City	1	Edmonton	002	0	
4	11426	84	NULL	StoreCh5	NULL	City	1	Chandler	008	0	
5	11427	84	NULL	StoreCh5	NULL	City	1	Augsburg	034	0	
6	11428	84	NULL	StoreCh5	NULL	City	1	Erlangen	035	0	
7	11429	84	NULL	StoreCh5	NULL	City	1	Frankfurt	036	0	
8	11430	84	NULL	StoreCh5	NULL	City	1	Grevenbroich	037	0	
9	11431	84	NULL	StoreCh5	NULL	City	1	Hof	038	0	
10	11432	84	NULL	StoreCh5	NULL	City	1	Ingolstadt	039	0	
11	11433	84	NULL	StoreCh5	NULL	City	1	Haney	018	0	
12	11434	84	NULL	StoreCh5	NULL	City	1	Langford	019	0	
13	11435	84	NULL	StoreCh5	NULL	City	1	Langley	020	0	
14	11436	84	NULL	StoreCh5	NULL	City	1	Metchosin	021	0	
15	11437	84	NULL	StoreCh5	NULL	City	1	N. Vancouver	022	0	

Errors in the staging process

If after invoking the staging process, it fails to complete successfully, the most common scenario is that the MDS database is not enabled for Service Broker. This means that any batches in the queue will never get processed. We can enable Service Broker on the MDS database using the following syntax:

```
-- Enable Service Broker:
ALTER DATABASE [Database Name] SET ENABLE_BROKER;
```

If the staging process completes successfully, but not all of your updates or additions appear in MDS as you would expect, it's possible that some of the rows failed to load. As shown in our previous examples of invoking the staging process using T-SQL, we can review the staging tables looking in particular for any rows that have a **Status_ID** of **2** indicating failure. Any row marked as such will also be marked with a code that indicates the reason for the failure (or success). The possible codes and their meanings are shown next.

Success codes

Any members marked with the following codes have been successfully loaded into the MDS repository:

Code	Description
ERR210000	The record was imported successfully.
ERR210012	A new non-mandatory explicit hierarchy relationship was created successfully.
ERR210013	A new collection member was created successfully.
ERR210014	The member was assigned as a child of MDMUNUSED successfully.

Warning codes

Any members marked with the following codes have been loaded into the MDS repository, but have been flagged with a warning as they either have made no changes or may have had data inserted into the field that wasn't required:

Code	Description
ERR210007	The assignment already exists. No changes were made.
ERR210030	The AttributeValue will not be assigned.
ERR210050	A hierarchy is not required when you are importing members into collections.

Error codes

Any members marked with the following codes have failed to load into the MDS repository. You should review the error codes and take appropriate action to resolve the issues:

Code	Description
ERR210001	The same MemberCode exists multiple times in the staging table. The first member with the MemberCode is created successfully, but the members with this error code are not.
ERR210003	The AttributeValue references a member that does not exist or is inactive. If you are updating a domain-based attribute, use a code instead of a name for AttributeValue.
ERR210004	The AttributeValue references a member that does not exist or is inactive.
ERR210006	The MemberCode is inactive.
ERR210008	The TargetCode is inactive.
ERR210009	The MemberCode does not exist.
ERR210010	The TargetCode does not exist.
ERR210011	When TargetType_ID is 1, the TargetCode cannot be a leaf member. It must be a collection or consolidated member.
ERR210015	For the non-mandatory hierarchy, the MemberCode exists multiple times in the staging table.
ERR210016	The relationship could not be created because it would cause a circular reference.
ERR210017	The UserName is not valid.
ERR210018	The ModelName is missing or not valid.
ERR210019	You must be a model administrator.

Code	Description
ERR210020	The EntityName is missing or is not valid.
ERR210021	The MemberType_ID is not valid. Use 1 for leaf, 2 for consolidated (parent), or 3 for collection.
ERR210022	You cannot update system attributes.
ERR210023	You cannot update file attributes.
ERR210024	The AttributeValue is too long.
ERR210025	The AttributeValue must be a number.
ERR210026	The AttributeValue must be a date.
ERR210027	The AttributeValue must be an integer.
ERR210028	The AttributeName is missing or is not valid.
ERR210029	The AttributeValue is missing.
ERR210031	When you change the MDMMemberStatus attribute, the AttributeValue must be either "Active" or "De-Activated".
ERR210032	The HierarchyName is required if MemberType_ID is 2. You must designate which explicit hierarchy the member belongs to.
ERR210033	The entity is not enabled for collections.
ERR210034	The MemberCode is a reserved word and is not valid.
ERR210035	Because a code generation business rule does not exist, the MemberCode is required.
ERR210036	Because a code generation business rule exists, the MemberCode is not required.
ERR210037	The MemberType_ID is not valid. Use 1 for leaf, 2 for consolidated (parent), or 3 for collection.
ERR210038	The HierarchyName is required when the MemberType_ID is 4. When you are updating relationships in an explicit hierarchy, you must include the hierarchy name.
ERR210039	The MemberType_ID must be 4 (hierarchy relationship) or 5 (collection relationship).
ERR210040	MemberCode is required.
ERR210041	ROOT is not a valid MemberCode.
ERR210042	MDMUNUSED is not a valid MemberCode.
ERR210043	The TargetType_ID must be 1 (parent) or 2 (sibling).
ERR210044	The TargetCode does not exist.
ERR210045	MDMUNUSED is a reserved word and is not valid.
ERR210046	The member cannot be a sibling of Root.
ERR210047	The member cannot be a sibling of Unused.
ERR210048	MemberCode and TargetCode cannot be the same.

Code	Description
ERR210049	The `TargetType_ID` must be 1 (parent) when staging collection relationships.
ERR210051	The `ObjectID` cannot be updated because it is a system attribute.
ERR210052	The `MemberCode` cannot be deactivated because it is used as a domain-based attribute value.
ERR210053	The relationship could not be created because it would cause a circular reference.
ERR210054	An unknown error occurred when staging attribute values.
ERR210055	An unknown error occurred when staging attribute members.
ERR300001	The file attribute cannot be saved.
ERR300002	The member code is not valid.
ERR300003	The member code already exists.

Automating the MDS load process with SSIS

Master Data Services does not include the functionality to import data itself. This can be carried out using another component of SQL Server: **SQL Server Integration Services** (**SSIS**). SSIS is an enterprise-level extract, transform, and load (ETL) tool that compliments MDS well. There are many books and a huge amount of information already available about SSIS, so we won't be covering any "how-to" information on the product itself. Instead, we will look at the process of building a package to load data into MDS and invoke the staging and validation processes. The exercise assumes you are competent in building basic SSIS packages.

The package will essentially follow the process we have already discussed in detail in this chapter— automating the SQL scripts already developed. As we have already loaded the new stores from the UK in our example, this time we will add new acquisitions from France into the store entity, and update the `City` (domain) and `PostalCode` (free-form) attributes of those stores. The build of the package has a number of steps, but once created it will provide a sound template for loading data into MDS:

1. Start a new SSIS project using Visual Studio, save in a suitable location, and rename the default package as required:

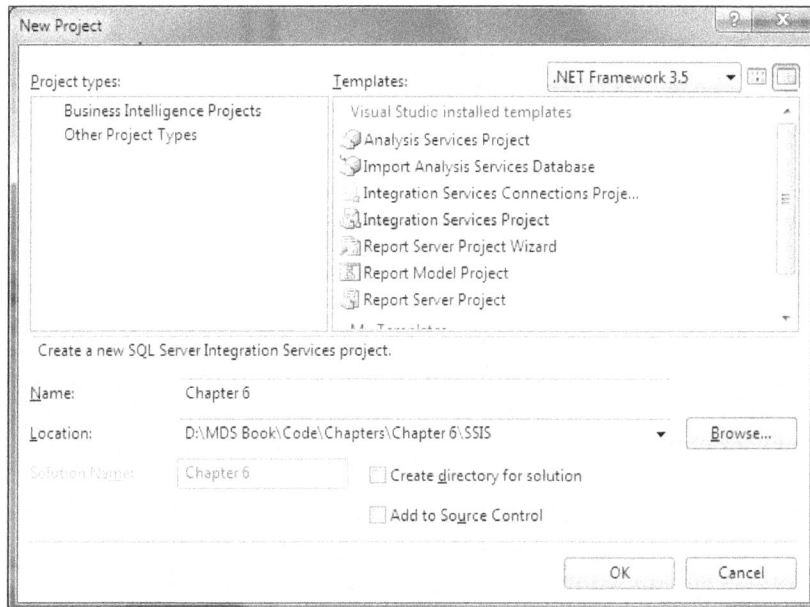

2. Create two new connection managers as follows:

Name:	AdventureWorksOLTP
Provider:	OLE DB
Server:	[Your SQL Server]
Database:	AdventureWorks2008R2

Name:	MDSRepository
Provider:	OLE DB
Server:	[Your SQL Server]
Database:	[Your MDS Database]

3. Create the following variables in your package:

Name	Scope	Data type	Value	Description
blnClearStage	Package	Boolean	False	Whether or not to clear the stage tables
dtMDSLoopTimer	Package	DateTime	[Empty]	Date for use with the staging process timeout
intMDSTimeout	Package	Int32	5	Timeout for the staging process to complete (minutes)
strMDSBatchStatus	Package	Byte		Used to store the batch Status_ID
strMDSEntityName	Package	String	Store	The name of the model we are staging
strMDSModel	Package	String	Store	The name of the entity we are staging
strMDSUser	Package	String	[Domain\User]	The domain and username of the MDS user running the package

As with our SQL examples, the first thing we need to do in the package is load the staging tables.

4. Add a data flow task to your control flow, rename it to "Load data to staging tables", and switch to the data flow tab.

5. Add two further variables to your package as follows:

Name	Scope	Data Type	Value	Description
strMDSAttribute1	Data flow	String	City	The name of the 1st attribute we will set
strMDSAttribute2	Data flow	String	PostalCode	The name of the 2nd attribute we will set

6. Add an OLE DB source to your data flow, set the properties as:

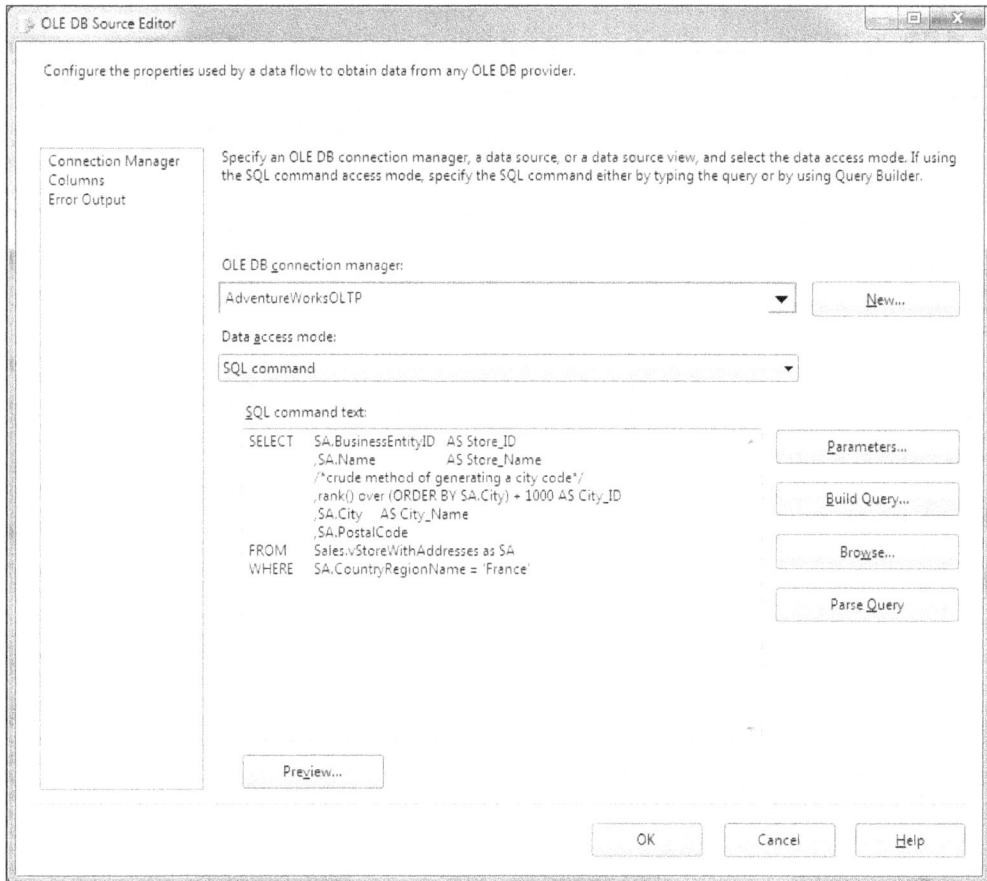

This will return the following columns to our data flow:

- ° `Store_ID`
- ° `Store_Name`
- ° `City_ID`
- ° `City_Name`
- ° `PostalCode`

> You can find this SQL syntax for the data source (and completed SSIS package) in the files that accompany this book.

To add any additional columns we need for all the staging tables, we will use a **Derived Column Transformation**.

7. Add a Derived Column Transform after the data source that will add the name of the model and the MDS user using the variables we created in step 3. Add the two new columns as shown:

Derived Column Name	Derived Column	Expression
Model_Name	<Add as new column>	@[User::strMDSModel]
User_Name	<Add as new column>	@[User::strMDSUser]

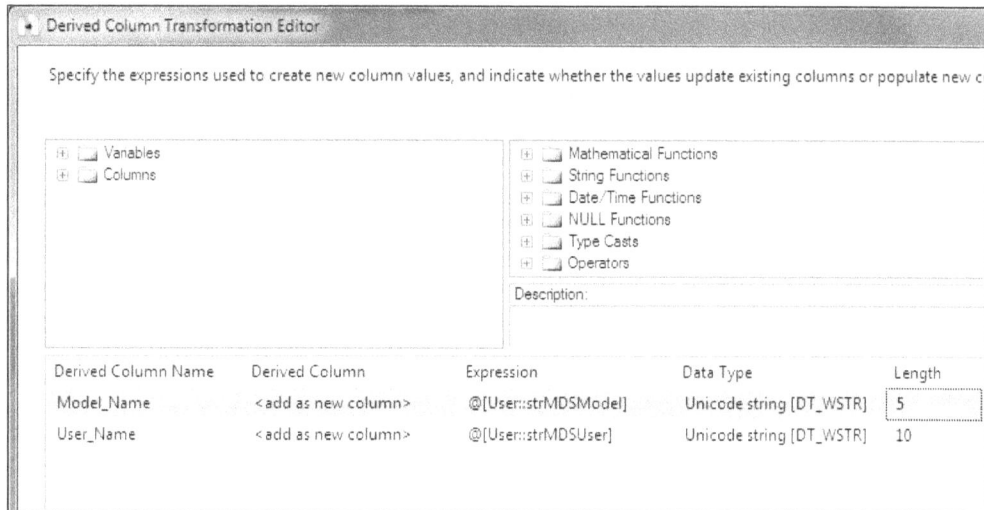

At this point we will "multicast" the data so that we can use the same source record to enter multiple target rows in our staging tables. We will use the output of the multicast four times (Store members, City members, City attribute of Store, PostalCode attribute of Store).

8. Add a Multicast Transformation following the Derived Column Transformation added in the previous step (no configuration necessary).At this point your data flow should appear as shown:

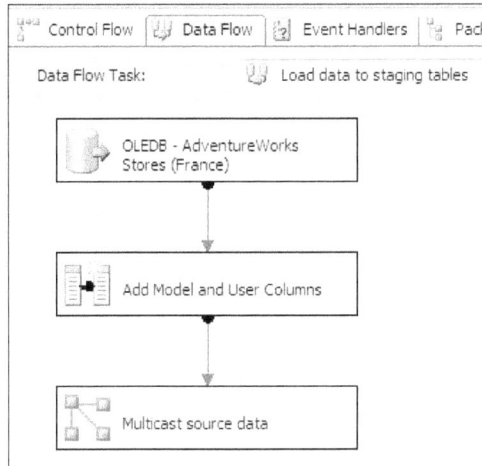

Next we need to add the additional columns required that are specific to each insert into the staging destinations.

9. Add a Derived Column Transformation to the first output of the Multicast. Rename the Transformation to "Add Store member Information" and set the derived column values as follows:

Derived Column Name	Derived Column	Expression
EntityName	<Add as new column>	@[User::strMDSEntityName]
MemberType_ID	<Add as new column>	1

10. Add a Derived Column Transformation to the second output of the Multicast. Rename the Transformation to "Add City member Information" and set the derived column values as follows:

Derived Column Name	Derived Column	Expression
EntityName	<Add as new column>	@[User::strMDSAttribute1]
MemberType_ID	<Add as new column>	1

11. Add a Derived Column Transformation to the third output of the Multicast. Rename the Transformation to "Add City attribute Information" and set the derived column values as follows:

Derived Column Name	Derived Column	Expression
AttributeName	<Add as new column>	@[User::strMDSAttribute1]
EntityName	<Add as new column>	@[User::strMDSEntityName]
MemberType_ID	<Add as new column>	1

12. Add a Derived Column Transformation to the fourth output of the Multicast. Rename the Transformation to "Add PostalCode attribute Information" and set the derived column values as follows:

Derived Column Name	Derived Column	Expression
AttributeName	<Add as new column>	@[User::strMDSAttribute2]
EntityName	<Add as new column>	@[User::strMDSEntityName]
MemberType_ID	<Add as new column>	1

We now have all the columns we need to insert data into the staging tables and can set up the (four) required Data destinations.

13. Add an OLE DB Data Destination to the first Derived Column Transformation "Add Store member Information" and set the properties to connect to `mdm.tblStgMember` in the MDS Repository using fast load as shown. This will add the records for our French stores:

13. Set the column mappings as follows:

Input Column	Destination Column
<ignore>	ID
<ignore>	Batch_ID
UserName	UserName
ModelName	ModelName
<ignore>	HierarchyName
EntityName	EntityName
MemberType_ID	MemberType_ID
Store_Name	MemberName
Store_ID	MemberCode
<ignore>	Status_ID
<ignore>	ErrorCode

14. Add an OLE DB Data Destination following the second Derived Column Transformation "Add City member Information" and set the properties to connect to `mdm.tblStgMember` in the MDS Repository using fast load as shown in step 13. This will add the records for the city members to so that we can set the City attribute of our French stores.

15. Set the column mappings as follows (note the change to member name and code to the city fields):

Input column	Destination column
<ignore>	ID
<ignore>	Batch_ID
UserName	UserName
ModelName	ModelName
<ignore>	HierarchyName
EntityName	EntityName
MemberType_ID	MemberType_ID
City_Name	MemberName
City_ID	MemberCode
<ignore>	Status_ID
<ignore>	ErrorCode

16. Add an OLE DB Data Destination following the third Derived Column Transformation "Add City attribute Information" and set the properties to connect to `mdm.tblStgMemberAttribute` in the MDS Repository using fast load as shown. This will add the records that will update the `City` attribute of our French stores:

17. Set the column mappings as follows (note the mapping of the `City_ID` to the `AttributeValue`):

Input column	Destination column
`<ignore>`	`ID`
`<ignore>`	`Batch_ID`
`UserName`	`UserName`
`ModelName`	`ModelName`
`EntityName`	`EntityName`
`MemberType_ID`	`MemberType_ID`
`Store_ID`	`MemberCode`
`AttributeName`	`AttributeName`
`City_ID`	`AttributeValue`
`<ignore>`	`Status_ID`
`<ignore>`	`ErrorCode`

18. Add an OLE DB Data Destination following the fourth Derived Column Transformation "Add PostalCode attribute Information" and set the properties to connect to `mdm.tblStgMemberAttribute` in the MDS Repository using fast load as shown in step 17. This will add the records that will update the `PostalCode` attribute of our French stores.

19. Set the column mappings as follows (note the mapping of `PostalCode` to the `AttributeValue`):

Input column	Destination column
`<ignore>`	`ID`
`<ignore>`	`Batch_ID`
`UserName`	`UserName`
`ModelName`	`ModelName`
`EntityName`	`EntityName`
`MemberType_ID`	`MemberType_ID`
`Store_ID`	`MemberCode`
`AttributeName`	`AttributeName`
`PostalCode`	`AttributeValue`
`<ignore>`	`Status_ID`
`<ignore>`	`ErrorCode`

Complete the data flow by resizing and laying out the tasks and adding appropriate annotations. Your final data flow should now appear similar to the following:

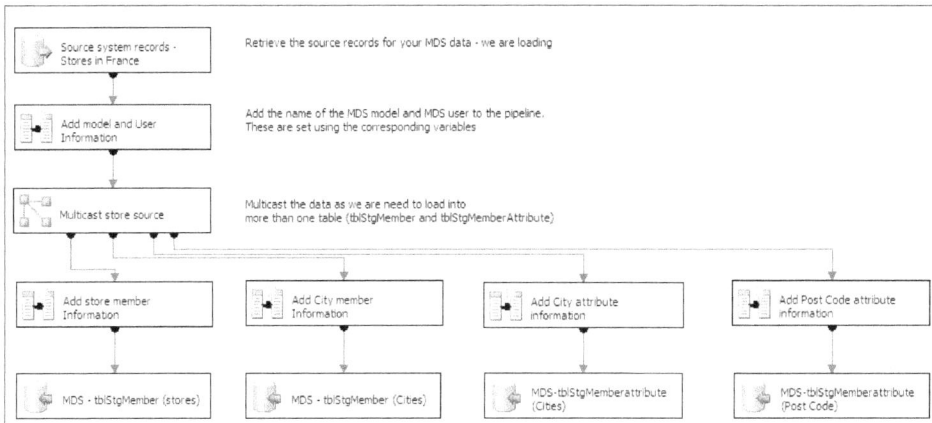

The completed data flow should see the staging tables loaded with all the relevant data leaving us to add the tasks to invoke the staging process and validate the data flow

20. Return to the control flow of the package.

21. Add an Execute SQL task to your control flow as a successor to your data flow. Rename this task " Invoke the Staging Process".

22. Configure the task to use the MDS Repository connection and set the SQLStatement property as follows:

```
DECLARE @ModelName nVarchar(50) = ?
DECLARE @UserName nvarchar(50)= ?
DECLARE @User_ID int
DECLARE @Version_ID int

SET @User_ID =      (SELECT ID
                     FROM  mdm.tblUser u
                     WHERE u.UserName = @UserName )

SET @Version_ID = (SELECT MAX(ID)
                     FROM mdm.viw_SYSTEM_SCHEMA_VERSION
                     WHERE Model_Name = @ModelName)


EXECUTE mdm.udpStagingSweep @User_ID, @Version_ID, 1
```

As you can see, this is almost identical to the syntax we used in our example to invoke the staging process earlier in the chapter. The only difference is the use of ? to indicate parameters in out SQL statement.

23. Configure the parameter mapping of the Execute SQL task as shown:

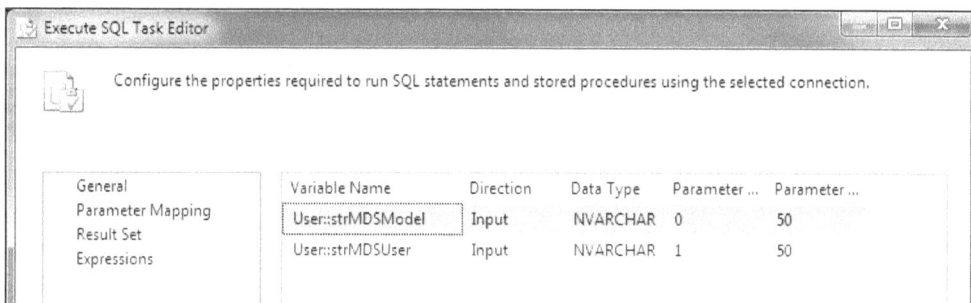

That is all that is required to start the staging process. As discussed previously, the staging process is asynchronous so before we can continue, we need to check the status of the process at regular intervals. There are a number of ways you can do this using SSIS—in our example, we will use a For Loop Container that will check the status of the batch by querying the batch table. To ensure that this loop doesn't run infinitely (if the process doesn't succeed) we will also add a timeout to the loop set using the intMDSTimeout variable created at the beginning of the package.

24. Add a `For Loop` Container to your control flow as a successor to the " Invoke the Staging Process" Execute SQL task.

25. Add an Execute SQL task inside the For Loop task and rename it "Get Batch Status".

26. Configure the task to use the `MDS Repository` connection, set the **Result Set** to a type of `Single Row`, and set the `SQLStatement` property as follows:

```
DECLARE @Version_ID int

--Get the current version name based on the model name
SET @Version_ID = (SELECT MAX(ID)
                   FROM mdm.viw_SYSTEM_SCHEMA_VERSION
                   WHERE Model_Name = ?)

--Get the status based on the version
SELECT TOP  1 Status_ID
FROM        mdm.tblStgBatch
WHERE       Version_ID = @Version_ID
ORDER BY    ID DESC
```

27. Set the parameter mapping of the task as shown below:

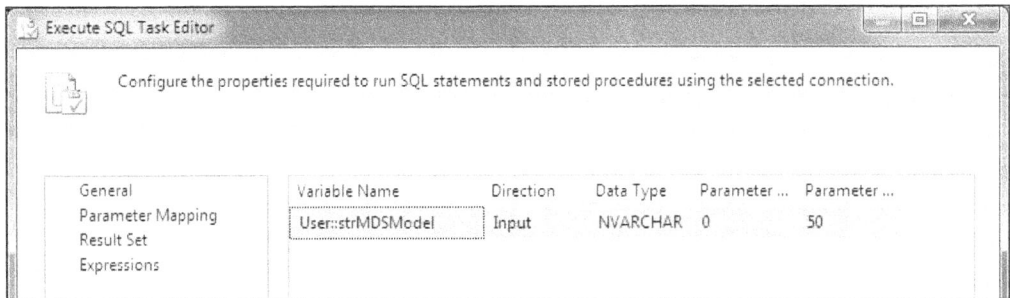

28. Set the **Result Set** to pass the **Status_ID** returned from the query to the `strMDSBatchStatus` variable we created earlier.

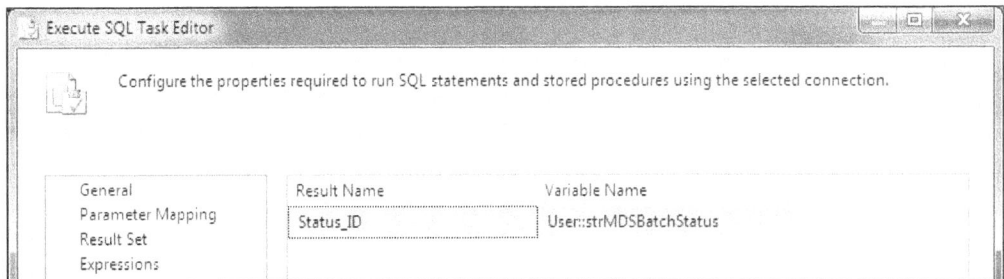

29. Configure the **Expressions** properties of the For Loop task as follows:

Expression	Value
InitExpression	@dtMDSLoopTimer = DATEADD("mi", @intMDSTimeout, GETDATE())
EvalExpression	@strMDSBatchStatus != 2 && @dtMDSLoopTimer > GETDATE()

The InitExpression value sets the @dtMDSLoopTimer to the current time + the interval set in our @intMDSTimeout variable.

The EvalExpression checks if either the @strMDSBatchStatus is either not equal to 2 (Success) or the timeout has expired.

The For Loop will only succeed if the status of the batch we are processing returns success. At this point we can add a final task to validate the model.

30. Add an Execute SQL task as a successor to the For Loop task and rename it "Invoke the Validation Process".

31. Configure the task to use the MDS Repository connection and set the SQLStatement property as follows:

```
DECLARE @ModelName nVarchar(50) = ?
DECLARE @UserName nvarchar(50)= ?
DECLARE @User_ID int DECLARE @Version_ID int
DECLARE @Model_id int

SET @User_ID =     (SELECT ID
                     FROM   mdm.tblUser u
                     WHERE u.UserName = @UserName )

SET @Version_ID = (SELECT MAX(ID)
                     FROM mdm.viw_SYSTEM_SCHEMA_VERSION
                     WHERE Model_Name = @ModelName)

SET @Model_ID =    (SELECT Model_ID
                     FROM mdm.viw_SYSTEM_SCHEMA_VERSION
                     WHERE Model_Name = @ModelName)

EXECUTE mdm.udpValidateModel @User_ID, @Model_ID, @Version_ID, 1
```

32. Finally, set the parameter mapping of the task as shown below:

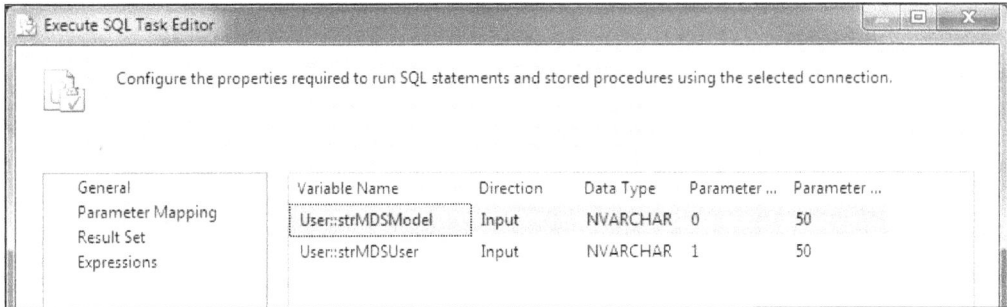

Execute SQL Task Editor						

Configure the properties required to run SQL statements and stored procedures using the selected connection.

	Variable Name	Direction	Data Type	Parameter ...	Parameter ...
General	User::strMDSModel	Input	NVARCHAR	0	50
Parameter Mapping	User::strMDSUser	Input	NVARCHAR	1	50
Result Set					
Expressions					

As we did with the data flow, tidy up the package by arranging and re-sizing the tasks appropriately, and adding annotations. Your finished package should look similar to the one in the following diagram:

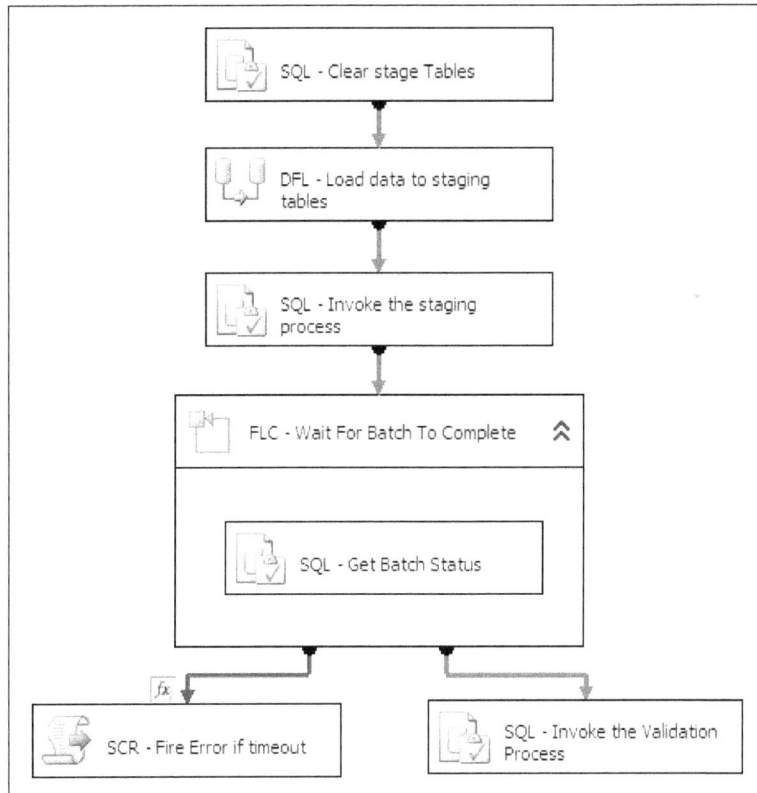

SQL - Clear stage Tables

DFL - Load data to staging tables

SQL - Invoke the staging process

FLC - Wait For Batch To Complete

SQL - Get Batch Status

SCR - Fire Error if timeout

SQL - Invoke the Validation Process

The sample package available in the code bundle has been enhanced to include a task to clear the staging tables if the package variable `blnClearStage` is set to true and a script task to fire an error if the staging process times out. The complete, working package can be found in the source files for the book.

Summary

In this chapter, we have covered a number of different examples of how to add, update, and delete data in the MDS repository. In particular, we have seen that:

- Loading data into MDS involves three core steps—loading, staging, and validation
- The majority of the technical effort is in populating the MDS staging tables correctly
- There are three staging tables, each with their own set of uses
- Other than loading the tables, almost all of the processes involved can be carried out either using the user interface or T-SQL stored procedures
- Comprehensive error codes allow easy diagnosis of rows that fail to load

Finally, we have seen that while MDS itself doesn't include any data loading functionality of its own, when complimented with T-SQL and SSIS (or indeed any other competent ETL tool), it is an extremely powerful combination for loading your MDS system with data from many different sources.

In the next chapter, we will look at the MDS features of business rules and workflow.

7
Business Rules and Workflow

One of the more powerful features of Master Data Services will be covered in this chapter, namely the business rules engine. We will look at the different types of business rules that can be created within MDS, covering the various conditions and actions that can help to make an MDS solution so flexible.

The example solution will be extended further to include business rules that modify the data, interact with the data validation, and send e-mail notifications. Implementation of workflow will also be covered, through the use of SharePoint 2010.

In this chapter, we will cover the following topics:

- Introduction to MDS business rules
- Conditions and actions
- Business rules user interface
- Creating business rules
- E-mails and notifications
- SharePoint workflow

Introduction to MDS business rules

The phrase "business rules" comes up often in Enterprise-level software solutions — whether you are working with Enterprise Resource Planning (ERP), Customer Relationship Management (CRM), Supply Chain Management (SCM), or a variety of other systems — there will generally always be a business rules module. The reason is that a business rules feature or module allows the implementation of custom logic within a platform or off-the-shelf product that gives organizations the ability to tailor the product to their exact needs.

Master Data Services is no different to the aforementioned technologies – it contains the ability to create business rules via the Master Data Manager front-end, which upon the occurrence of certain events, are then executed in the MDS business rules engine.

The business rules that you create in MDS take the form IF *condition* THEN *action*. It is possible to choose from a number of different conditions, each of which can perform different logical checks on the various attributes of a member. If the condition resolves to true, then the action will be fired, producing the desired effect.

At the simplest level, the idea behind business rules in MDS is that values for an attribute can be set to a given value, based on a condition. For example, in a Product Entity, we may decide to set the Dealer Price attribute to be 30% higher than the Product Cost attribute, if the Product is in a certain category.

Using business rules to generate values is useful, as time can be saved by getting a system to determine attribute values. However, instead of just generating values, we may also want to use business rules to ensure the quality of our master data. Using the same Product Entity as an example, we may want to use a business rule to ensure that our Product Cost attribute cannot be set to a negative value. Using the business rules in this way will mean that any downstream applications consuming data will benefit from a high level of data quality.

Running business rules

Business rules in MDS can be run in several different ways, namely:

- When model validation occurs, either from the **Validate Version** page in Master Data Manager, via the MDS stored procedures, or via the MDS API
- When a member is edited or created
- Manually, for one or more members, via a button on the Explorer grid

Technical overview

The business rules are physically run against the members of an Entity by running stored procedures that exist within the MDS SQL Server relational database.

The stored procedure that is used to run the business rules for an entity is actually generated each time that a rule is created or changed, and contains the translation of the aforementioned conditions and actions into Transact SQL code. An additional stored procedure will be created by MDS if there are business rules for Consolidated Members.

When a member is edited or created, the stored procedures are called directly in order to run the business rules. However, when model validation occurs, thousands of members potentially need to be validated, so Service Broker is used in order to run the business rules asynchronously.

Service Broker is also used in the process of sending data to SharePoint, as one of the actions available in MDS business rules is to activate a SharePoint workflow. When business rules with such an action actually fire, Master Data Services places a message on the Service Broker External Action queue, within the MDS database. There is then a Windows Service, known as the SQL Server MDS Workflow Integration service, which takes the message from the aforementioned queue and sends it to SharePoint.

The technical architecture of Master Data Services business rules can be summarized by the following diagram:

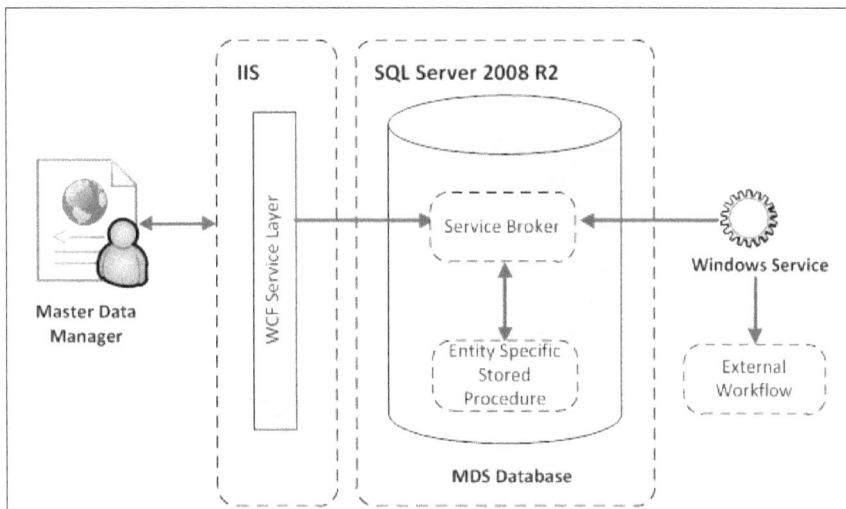

Conditions and actions

As mentioned, the conditions and actions are the components that make up MDS business rules. We will now cover the conditions and actions that are available in MDS, before we encounter them when creating our own business rules.

Conditions

There are a variety of different conditions in MDS, as different businesses will need rules to be triggered in different ways. While the conditions are a key part of the business rules, they are actually optional. If a condition is omitted, this will effectively create a business rule with an action that is executed every time the business rules are run.

The full list of conditions supported by MDS is shown below:

Condition	Description
Is equal to	Checks if an attribute is equal to a given value, another attribute, or blank.
Is not equal to	Checks if an attribute is not equal to a given value, another attribute, or blank.
Is greater than	Checks if an attribute is greater than a given value, another attribute, or blank.
Is greater than or equal to	Checks if an attribute is greater than or equal to a given value, another attribute, or blank.
Is less than	Checks if an attribute is less than a given value, another attribute, or blank.
Is less than or equal to	Checks if an attribute is less than or equal to a given value, another attribute, or blank.
Starts with	Checks if the first character of an attribute starts with a given value, the value of another attribute, or is blank.
Ends with	Checks if the last character of an attribute is a given value, the value of another attribute, or is blank.
Contains	Checks if an attribute contains a given value, the value of another attribute, or is blank.
Contains the pattern	Checks if an attribute contains a given regular expression, the value of another attribute, or is blank.
Contains the subset	Checks if an attribute contains a value or attribute value at a specified position.
Has changed	Checks if the value of a given attribute has changed since the last time the business rule was run.
Is between	Checks if the value of a given attribute is between the values of two other attributes in the Entity.

Actions

There are several different types of actions in MDS, all of which have different behavior. We will look at each action type in turn, before looking at the full list of actions available.

Default Value

Actions of this type will set the value of a target member attribute, but will only do so if the attribute has not been populated before, or is currently blank.

Change Value

The Change Value actions will set the value of a target member attribute, but unlike the Default Value actions, the Change Value actions will always change the target attribute any time that the condition is satisfied.

Validation

Validation actions affect the validation status of a given member, causing the member to be invalid if the action fires. In addition, when the Validation actions do fire, they are the only action type that will cause notifications to fire.

External Action

There is only one external action, namely "Start Workflow". The default behavior for this action is to initiate a user-specified SharePoint workflow, although it supports use of custom actions, as long as they adhere to the IWorkflowTypeExtender interface.

The full list of actions supported by MDS is shown below:

Action type	Action	Description
Default Value	Defaults to	Sets a target attribute to a given value, only if the target attribute is blank
Default Value	Defaults to a generated value	Sets a target attribute to a generated numeric value, only if the target attribute is blank. The generated value is an incrementing value, starting at a given value, and incrementing each time the condition is true by a chosen increment value
Default Value	Defaults to a concatenated value	Sets a target attribute to a concatenated value, only if the target attribute is blank. The concatenated value can be made up of substrings of attributes, as well as free form text
Change Value	Equals	Sets a target attribute to a given value
Change Value	Equals a concatenated value	Sets a target attribute to a concatenated value

Action type	Action	Description
Validation	Is required	Sets a member's validation status to failed if a given member attribute is blank
Validation	Is not valid	Sets a member's validation status to failed
Validation	Must contain the pattern	Sets a member's validation status to failed if an attribute does not contain the specified pattern
Validation	Must be unique	Sets a member's validation status to failed if an attribute is not unique
Validation	Must have one of the following values	Sets a member's validation status to failed if it does not contain one of the specified values
Validation	Must be greater than	Sets a member's validation status to failed if it is not greater than a given value
Validation	Must be equal to	Sets a member's validation status to failed if it is not equal to a given value
Validation	Must be greater than or equal to	Sets a member's validation status to failed if it is not greater than or equal to a given value
Validation	Must be less than	Sets a member's validation status to failed if it is not less than a given value
Validation	Must be less than or equal to	Sets a member's validation status to failed if it is not less than or equal to a given value
Validation	Must be between	Sets a member's validation status to failed if it is not between two values
Validation	Must have a minimum length of	Sets a member's validation status to failed if the length of a text-based attribute is less than the number specified
Validation	Must have a maximum length of	Sets a member's validation status to failed if the length of a text-based attribute is greater than the number specified
External Action	Start workflow	Passes member data to an external workflow, via service broker, and then a Windows Service

Business rules user interface

MDS business rules are created within a model for a given entity, member type (leaf or consolidated), and attribute combination. All of this is carried out in the System Administration function, which exposes the familiar MDS grid-based interface to hold the created business rules. Although our Store model does not contain any business rules yet, an example of the business rules user interface for the sample Product model is shown next:

Business Rule Maintenance

Model:
Product ▾

Entity:
Product ▾

Member type:
Leaf ▾

Attribute:
All ▾

➕ 🔗 ✏️ ✖️

Priority	Excluded	Name	Description	Expression	Status	Notification
10	☐	Required fields	Required fields	🔲	Active	
20	☐	DaysToManufacture	Days to manufacture	🔲	Active	
30	☑	Std Cost	Std cost must be &gt ; 0	🔲	Excluded	
40	☑	FG MSRP Cost	FG's must have msrp & d ealer cost	🔲	Excluded	

The buttons above the grid are explained next from left to right:

➕	The familiar green plus icon that is shown is how the business rules are created, much like the other MDS objects that we've looked at so far.
🔗	The business rules contain a concept called publishing that involves creating or editing the business rules offline, before clicking this button to make the rules active on the server.
✏️	This edit button is how the business rules are designed, whether creating a new rule or editing an existing rule.
✖️	The familiar delete icon is how business rules are deleted. However, as with creating or editing a rule, the change must be published for an active rule to be deleted from the run time rule set.

As with some of the other grids that can be found within MDS, the business rules grid can be edited directly, in order to edit the following key columns:

- **Priority**—Each business rule is given a priority that controls the order in which the business rules fire. The rules fire in order of priority, with the rules that have the lower numbers firing first.

- **Excluded**—Instead of deleting a business rule, it is possible to mark a business rule as being inactive by checking the **Excluded** checkbox.

- **Notification**—When a business rule causes an e-mail notification to be sent, editing this column sets who the e-mail will be sent to.

Creating business rules

We will now extend our sample Store model to include some new business rules, while drilling deeper into the various conditions and actions that are available in the business rules editor.

Creating the required attributes business rule

We will start off the examples in this chapter with something simple—namely enforcing that a number of attributes in our Store entity must be completed. This can be carried out by creating a business rule that has a *Validation* action, as we will now see by covering the steps outlined next:

1.   Navigate to the MDS home page and click on the **System Administration** function.

2.   Hover over the **Manage** menu and choose the **Business Rules** menu item.

3.   Click on the green plus icon to add a new business rule that will insert one line into the grid that will appear below.

4.   Click on the edit business rules button, which will cause the **Edit Business Rule** window to appear, as shown below:

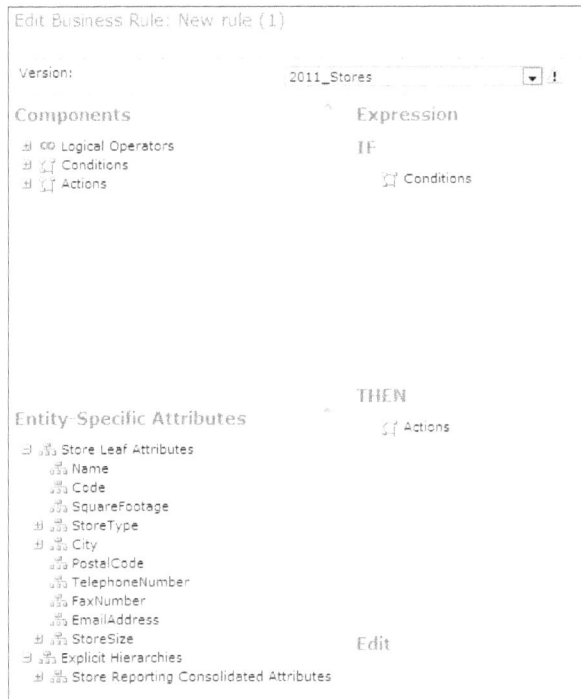

5. The **Components** pane in the top-left hand corner of the previous image is where we can pick our **Conditions** and **Actions** and then drag them onto the **IF** or the **THEN** part of the **Expression** pane, on the right-hand side. The rule that we need to create is an example of a rule that does not require a **Condition**, so we will go straight to picking an **Action**. Expand the **Actions** node to show the following list of actions:

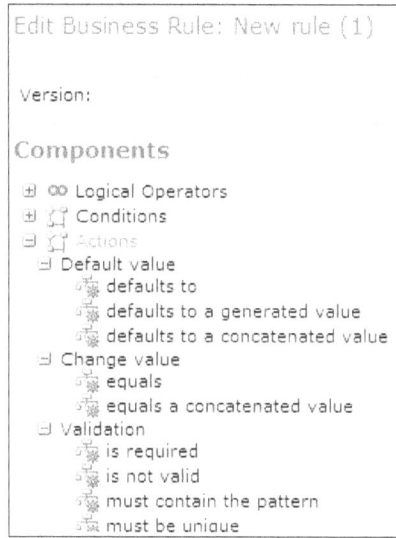

6. The **Action** that we want to pick is the **is required** action. This will enforce that a particular attribute cannot be null or blank, marking the member as invalid if a null or blank is detected. Click on the **is required** action and drag it over to the right-hand side of the screen, dropping it onto the **Actions** node that is under the **THEN** pane, which will produce the following results:

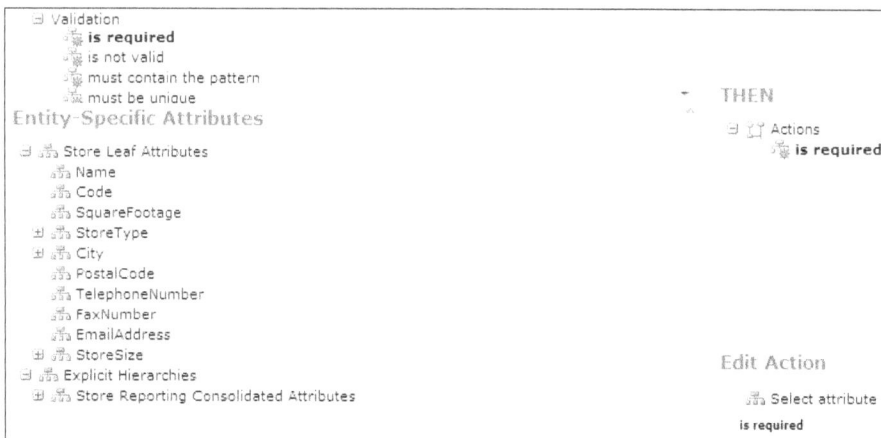

7. This has caused the **Edit Action** pane to appear, as we must tell the **Action** which attribute to operate on. Click on the **Name** attribute that is shown in the **Entity-Specific Attributes** section and drag it onto the **Select attribute** node that has appeared in the **Edit Action** pane:

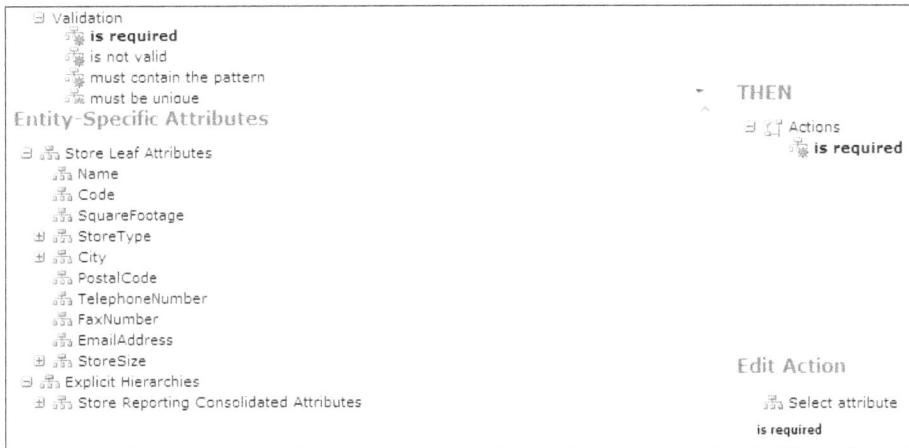

8. Click on the save icon that will save our action and update the **THEN** pane:

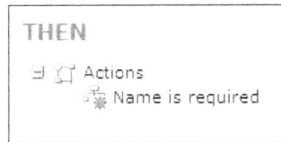

9. This completes the setup for us to enforce that the **Name** attribute must be entered. Before we finish though, we will add another action to our rule, as rules can have multiple conditions and actions. We also want to ensure that the **City** attribute is completed. Therefore, repeat the process that we have just gone through, by dragging a second **is required** action onto the **Actions** node that exists in the **THEN** pane, but using the **City** attribute as the action's input. Once completed, the **THEN** pane should look as follows:

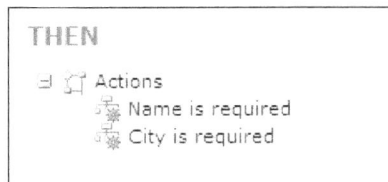

10. In reality, we may want to mark more attributes as required, but this will do for our example. Therefore, click the green back arrow at the top of the screen, to return to the **Business Rules Maintenance** screen.

11. Double-click in the **Name** column to edit the business rule name. Give the business rule the name of **Required Fields** and then click outside the grid to save this change. Double-click on the **Description** column to give the rule the description of **Enforces required fields**, and then click outside the grid. The grid will now look as follows:

12. The **Status** of the rule is **Activation Pending**, indicating that the rule is complete, but has not been activated yet. The final step is to publish our rule, so click the **Publish** button (second from the left) in order to deploy the rule.

13. Verify that the **Status** of the rule is **Active** after publishing has occurred.

We now need to test our rule to verify that it has the desired effect of enforcing our required fields. Remember, one of the ways in which business rules fire is when we add a new member, so we will do this now by carrying out the following steps:

1. Navigate to the MDS home page and choose the **Explorer** function.

2. Click the green plus icon at the top of the screen, and choose **Add Leaf** from the small drop-down that will appear, in order to immediately add a new member.

3. Enter **053** as the **Code**, leave the **Name** blank, and then click on the save icon.

4. As we saw in *Chapter 4, Creating and Using Models*, saving a member and saving its attributes are separate steps when creating a member, and the business rules are run on both of these events. Therefore, our business rule has been run, and has returned two validation issues, as shown at the bottom of the screen:

5. Instead of rectifying the issues, click the green back arrow, and then click the pencil edit icon to get to the Explorer grid.

6. Scroll down to the bottom of the grid and note the icon next to the new member that we have created:

As we can see in the previous image, the new member has a validation status of Validation Failed that was caused by the action on our business rule. As we learnt in *Chapter 5, Version Management*, the member still gets created, but just gets marked with a different validation status.

Also note the validation status of the other members. They are all marked with a yellow question mark that corresponds to a status of Awaiting Validation. This will happen whenever the business rules get published. These members have the yellow question mark as the business rules have only been run for the new member that we created. At some point we need to run validation for all the members that we will see later in this chapter.

As a final step, delete the store that we have just created, as we don't actually need it to be part of our model. For reference, we covered how to delete members in *Chapter 4*.

Model setup

We now need to create some more complex business rules, but in order to do so, we need to make some changes to our model structure.

Our model requires two new domain attributes, namely StoreSize and StoreStatus, which in turn require new populated entities behind them.

Our first step is to create our new entities that we will do by carrying out the following steps:

1. Navigate to the **System Administration** function.
2. Hover over the **Manage** menu and click on the **Entities** menu item.
3. Ensure that the **Store** model is selected from the **Model** drop-down.
4. Click the green plus icon. This will open the **Add Entity** screen.
5. Enter **StoreSize** as the name of the **Entity**.
6. Choose **No** to not **Enable Explicit Hierarchies and Collections.**
7. Click the save button to return to the **Entity Maintenance** screen.
8. Repeat the above process to create the **StoreStatus** Entity.
9. We now need to edit the Store entity to get its new attributes. Remaining on the **Entity Maintenance** screen, click on the Store entity within the grid, and then click the pencil icon to edit the entity.
10. Click the green plus icon for the **Leaf Attributes** section to open the **Add Attribute** screen.

11. Create a new **Domain-based** attribute, entering the information shown below:

```
Entity: Store
Add Attribute


  ⚪ Free-form
  ◉ Domain-based
  ⚪ File

Name:
  StoreSize
Display pixel width:
       100 ▲▼
Entity:
  StoreSize                    ▼
Enable change tracking: ☑

Change tracking group:
        1 ▲▼
```

12. Click the save icon to save the new **Attribute**, which will return us to the **Edit Entity** screen.

13. Repeat this process for the StoreStatus Domain-based attribute

14. Click the save icon to return to the **Entity Maintenance** screen.

As we set the Store model up to use Attribute Groups, we now need to add the new attribute to an Attribute Group in order to display it correctly to users. Carry out the following steps to make the changes:

1. Remaining in the **System Administration** function, hover over the **Manage** menu, and choose the **Attribute Groups** menu item.

2. Ensure that the Store **Model** and the Store **Entity** are selected from the drop-downs.

3. Expand the **General Attribute Group**, and then click on the **Attributes** node so that it is highlighted in bold.

4. Click the pencil edit icon.

5. Move both the **StoreSize** and the **StoreStatus** attributes from the **Available** list box to the **Assigned** list box, using the arrow buttons in between the two list boxes. Once this has been carried out, the two list boxes should be as follows:

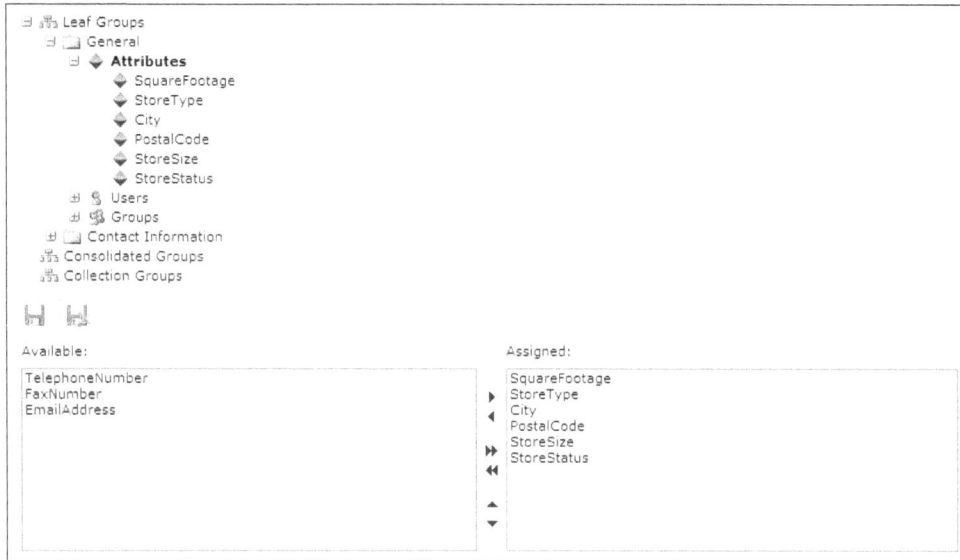

6. Click the save icon to save the changes to the Attribute Group.

Now having created our new entities and attributes, we need to create some members for the new entities in order to continue with our example. To create the new Store Size members, carry out the following instructions:

1. Navigate to the MDS home page and click on the Explorer function.

2. Hover over the **Entities** menu and choose the StoreSize menu item.

3. Click the green plus icon, to add a Leaf member.

4. Enter **Small** as both the **Name** and the **Code** of the new member.

5. Click the save icon.

6. Repeat the process in order to add two additional members, namely **Medium** and **Large**.

Once completed, the Explorer grid for the **StoreSize** entity should look as follows:

Finally, we need to populate the StoreStatus entity. Repeat the aforementioned steps, but within the StoreStatus entity, ensuring that the members created are as follows:

Creating the Store Size business rules

Now that we have made our structural model changes, we are in a position to create some more complex business rules, the first of which will involve our new Store Size attribute.

The idea behind the Store Size attribute is to provide an easy to understand sizing guide to our end consumers, instead of quoting the size in square feet, which some people may not be able to understand. We do, of course, already have the size in square feet, so we will write a set of business rules that set the Store Size based on the Square Footage attribute.

Now having made our model changes, we will find that the existing Store members do not have a value for the new Store Size attribute. This is precisely where the business rule will be used – to set the Store Size based on the Square Footage. The business rule will require the following logic:

- If the Square Footage is less than or equal to 2,000, then the Store Size should be Small.

- If the Square Footage is greater than 2,000 but less than or equal to 4,000, then the Store Size should be Medium.

- If the Square Footage is greater than 4,000, then the Store Size should be Large.

The business rules in MDS do not allow an ELSE as part of the IF...THEN logic, nor are CASE statements available, meaning we need to create three separate rules to satisfy the above requirement. Carry out the following steps to create the first business rule:

1. Navigate to the MDS home page and click on the **System Administration** function.

2. Hover over the **Manage** menu and choose the **Business Rules** menu item.

3. Click on the green plus icon to add a new business rule, which will insert one line into the grid below.

4. Click on the edit business rules button, which will cause the **Edit Business Rule** window to appear.

5. Expand the **Conditions** tree view section and then the **Value** comparison node, both of which are available in the top-left hand corner of the screen, in order to reveal the following **Conditions** that are available to us:

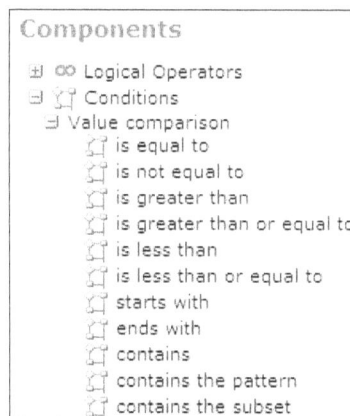

6. Having expanded the **Value** comparison node, drag the **Is less Than or Equal** to condition from the **Components** pane and drop it on the **Conditions** node that exists on the right hand side of the screen, on the **IF** pane. The screen should now look as follows:

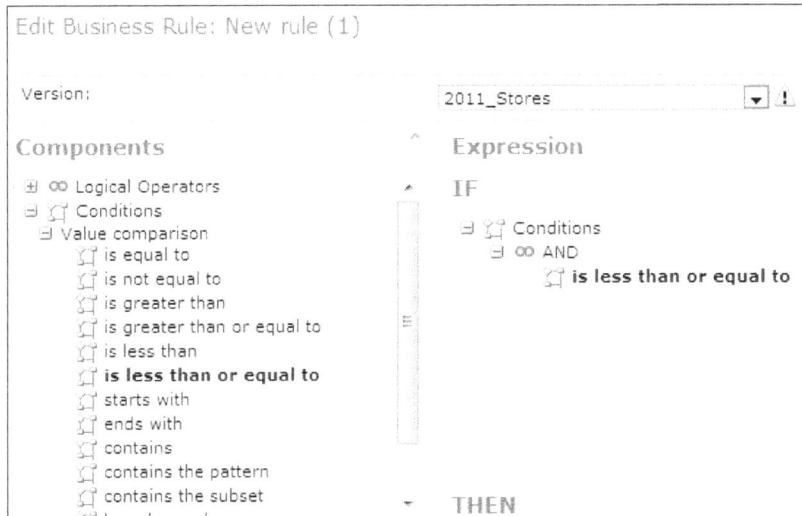

```
Edit Business Rule: New rule (1)

Version:                              2011_Stores              ▾ ⬇

Components                      ⌃     Expression

 ⊞ ∞ Logical Operators          ▴     IF
 ⊟ ⟁ Conditions
   ⊟ Value comparison                  ⊟ ⟁ Conditions
     ⟁ is equal to                        ⊟ ∞ AND
     ⟁ is not equal to                        ⟁ is less than or equal to
     ⟁ is greater than
     ⟁ is greater than or equal to   ⬚
     ⟁ is less than
     ⟁ is less than or equal to
     ⟁ starts with
     ⟁ ends with
     ⟁ contains
     ⟁ contains the pattern
     ⟁ contains the subset       ▾     THEN
```

7. Notice that the **Edit Condition** pane is now populated at the bottom of the screen. Drag the **SquareFootage** attribute from the **Entity-Specific Attributes** pane onto the **Select attribute** node that exists in the **Edit Condition** pane. The screen should now look as follows:

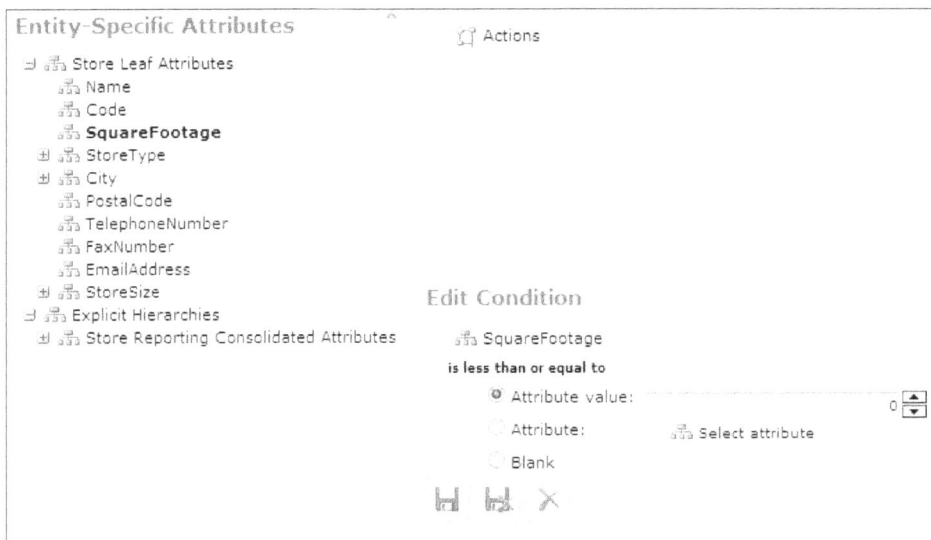

```
Entity-Specific Attributes        ⌃      ⟁ Actions

 ⊟ ⧈ Store Leaf Attributes
     ⧈ Name
     ⧈ Code
     ⧈ SquareFootage
   ⊞ ⧈ StoreType
   ⊞ ⧈ City
     ⧈ PostalCode
     ⧈ TelephoneNumber
     ⧈ FaxNumber
     ⧈ EmailAddress
   ⊞ ⧈ StoreSize                         Edit Condition
 ⊟ ⧈ Explicit Hierarchies
   ⊞ ⧈ Store Reporting Consolidated Attributes    ⧈ SquareFootage
                                          is less than or equal to
                                           ⦿ Attribute value: ─────────── 0 ⬆⬇
                                           ⦾ Attribute:      ⧈ Select attribute
                                           ⦾ Blank

                                          ⊢⊣  ⊢⊣  ✕
```

8. Within the **Edit Condition** pane, we can choose to compare the **SquareFootage** attribute to a value, to the value of another attribute or to a **blank** value. In this case, we wish to compare **SquareFootage** against a value, so therefore leave the radio button selected against **Attribute value**. Enter 2000 into the **Attribute value** textbox, then click the save icon at the bottom of the screen. The **IF** pane at the top of the screen should now be updated, as follows:

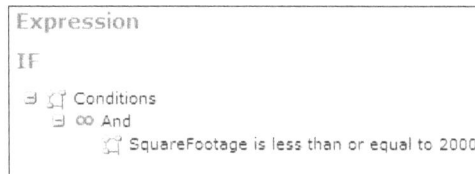

9. We now need to produce the action part of the business rule. Go back to the **Components** section of the editor and expand the **Actions** node, as shown next:

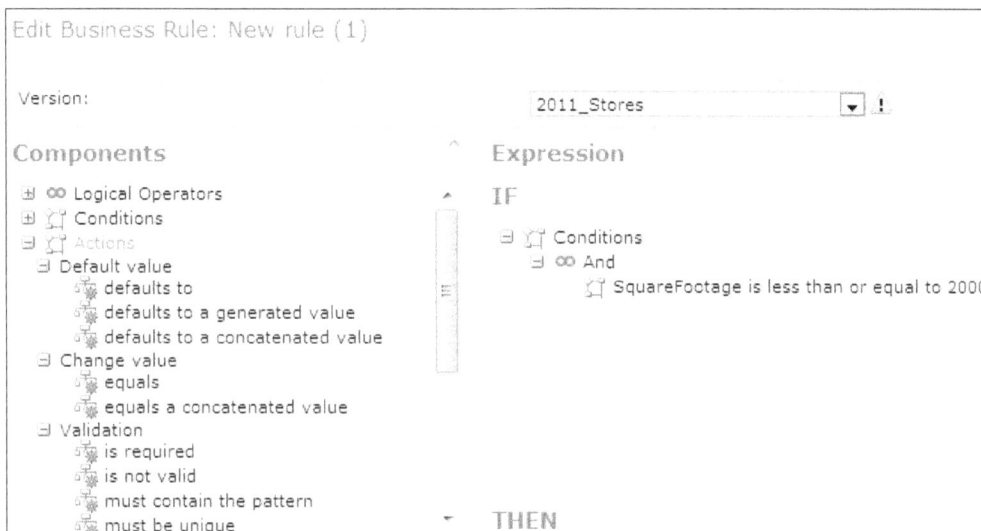

10. Drag the **Equals** action from the **Components** section onto the **Actions** node that is found in the **THEN** pane. The lower half of the screen should be as follows:

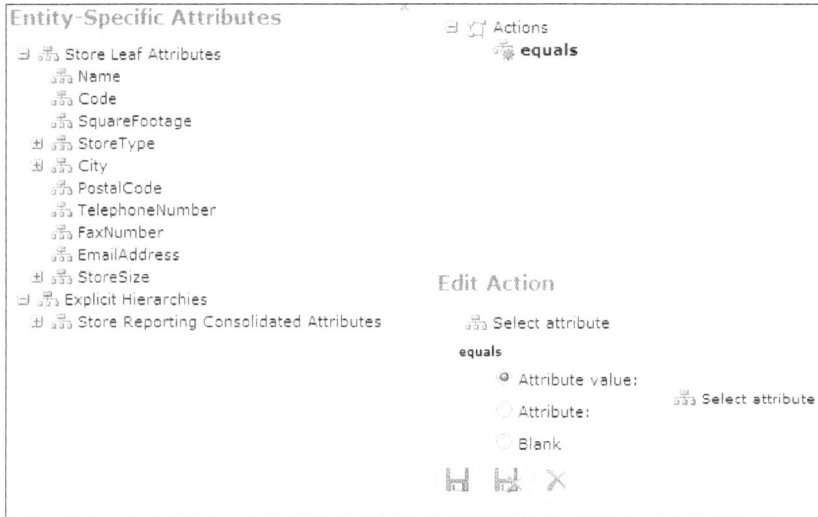

11. Now drag the **StoreSize** attribute from the **Entity-Specific Attributes** section onto to the **Select attribute** node that exists in the **Edit Action** pane. As the **StoreSize** attribute is a Domain-attribute, the **Attribute value** option in the **Edit Action** pane will expose a drop-down of possible attribute values. Select the value of **Small**, as shown below:

12. Click on the save icon at the bottom of the screen.

13. Click the green back arrow to return to the **Business Rules Maintenance** screen. Hover over the **Expression** column and verify that it is **IF SquareFootage is less than or equal to 2000 THEN StoreSize equals Small**.

14. Double-click on the **Name** column in order to rename the rule from the default. Call the rule **StoreSize small**, and enter an appropriate description in the adjacent column.

15. Now we need to create two more rules, in order to cover the Medium and Large stores. Repeat this process, entering the following settings for the two rules:

Property	Rule 1	Rule 2
Rule name	Store Size Medium	Store Size Large
Rule description	Set the store size to Medium	Set the store size to large
Condition 1	Greater Than	Greater Than
Condition 1 attribute	SquareFootage	SquareFootage
Condition 1 value	2000	4000
Condition 2 *	Less Than or Equal to	N/A
Condition 2 attribute	SquareFootage	N/A
Condition value	4000	N/A
Action	Equals	Equals
Action attribute	StoreSize	StoreSize
Action value	Medium	Small

*— The rule called Store Size Medium requires two conditions, whereas the rule we created before just had one condition. Adding a second condition to a rule is carried out simply by dragging another condition onto the **And** node that is shown in the IF pane, as shown below:

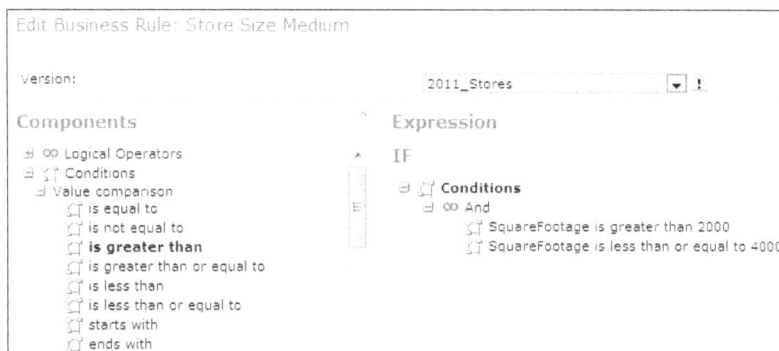

16. After the two new rules have been created, the four rules should be present as follows on the **Business Rules Maintenance** screen:

Business Rule Maintenance

Model:
Store

Entity:
Store

Member type:
Leaf

Attribute:
All

Priority	Excluded	Name	Description	Expression	Status
10	☐	Required Fields	Enforces required fields		Active
20	☐	Store Size Small	Set the store size to small		Activation pending
30	☐	Store Size Medium	Set the store size to medium		Activation pending
40	☐	Store Size Large	Set the store size to large		Activation pending

17. As with the **Required Fields** rule that we created, the **Status** of each of the rules is **Activation Pending**. The final step is to publish our rules, so click the **Publish** button that will deploy the rules.

Publishing will set the **Status** of the rules to **Active**, which concludes creating our first set of rules.

Running the Store Size business rules

As the business rules have the potential to mark entity members as invalid, each member in each entity of the model is marked as requiring validation once the business rules have been published. This is the case for us after creating our rules — we need to validate the model to re-validate the members in each of the entities.

As the business rules are run when validating a model, our new rules will run, and we will see our new Store Size attribute populated correctly. Carry out the following steps to validate our model:

1. Navigate to the MDS home page and click on the **Explorer** function.

2. Click on the edit pencil icon and note that each member requires validation and that the new **StoreSize** attribute is blank for each member, as shown:

3. Navigate to the MDS home page and click on the **Version Management** function.

4. Once in the **Version Management** function, click on the **Validate Version** menu item.

5. Ensure that the **Model** selected is called **Store** and the **Version** selected is called **2011_Stores**.

6. Click on the **Validate Version** button.

7. As we discussed in *Chapter 5*, the validation process will happen asynchronously, so it will not be finished immediately. Once it does finish, return to the Explorer grid to look at the new **StoreSize** attribute.

8. The **StoreSize** attribute will now be populated as shown, which concludes running our business rules:

Notifications

As we saw when we covered versions in *Chapter 5*, MDS has the ability to send e-mail notifications. Business rules in MDS also have the ability to send notifications that can be useful to flag up issues in data quality, for example, to relevant users.

There is only one category of action that can cause the business rules to send notifications, namely the validation actions. When a validation action is invoked, if the rule has a notification user assigned, then a notification e-mail will be sent.

We will now walk through how to configure one of our existing rules to send a notification:

1. Navigate to the MDS home page and click on the **System Administration** function.

2. Hover over the **Manage** menu and select the **Business Rules** option.

3. We originally set up a business rule called Required Fields, which enforces that the Name and City attributes cannot be missing. If a user is adding a member in the front-end, then we probably don't need a notification. On the other hand, if we're receiving stores in from an external data source, via SSIS, then it may be useful to know that some fields were missing. Therefore, double-click on the **Notification** column and select your domain/username combination:

Priority	Excluded	Name	Description	Expression	Status	Notification
10	☐	Required Fields	Enforces required fields		Changes pending	DOMAIN\User
20	☐	Store Size Small	Set the store size to small		Active	
30	☐	Store Size Medium	Set the store size to medium		Active	
40	☐	Store Size Large	Set the store size to large		Active	

Given that the **Status** of the rule is now at **Changes Pending**, click on the publish button to publish the rule.

We now need to walk through the process of the notification firing. To do this, carry out the following:

1. Navigate to the MDS home page and click on the **Explorer** function.

2. Click on the green plus icon to add a leaf member.

3. Enter a **Code** of **053**, but leave the **Name** blank, and click on the save button.

4. As before, the validation issues should appear at the bottom of the page. Instead of editing the attributes, click the green back arrow and verify that the member is invalid in the member grid.

We now need to wait for the notifications to be sent. The e-mail sending frequency is defined by a system setting called Notification E-mail Setting, which by default is 120 seconds. Once this time has passed, logging into the e-mail client should display an e-mail with the following notification:

Finally, click on one of the links within the notification e-mail and verify that the **Edit Member** page is loaded for the invalid member. This gives the user responsible a quick method of responding to notification issues.

Workflow and SharePoint

So far in our examples, we've been changing our master data as and when we wish. In the real world, this would be much more controlled with security, and might even require approval from a business owner or stakeholder before the change is accepted.

MDS business rules can help with this scenario, as, with a bit of creativity, it's possible to use attributes, business rules, and notifications to create a simple workflow. Essentially we would create an additional attribute, called "MemberStatus", that relevant users can change to Approved or Rejected. If we check for a condition of "MemberStatus = Rejected", then we can have an *Is Invalid* validation action that we know from the previous section will cause a notification to be sent.

There is a good blog post on how to configure basic workflow in this way at the following address: `http://sqlblog.com/blogs/mds_team/archive/2010/02/15/ enabling-human-workflow-part-1-changing-your-model.aspx`.

While the business rules and notifications are useful for simple workflow scenarios, if we require a multi-level approval structure, or perhaps some complex conditions or actions, then we can get the assistance of a SharePoint 2010 workflow.

As we touched on when looking at the different types of actions, an MDS business rule can have an external action that can initiate a SharePoint 2010 workflow.

The workflow functionality in SharePoint is built on the Windows Workflow Foundation (WF) .Net functionality, and offers a number of controls that help model a business process via workflow.

We will now extend our example scenario so that the business rules connect to a SharePoint workflow that we will develop.

Setup

For us to develop and initiate a SharePoint 2010 workflow from MDS, we need to install two additional products, namely:

- SharePoint 2010 Foundation or SharePoint Server 2010
- Microsoft Visual Studio 2010 Professional

Installing both SharePoint and Visual Studio are outside the scope of this book. There are, however, useful guides available for both:

- SharePoint—`http://msdn.microsoft.com/en-us/library/ee554869(office.14).aspx`
- Visual Studio—`http://msdn.microsoft.com/en-us/library/e2h7fzkw.aspx`

SharePoint site creation

Once SharePoint has been installed, we need to make some specific changes to ensure that our example workflow will function correctly. Ensure that a SharePoint site exists that is configured in the following manner:

- The web application that runs the site is configured to run on a different port than the port used by MDS.
- The SharePoint site that gets created gets created with the Document Workspace template.

Store approval business rule

Now that SharePoint is installed and configured, we are in a position to create a business rule for store approval. There is a requirement in our example scenario to ensure that all stores that get added to MDS are approved first by a Regional Manager, and finally by a Head Office Manager.

To enable this scenario, we will have to carry out three high level steps, namely:

1. Create a new MDS business rule.
2. Create a custom column in a SharePoint task list.
3. Create a SharePoint workflow.

We will now cover each of these tasks in detail:

Creating the Store approval business rule

The SharePoint workflow that we will create shortly will carry out all the work for our approval process, but the MDS business rule needs to initiate the workflow. The basic logic to our business rule will be—if the MemberStatus is blank, then the store will be new, so initiate the workflow. This will only handle new stores, but will do fine as an example to demonstrate a SharePoint workflow.

To create the new MDS business rule, carry out the following steps:

1. Navigate to the MDS home page and click on the **System Administration** function.

2. Hover over the **Manage** menu and choose the **Business Rules** menu item.

3. .Click on the green plus icon to add a new business rule that will insert one line into the grid below.

4. Double-click on the appropriate columns to give the following values for the **Name** and **Description**:

    ° **Name—Initiate Approval**

    ° **Description—Fire the SharePoint workflow**

5. Click on the **Edit** button to begin editing the new business rule.

6. Expand the **Conditions** node on the left-hand side and drag the **Is Equal To** item over to the **Conditions** node that exists on the right-hand side of the page.

7. Drag the **StoreStatus** attribute from **Entity Specific Attributes** pane onto the **Select Attribute** node that will have appeared in the **Edit Condition** page.

8. Remaining in the **Edit Condition** pane, change the radio button to the **Blank** option, and then click the **Save** button. The **IF** pane should look as follows:

```
Expression

IF

⊟ ⟨⟩ Conditions
   ⊟ ∞ And
         ⟨⟩ StoreStatus is equal to Blank
```

9. Now we need to include an action for our rule. Expand the **Actions** node in the top-left hand side of the page, and drag the **Start Workflow** action on top of the **Actions** node in the bottom-right hand side of the page. Enter the following information in the **Edit Action** pane:

   ○ **Workflow Type** – Leave this as **SPWF**.

   ○ **Include Member Data in the Message** – **Checked**. This will include details of the member, such as the Code and Name in the message that is passed to SharePoint.

   ○ **Workflow Site** – Enter the address of your SharePoint site, including the port number. The address should be the SharePoint site where you are happy to create the SharePoint workflow. As an example, if you are using a local SharePoint Server, and you created the site on port number 8888, then the address should be **http://localhost:8888/**.

   ○ **Workflow Name** – Enter **StoreApprovalWorkflow**. This is the name that we will give our workflow when we create it.

10. Drag the **StoreSize** attribute onto the **Select Attribute** node. We can include one additional attribute in the message that gets sent to SharePoint, and it may be useful for us to let the approver know how big the store is.

11. Click on the **Save** button. The **THEN** pane should now look as follows:

```
THEN

 ⊐ ⟨ᴸ Actions
      ⚙ StoreSize start Workflow http://localhost:8888/ StoreApprovalWorkflow SPWF True
```

12. Click the green back arrow at the top of the screen, in order to return to the business rules editor.

Workflow priority

At the time of writing, business rules that have an action of *Start Workflow* do not obey the business rules priority firing order. Business rules with other actions will fire in priority order, but a business rule with an action of Start Workflow will always fire after the other business rules.

If you require logic to occur after a Start Workflow action has occurred, then a workaround is to move that logic to the SharePoint Workflow itself. This is a bug with the current release, and may be fixed in a future update.

We're almost ready to publish our business rule. Before we do though, we need to change the StoreStatus values for the existing stores. They are all currently blank, which means they will all hit the SharePoint workflow when we create it. To keep things simple, we want our SharePoint workflow to work on only one Store, instead of 50 plus. We can go to the Explorer grid and set the StoreStatus for our existing stores to "Approved" with a few clicks. To complete this, carry out the following:

1. Navigate to the MDS home page and choose the **Explorer** function.

2. Click on the edit pencil icon to get to the **Explorer** grid.

3. Click on the small X in the top-left hand corner of the grid to select all of the members on the page:

4. Double-click on the **StoreStatus** attribute of the first member. When the drop-down appears, choose **Approved**, and then click out of the cell. As all members on the page are selected, this will change **StoreStatus** of all selected members to **Approved**.

5. Repeat the process on the members that are shown on the second page, and verify that all members now have a **StoreStatus** of **Approved**.

6. Now return to the **Business Rules Maintenance** screen and publish the rules that we have just created.

Creating the SharePoint custom column

Our SharePoint workflow will create a new task in our basic SharePoint task list. While the default task is useful, we can extend it to help with the approval process by creating a custom column to hold the approval status. The idea is then that the Regional Manager and Head Office Manager can approve a new store by simply selecting from a drop-down. This will work well for our example, although it is only scratching the surface of what can be achieved with SharePoint. Although out of the scope of this book, the scenario could be taken further by rendering a custom InfoPath form to the user, displaying all attributes of the new member, as well as customizing the appearance.

We will create our custom column in a SharePoint object called a Content Type, which is a container object that defines the content of another SharePoint object. If we want a custom column in any sort of object in SharePoint, then we edit a Content Type to define that column. By default, the task item that gets created in SharePoint workflow uses the Workflow Task Content Type. It's possible to create custom content types in SharePoint, and specify to use these in our Workflow, but we'll keep things simple for the moment and edit the default Content Type.

Carry out the following in order to edit the Workflow Task Content Type:

1. Within the SharePoint site, navigate to the following address: `http://YourServer:Port/_layouts/ManageContentType.aspx?ctype=0x010801`.

2. Click on the link at the bottom of the page called **Add from new site column**.

3. Enter the **Column Name** as **Approval Status**, and pick **Choice** from the radio buttons as shown:

4. Scroll down the page to the **Additional Column Settings** section and enter the column choices, as shown next:

```
Require that this column contains information:
   Yes   ⦿ No
Type each choice on a separate line:
Approved
Awaiting Approval
Rejected
```

5. Scroll down the page to the **Default Value** textbox and enter **Awaiting Approval** in the textbox.

6. Click **OK** to finish creating the custom column.

Creating the Visual Studio project

We are now ready to start building the SharePoint workflow. Carry out the following instructions to create the Visual Studio project:

1. Open Visual Studio 2010.

2. From the start page, click on the **New Project** link.

3. Navigate the **Installed Templates** structure on the left-hand side of the pop-up window, and choose **Sequential Workflow** under **Visual C# | SharePoint | 2010**. Enter a **Name** and **Location** of your choice:

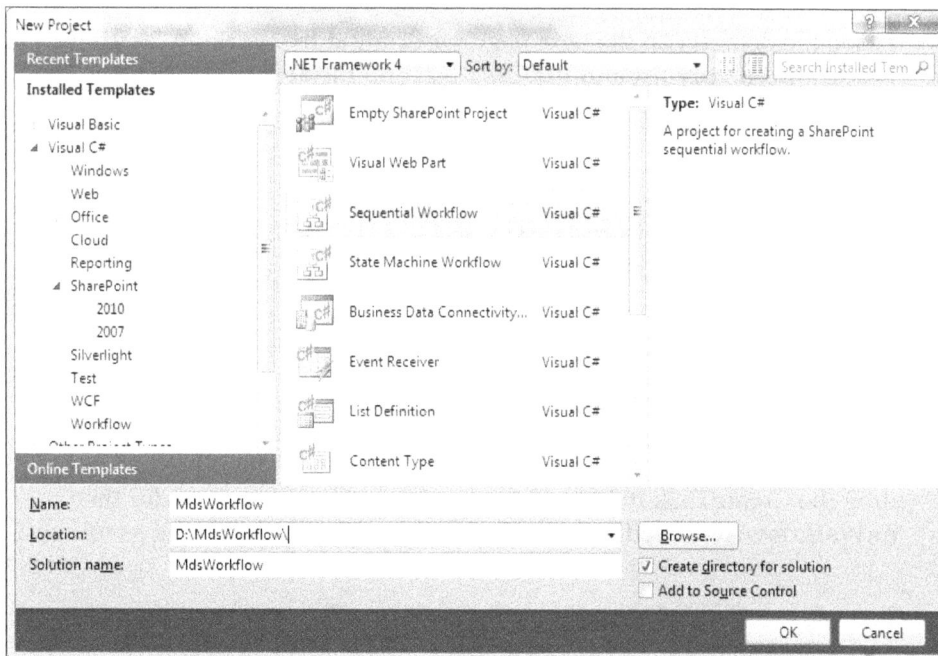

4. Click on the **OK** button that will cause a wizard to appear.

5. Enter the correct path for your SharePoint site, for example, `http://YourServerAndPort/`, and then click the **Next** button.

6. Enter the name of the workflow as **StoreApprovalWorkflow** and choose **Site Workflow** from the radio buttons, as shown below:

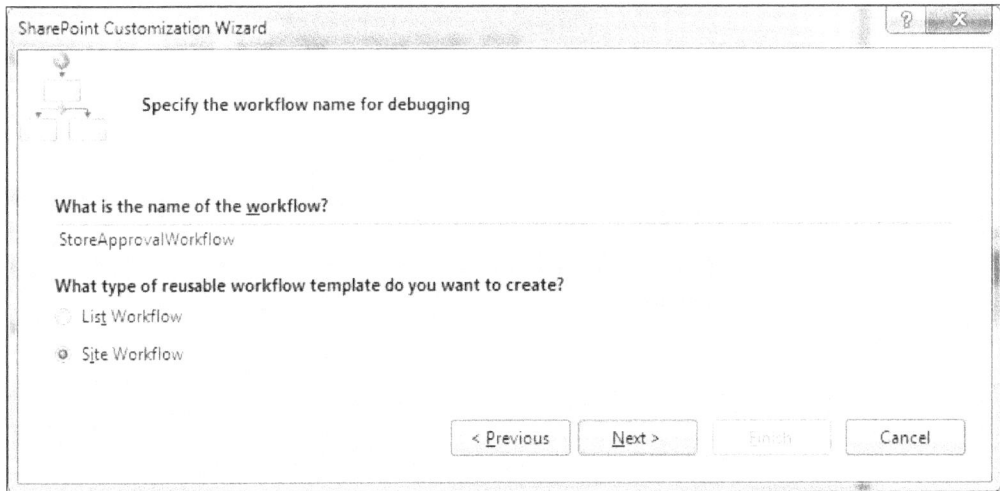

7. Click on the **Next** button to continue.

8. Leave the defaults on the next page, associating the workflow with the **Workflow History** list and the **Task** list, and then click on **Next**.

9. Leave the default selection on the final screen, and then click on **Finish**.

Designing the SharePoint workflow

Now that we have exited the wizard, Visual Studio will display a design window for the Sequential Workflow. We will now build the logical flow of our workflow, by dragging items from the toolbox, before configuring them appropriately:

1. The first piece of functionality that we want in our workflow is to create a new SharePoint task for the Regional Manager, alerting him or her that they have to approve a store. To do this go to the toolbox, and drag the **CreateTask** item onto the workflow, dropping it under the **onWorkflowActivated1** object. The designer should now look as follows:

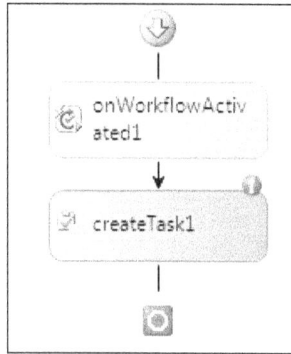

2. Do not worry about the red warnings that have now appeared in the designer; we will correct these after we design the workflow. Navigate to the top of the toolbox and expand the **Windows Workflow v3.0** section. Drag the **While** item onto the designer, below the **createTask1** object.

3. Return to the **SharePoint Workflow** section of the toolbox and drag the **OnTaskChanged** item onto the designer, inside the **whileActivity1** object. The designer should now look as follows:

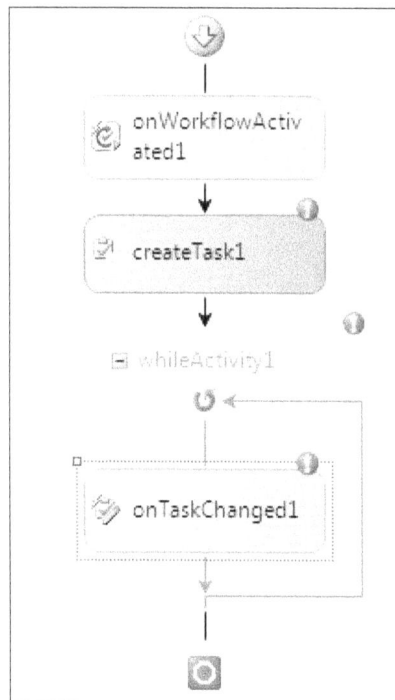

4. Return to the **Windows Workflow v3.0** section in the toolbox and drag on the **IfElse** control, below **whileActivity1**.

5. This time from the SharePoint workflow section of the toolbox, drag on a **CompleteTask** control and then another **CreateTask** control, both into the leftmost branch of the **IfElseActivity1** control. The designer should now look as follows:

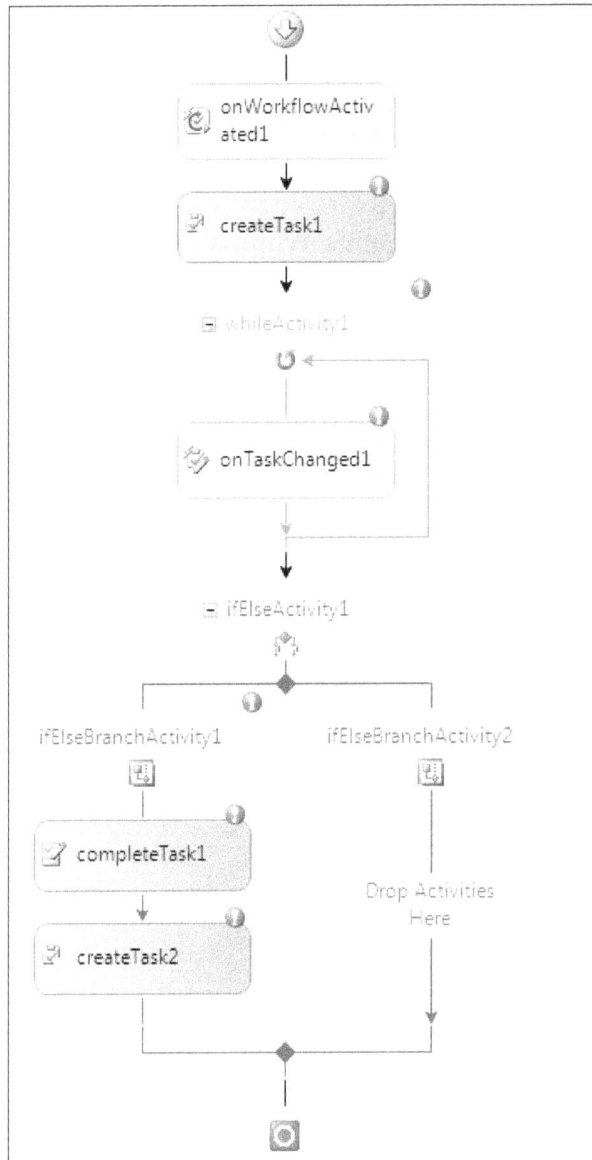

6. Remaining inside the leftmost branch of **IfElseActivity1**, drag on another **While** activity, and then drop another **OnTaskChanged** activity inside **whileActivity1**.

7. Still within the leftmost branch of **ifElseActivity1**, drag on another **IfElse** activity, and place it directly below **whileActivity2**.

8. Finally, drag a **CompleteTask** activity into the leftmost branch of activity. The final design of our workflow should be as follows:

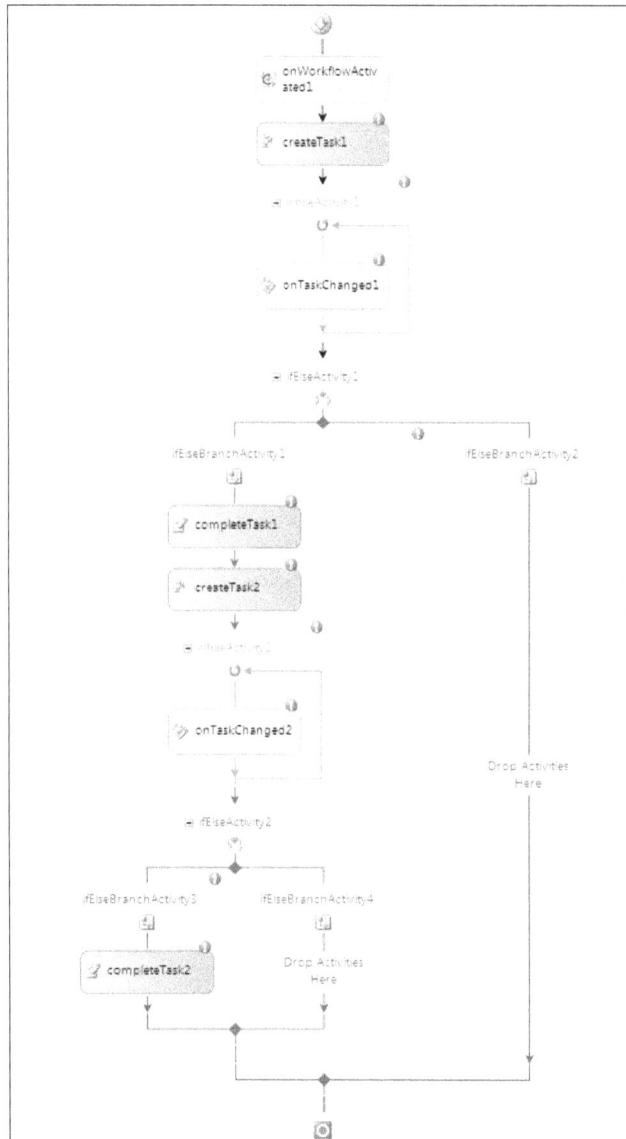

The logic of the workflow shown previously is to first create a SharePoint task that will be assigned to the Regional Manager, requesting approval. The while loop below will wait until the Regional Manager makes a change to the Approval Status field, which will then hit the If-Else activity. If the Regional Manager approved the new Store, then the task will be set to complete, and a new task created for the Head Office Manager. A similar while activity will occur, waiting until the Head Office Manager changes the approval status of the second task. If the task is marked as approved, then the second task will be marked as complete.

Note that we are not dealing with rejection of either the first or second task, in the interests of keeping things simple for this example. We will, however, extend this example in *Chapter 8, Extracting Data From Master Data Services*, using the MDS API to write data back to MDS itself.

For the moment, we will now make the changes needed to the activities that we have added:

1. Click on **createTask1** and change its **CorrelationToken** property to be **firstTask**, and ensure that its **OwnerActivityName** is **Workflow1**, as shown below:

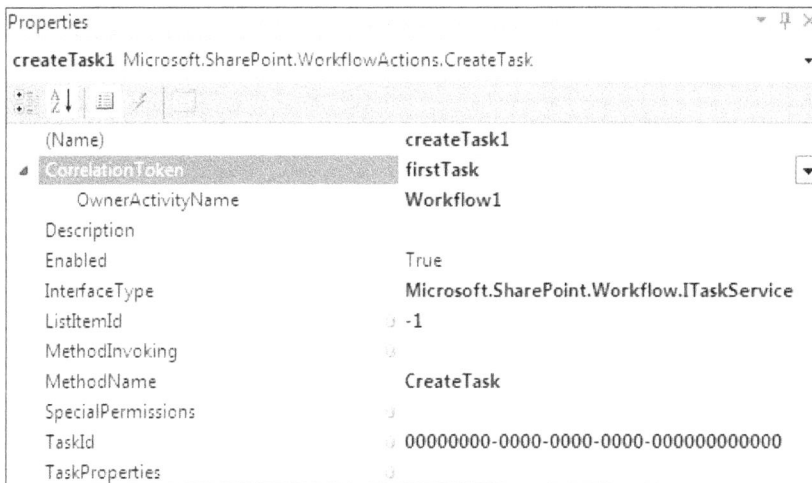

Properties		▼ ╄ ✕
createTask1 Microsoft.SharePoint.WorkflowActions.CreateTask		▼
(Name)	createTask1	
CorrelationToken	firstTask	▼
OwnerActivityName	Workflow1	
Description		
Enabled	True	
InterfaceType	Microsoft.SharePoint.Workflow.ITaskService	
ListItemId	-1	
MethodInvoking		
MethodName	CreateTask	
SpecialPermissions		
TaskId	00000000-0000-0000-0000-000000000000	
TaskProperties		

2. Double-click on **createTask1** to create its **MethodInvoking** method that we will be using later.

3. While in the file **Workflow1.cs**, insert the two variables that are highlighted next:

```
public sealed partial class Workflow1 :
SequentialWorkflowActivity
    {
```

```
public Workflow1()
{
    InitializeComponent();
}


//Code created by the designer
public Guid workflowId = default(System.Guid);
public SPWorkflowActivationProperties workflowProperties =
new SPWorkflowActivationProperties();


//Used to track the approval status of each task
private string firstTaskApprovalStatus = "Awaiting
Approval";
private string secondTaskApprovalStatus = "Awaiting
Approval";
```

4. Return to the designer. Change the name of **whileActivity1** to **whileFirstTaskWaiting**. Go to the properties of the while activity. Change its **Condition** property to **Declarative Rule Condition**. Expand the **Condition** property and click on the ellipsis button in the **ConditionName** property.

5. In the **Select Condition** window that will appear, click on the **New** button, and enter the **Condition** as shown below:

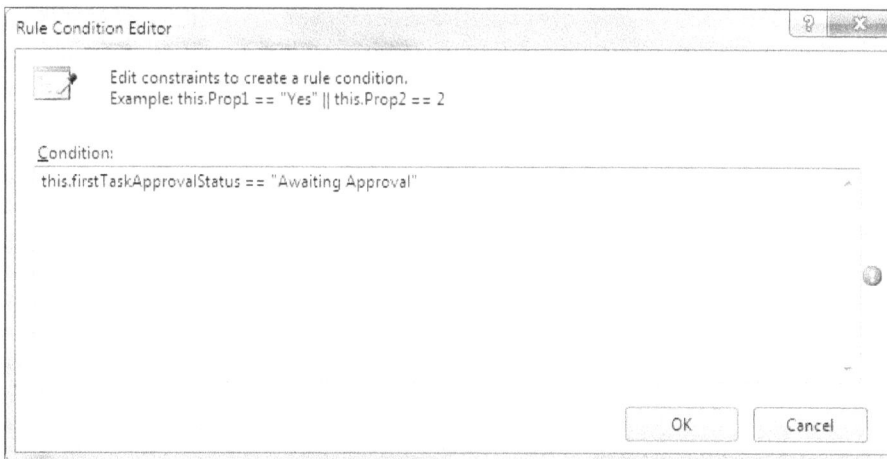

6. Click on **OK** and then rename the condition to **First Task Awaiting Approval**, before clicking **OK** to close the **Select Condition** window.

7. Click on **onTaskChanged1** and set its **CorrelationToken** property to **firstTask**.

8. Double-click on **onTaskChanged1** to generate its **Invoked** method.

9. Return to the designer and click the ellipsis on the **AfterProperties** property of **onTaskChanged1**. Click the **Bind to a new member** tab and choose the **Create Field** option. Set the name as **onTaskChanged1_AfterProperties**, as shown:

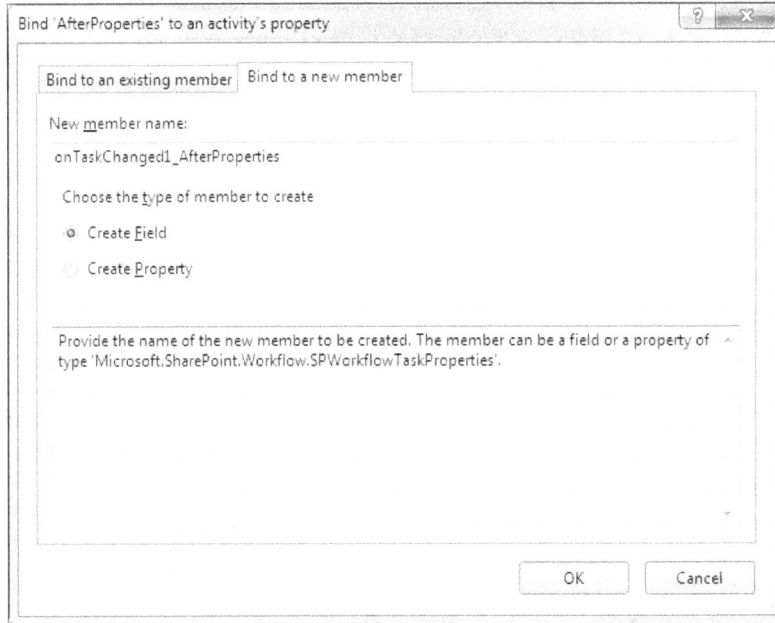

10. Click on **OK** to close the window and return to the designer.

11. Now select **ifElseActivity1**. Rename it to **ifElseFirstTaskApproved**.

12. Click on **ifElseBranchActivity** and rename it to **ifFirstTaskApproved**. Set its **Condition** to be a **Declarative Rule Condition** and click on the ellipsis button in the **ConditionName** property.

13. Click on the **New** button, and add a new Declarative Rule **Condition** with the following code: `this.firstTaskApprovalStatus == "Approved"`. Rename the Condition to **First Task Approved** and return to the designer.

14. Click on **completeTask1** and change its **CorrelationToken** property to **firstTask**.

15. Click on the ellipsis icon of the **TaskId** property of **completeTask1**. Expand **createTask1**, select **TaskId**, and then click on **OK**. This will bind the complete activity to first task that we created.

16. Click on **createTask2** and create a new **CorrelationToken** called **secondTask**. Also set its **OwnerActivityName** to **Workflow1**.

17. Go to the properties of **whileActivity2** and change its name to **whileSecondTaskWaiting**. Change its condition to a Declarative rule condition, and create a new condition called **Second Task Awaiting Approval** with the code: `this.secondTaskApprovalStatus == "Awaiting Approval"`.

18. Double-click on **onTaskChanged2** to create its **Invoked** method.

19. Return to the designer and change the **CorrelationToken** of **onTaskChanged2** to **secondTask**.

20. Remaining in the properties of **onTaskChanged2**, click on the **AfterProperties** ellipsis. As with the first task, click on the **Bind to a** member tab. Give the member a name of **onTaskChanged2_AfterProperties** and change the option to **Create Field** before clicking on **OK**.

21. Move to **ifElseActivity3** and rename it to **ifElseSecondTaskApproved**.

22. Click on **ifElseBranchActivity3** and rename it to **ifSecondTaskApproved**. Set its condition to be a **Declarative Rule Condition** and create a new condition called **Second Task Approved** with the code: `this. secondTaskApprovalStatus == "Approved"`.

23. Click on **completedTask2** and set its **CorrelationToken** property to **secondTask**.

24. Finally, click on the **TaskId** property of **completedTask2** and set it to the **TaskId** property of **createTask2**.

Adding code to the workflow

At this point we've successfully designed our workflow, but now we need to add some code to complete the solution.

The code is available in the file called `0509_07_Workflow.cs`, if you prefer to copy and paste it, or it is explained next:

Using section

We need to use the Xml class, so add a reference to the System.Xml namespace in the using section:

```
using System.Xml;
```

Declaration section

```
//Code created by the designer
public Guid workflowId = default(System.Guid);
public SPWorkflowActivationProperties workflowProperties = new
SPWorkflowActivationProperties();
public SPWorkflowTaskProperties onTaskChanged1_AfterProperties
= new Microsoft.SharePoint.Workflow.SPWorkflowTaskProperties();
public SPWorkflowTaskProperties onTaskChanged2_AfterProperties
= new Microsoft.SharePoint.Workflow.SPWorkflowTaskProperties();


//Used to track the approval status of each task
private string firstTaskApprovalStatus = "Awaiting Approval";
private string secondTaskApprovalStatus = "Awaiting Approval";
//Hold the store name from the MDS XML
private string storeName;
//Hold the GUID of the custom column
Guid approvalField;
```

The above code contains objects created by the designer, such as workflowProperties, which is the object that holds the workflow level properties. In addition, the variables that are declared hold values that we need to use throughout the code, such as the store name.

createTask1_MethodInvoking

```
private void createTask1_MethodInvoking(object sender, EventArgs e)
    {
        //Pick up the XML sent by MDS
        XmlDocument mdsXml = new XmlDocument();
        mdsXml.LoadXml(workflowProperties.InitiationData);
        //Create the new task
        createTask1.TaskId = Guid.NewGuid();
        createTask1.TaskProperties = new
SPWorkflowTaskProperties();
        //Replace with your domain/user
        createTask1.TaskProperties.AssignedTo = "DOMAIN\\User";
        createTask1.TaskProperties.DueDate = DateTime.Now.
AddDays(1);
        createTask1.TaskProperties.Title = "Approve New Store";
        storeName = mdsXml.SelectNodes("ExternalAction/MemberData/
Name")[0].InnerXml;
        createTask1.TaskProperties.Description = "A store with the
name " + storeName + " has been added to MDS. Approval is required.";
        //Approval Status is a custom field. Get its GUID, which
we need to pick up the columns value later on
```

```
        approvalField = workflowProperties.TaskList.
Fields["Approval Status"].Id;
        }
```

Our first task is to pick up the data that has been sent by MDS to the SharePoint workflow that is held in the `workflowProperties.InitiationData` property. We pick up the store name by using XPath to navigate the XML, before creating a new task, and setting all of its properties. One of the properties is the user that the task is assigned to. In a production system, we would want this to be the Regional Manager, but replace this with your own domain and username for our testing purposes.

onTaskChanged1_Invoked

```
private void onTaskChanged1_Invoked(object sender,
ExternalDataEventArgs e)
        {
            //Get the approval status (waiting/approved/rejected)
            firstTaskApprovalStatus = onTaskChanged1_AfterProperties.
ExtendedProperties[approvalField].ToString();
        }
```

When the invoked method of `onTaskChanged1` fires, we need to pick up the approval status. Our while loop will wait until this property does not equal **Awaiting Approval**, but we need to check it each time the task changes. This is achieved by using the `ExtendedProperties` of the task, where we can pick up the custom column that we added.

createTask2_MethodInvoking

```
private void createTask2_MethodInvoking(object sender, EventArgs e)
        {
            //Create the second task
            createTask2.TaskId = Guid.NewGuid();
            createTask2.TaskProperties = new
SPWorkflowTaskProperties();
            createTask2.TaskProperties.AssignedTo = "DOMAIN\\User";
            createTask2.TaskProperties.DueDate = DateTime.Now.
AddDays(1);
            createTask2.TaskProperties.Title = "Final Approval New
Store";
            createTask2.TaskProperties.Description = "A store with the
name " + storeName + " has been added to MDS. Approval is required.";
        }
```

The MethodInvoking method of createTask2 is very similar to the task we created before. Again, we create a new task, setting all of its properties. The one point to note is that we again need to edit the user that the final task will be assigned to — this can be the same user or a different user, as long as the user has been added to the SharePoint site.

onTaskChanged2_Invoked

```
private void onTaskChanged2_Invoked(object sender,
ExternalDataEventArgs e)
        {
            //Get the approval status (waiting/approved/rejceted)
            secondTaskApprovalStatus = onTaskChanged1_AfterProperties.
ExtendedProperties[approvalField].ToString();
        }
```

Our final piece of code checks the approval status of the final task and stores it in the secondTaskApprovalStatus variable. This is the last piece of code that is needed, as an **Approval Status** of **Approved** will cause the while activity to exit, meaning the workflow will continue and mark the task as approved.

Deploying the workflow solution

Now that the design and coding of the workflow is complete, we are ready to deploy the solution to SharePoint. Carry out the following in order to deploy:

1. Remaining within Visual Studio, click on the **Build** menu and choose the **Build** menu item.

2. Verify that **Build Succeeded** is shown in the bottom-left hand corner, or address any errors that are shown in the **Error List**.

3. Click on the **Build** menu again and choose the **Deploy** option to deploy to SharePoint.

4. Go to Windows **Services** in **Administrative Tools** and locate the service called **SQL Server MDS Workflow Integration**. Restart this service if it's started, or start it if it is currently stopped.

5. Verify that the workflow has been successfully deployed to SharePoint by clicking on **All Site Content** and then clicking on the **Site Workflows** item. If the workflow has been deployed correctly, then it should be available in the **Start a New Workflow** section. We don't want to start it yet; instead we want MDS to start the workflow in the next section.

Running the SharePoint workflow

We are now in a position to test our SharePoint workflow. We will do this by creating a new Store in Master Data Manager, and then verifying that a series of tasks get created in SharePoint. Carry out the following to test the workflow:

1. To begin, go to Master Data Manager, and navigate to the **Explorer** function.

2. Click on the green plus icon to add a new leaf level member. Enter the following information for the new member:
   - **Name — AW Seattle**
   - **Code — 054**

3. Click on the save button that will cause the business rule to run.

4. Click on the edit button in the attributes section and complete the remaining attributes with appropriate values, before clicking on save.

Now that we have created the new member, we need to have a look in SharePoint to see what has been created. We will now walk through the changes that have been made to SharePoint. To start off, if we go to the task list, we should now see the following:

		Type	Title	Assigned To	Status
☐			Approve New Store NEW	Jeremy Kashel	Not Started
⊕ Add new item					

Clicking on the task and then choosing **Edit Item** will allow us to edit the **Approval Status** (and other properties) as shown:

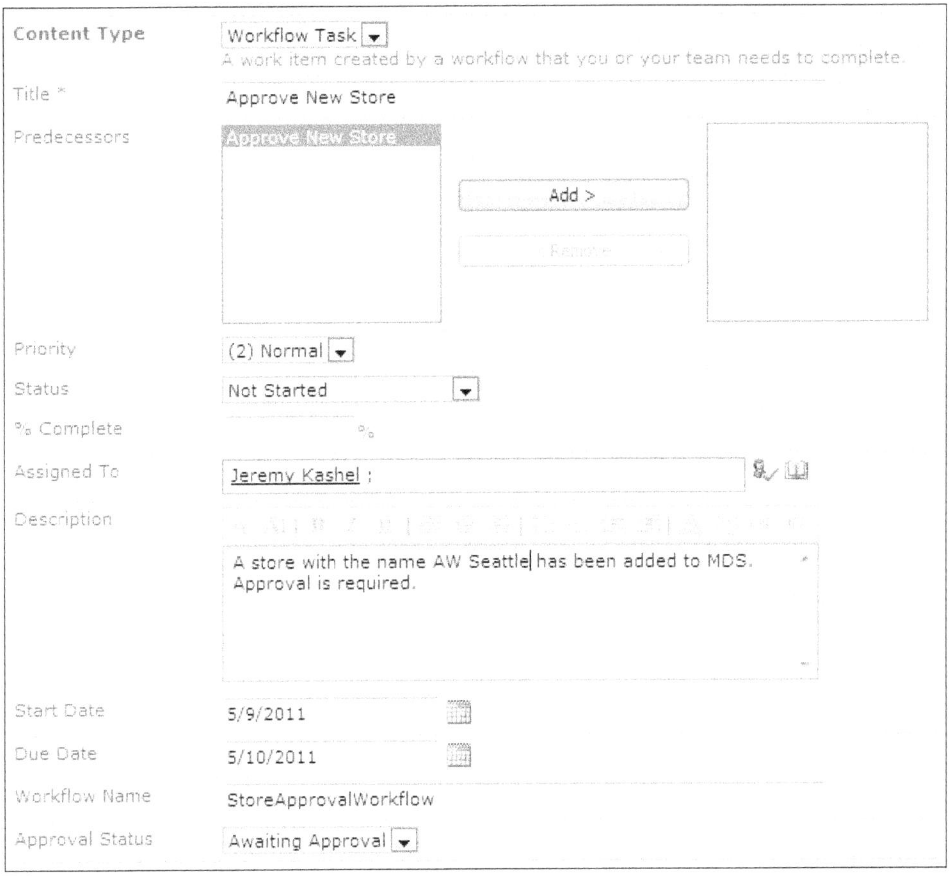

Change the **Approval Status** to **Approved** and click **Save**. Refresh the task view and notice that we now have a second task that of course is for the Head Office Manager:

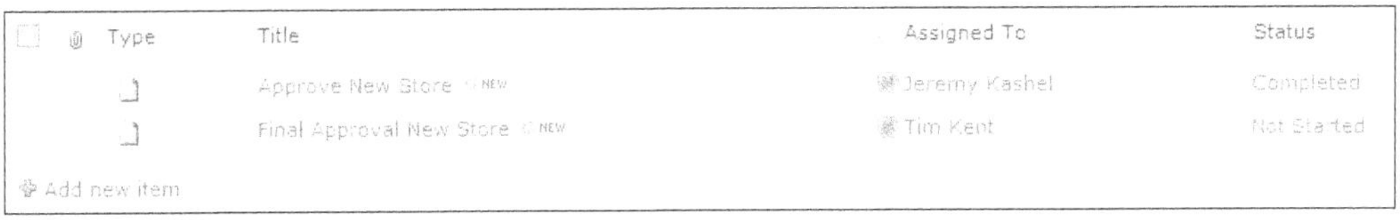

The second task has been generated because the first while activity in our workflow exited, causing the next activity, namely the creation of the second task, to be run. At this point the workflow is currently still in progress, and will remain this way until the second task is approved by the Head Office Manager.

Although the development of our approval process is not quite complete, it shows an idea of what can be achieved with MDS and SharePoint. We will extend this example further in *Chapter 9, Application Programming Interface,* when we look at the API.

Summary

We've covered a lot of ground in this chapter that can be summarized by the following key points:

- Business rule in MDS are If/Then expressions that are made up of conditions and actions
- The business rules are run on the following events:
  - Creating a member
  - Editing a member
  - Validating a version that can be carried out from the front-end using a stored procedure or using the API
- Actions can change the value of member attributes, generate member values, and cause a member to be invalid
- E-mail notifications are sent when a validation action is invoked
- External actions can initiate a SharePoint workflow that can be used for complex approval processes

Looking ahead to the next chapter, we will cover using the Master Data Services API, and see how it can be used to create custom .Net solutions.

8

Extracting Data from Master Data Services

We will start to look outside Master Data Services in this chapter, examining how master data can be fed to other systems. Our focus will be to look at the MDS objects that need to be created in order to support extracting data from MDS, which we will do by going through a number of examples.

A final, optional, part of the chapter will then be to create a BizTalk application that will deliver our Store data to an example subscribing system.

In this chapter, we will cover the following topics:

- Introduction
- Subscription Views
- Delivering master data using BizTalk

Introduction

The method of extracting data from MDS will depend on the requirements of the system that is consuming the data. For Operational MDM, there may be a need to make master data available to an application in near real time. On the other hand, for Analytical MDM, the general requirement will probably be to feed data to a data warehouse on a daily basis, rather than in real time.

MDS provides two core methods of extracting data, namely:

- Subscription Views
- Application Programming Interface (API)

The Subscription Views are MDS objects, created in Master Data Manager or via the API, that allow the extraction of data by implementing physical views in the MDS database.

MDS provides a Web Service API that allows a developer to access all of the functionality of MDS via code. Anything that can be done in the Master Data Manager front-end can also be done via the Web Service API, including the ability to retrieve the members of an entity.

This chapter will focus on Subscription Views as we will cover the API in detail in *Chapter 9*.

Master data delivery

Both the Subscription Views and the API can, in theory, be used by downstream systems to directly connect to Master Data Services (for example, in the transaction hub architecture that we covered in *Chapter 1*).

In other MDM architectures, such as the hybrid architecture that we also covered in *Chapter 1*, there may be a need for integration software to assist with the integration and synchronization of data to the subscribing systems. In an Operational MDM scenario, the integration will probably need to happen in real time, whereas in an Analytical MDM scenario, such integration is more likely be required on a daily scheduled basis.

If real time integration is needed, then this is where an Enterprise Application Integration tool, such as Microsoft BizTalk Server can help. BizTalk will be able to wait for a change to occur in an operational system (such as the update to a customer contact in the CRM system), and then send the change to Master Data Services. BizTalk will then wait for MDS to update its version of the customer contact, before sending the update out to all affected systems.

With Analytical MDM operations, such as transferring data to a data warehouse, the data transfer from MDS to the data warehouse will most likely not need to be so frequent. SQL Server Integration Services (SSIS) will often be the tool of choice in a Microsoft data warehouse, as a set of scheduled SSIS packages can take data from MDS and load into the warehouse. Although MDM will greatly reduce the need for the data warehouse to carry out data cleaning on the dimensions, some transformations may need to happen, such as the process of slowly changing dimensions, which SSIS would still need to handle.

Subscription Views

There are several different types of Subscription Views that can be created in MDS, in order to deliver data in the appropriate way for external systems.

The Subscription Views are model-level objects that are bound to either a version or a version flag. Binding the Subscription View to a version will mean that the resulting SQL Server view only contains data for that version (for example, our 2011_Stores Version). On the other hand, binding to a version flag will mean that it is always possible to extract a version dynamically, as the subscription view is bound to a version flag and the version flag is then bound to a version.

All of the objects that we covered back in *Chapter 4* can be extracted, namely Entities, Derived Hierarchies, Explicit Hierarchies, and Collections.

Formats

The choice in Master Data Manager is to bind the Subscription View to an Entity or a Derived Hierarchy, which then drives the structure of the resulting SQL Server view, by specifying a format. The formats that can be picked are shown below:

Entity / Derived Hierarchy	Format	Description
Entity	Leaf attributes	The leaf members of an entity along with all leaf attributes
Entity	Consolidated attributes	The consolidated members of an entity along with all consolidated attributes
Entity	Collection attributes	The collection level attributes of a collection, such as its Code and Name
Entity	Collections	An extract of the members that exist within a collection
Entity	Explicit parent child	Contains members of an explicit hierarchy with each member given a pointer to its parent
Entity	Explicit levels	A de-normalized representation of the levels of an explicit hierarchy
Derived Hierarchy	Derived parent child	A parent-child representation of a derived hierarchy
Derived Hierarchy	Derived levels	A de-normalized representation of the levels of a derived hierarchy

Creating Subscription Views

We will now create several different Subscription Views in our Store model, in order to explore the different formats that can be created.

Extracting leaf and consolidated members

The leaf attributes and consolidated attributes formats provide methods to extract leaf members and consolidated members respectively, containing either the leaf attributes or the consolidated attributes of each member.

We will start by looking how to create a Subscription View containing leaf members:

1. Navigate to the MDS home page and choose the **Integration Management** function.

2. Click on the **Export** menu at the top of the page. The Subscription Views page will now be shown, which by default will show an empty grid at the top of the page, along with the standard MDS buttons that we have been working with. The grid holds the Subscription Views that have been created across all Models in the system.

3. Click on the green plus icon, which will show the following:

4. Enter **StoreLeafAttributes** as the **Name** for the Subscription View, and then select **Store** from the **Model** drop-down.

5. Choose **2011_Stores** from the **Version** drop-down. We will initially create our Subscription View mapped to a specific version, rather than a version flag.

6. Choose **Store** from the **Entity** drop-down. As the Store entity contains both leaf and consolidated members, plus collections and explicit hierarchies, we get a variety of choices in the **Format** drop-down.

7. Pick **Leaf Attributes** from the **Format** drop-down and then click the save button, which is highlighted next:

The Subscription View will now be created, and will be shown in the grid at the top of the page. In addition, the SQL Server view will now be created, which we will now look at.

Using SQL Server Management Studio (SSMS), connect to the SQL Server instance where your MDS database is located, and expand the Views folder. There should now be a view in the mdm schema called **StoreLeafAttributes**, as shown:

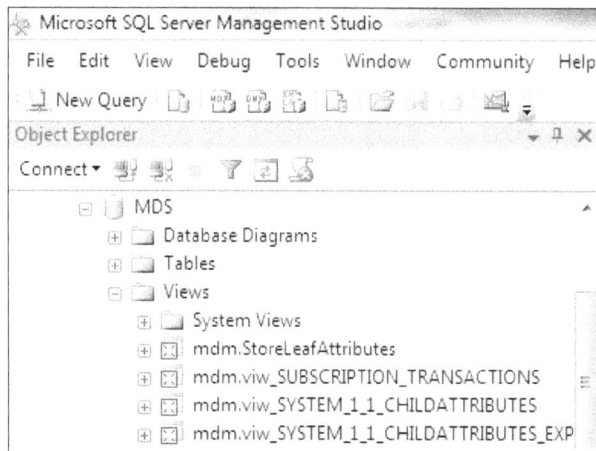

Right click on the **mdm.StoreLeafAttributes** view and click on **Select Top 1000 Rows**. All of the Store Leaf Entity members will now be displayed, along with their attributes:

Downstream applications, such as an Enterprise Resource Planning (ERP) system, or integration tools, for example, SSIS, can now connect directly to the view in order to extract the Stores.

We will now see how the consolidated members can be extracted. Repeat this process, creating a Subscription View with the following options:

Name	StoreConsolidatedAttributes
Version	2011_Stores
Entity	Store
Format	Consolidated Attributes

From within SSMS, right-click on the **mdm. StoreConsolidatedAttributes** and choose **Select Top 1000 Rows.** The results below show all the consolidated members that exist in the Store entity:

The interesting point to note here is the inclusion of a column in the view called **Hierarchy**. As we learnt in *Chapter 4*, consolidated members can only belong to one hierarchy, so therefore, as the mapping is a one-to-one, the Hierarchy name is included in the view.

Extracting Explicit Hierarchies

As we saw in *Chapter 4*, Explicit Hierarchies can contain a mix of consolidated and leaf members, with the scope for the hierarchy to be ragged. For this reason, Explicit Hierarchies can be extracted in two formats, namely *Explicit Parent Child* and *Explicit Levels*.

The Explicit Parent Child format results in each hierarchy member getting a column containing a pointer to its parent, with members at the top of the hierarchy simply getting a pointer of ROOT.

In contrast, the Explicit Levels format results in the hierarchy being output in a de-normalized structure, with NULL values appearing where the structure is ragged.

We will now create two new Subscription Views with the above formats. Repeat the process that we have been through already, entering the following properties for each Subscription View:

	Subscription View 1	Subscription View 2
Name	StoreExplicitParentChild	StoreExplicitLevels
Version	2011_Stores	2011_Stores
Entity	Store	Store
Format	Explicit Parent Child	Explicit Levels
Level *	N/A	3

* - Note: When the Explicit Levels format is chosen, it's necessary to pick the number of levels that are needed in the view. We have three levels in our Store Reporting Explicit Hierarchy, so we are OK to pick three. In a production environment there is a danger that setting this property too low could cause some members to be omitted from the SQL Server view if, for example, a user adds a new level in the hierarchy. If users are likely to cause such a change, then a good idea is to increase the number of levels beyond the maximum actual levels, which just means that some NULL columns are output in the view.

Once the two new Subscription Views have been created, we need to return to SSMS to have a look at the results. Opening the first view, **StoreExplicitParentChild**, will give the following results:

	VersionName	VersionNumber	VersionFlag	Hierarchy	ParentCode	ParentName	ChildCode	ChildName	ChildSortOrder	ChildLevelNumber	EnterDateTime
1	2011_Stores	2	NULL	Store Reporting	E	East	006	AW Baltimore	3	2	2010-12-02 20:28:29.067
2	2011_Stores	2	NULL	Store Reporting	S	South	011	AW Baytown	4	2	2010-12-02 20:28:29.067
3	2011_Stores	2	NULL	Store Reporting	HO	Head Office	050	AW Bellevue	9	1	2010-12-02 20:28:29.067
4	2011_Stores	2	NULL	Store Reporting	N	North	048	AW Billings	11	2	2010-12-02 20:28:29.067
5	2011_Stores	2	NULL	Store Reporting	S	South	037	AW Biloxi	11	2	2010-12-02 20:28:29.067
6	2011_Stores	2	NULL	Store Reporting	S	South	029	AW Birmingham	7	2	2010-12-02 20:28:29.067
7	2011_Stores	2	NULL	Store Reporting	S	South	019	AW Bluffton	6	2	2010-12-02 20:28:29.067
8	2011_Stores	2	NULL	Store Reporting	W	West	017	AW Bountiful	4	2	2010-12-02 20:28:29.067
9	2011_Stores	2	NULL	Store Reporting	S	South	044	AW Bradenton	12	2	2010-12-02 20:28:29.067
10	2011_Stores	2	NULL	Store Reporting	E	East	015	AW Braintree	4	2	2010-12-02 20:28:29.067
11	2011_Stores	2	NULL	Store Reporting	N	North	046	AW Branch	10	2	2010-12-02 20:28:29.067
12	2011_Stores	2	NULL	Store Reporting	C	Central	014	AW Branson	1	2	2010-12-02 20:28:29.067
13	2011_Stores	2	NULL	Store Reporting	W	West	013	AW Burbank	2	2	2010-12-02 20:28:29.067
14	2011_Stores	2	NULL	Store Reporting	W	West	016	AW Burbank 2	3	2	2010-12-02 20:28:29.067
15	2011_Stores	2	NULL	Store Reporting	S	South	036	AW Byron	10	2	2010-12-02 20:28:29.067
16	2011_Stores	2	NULL	Store Reporting	E	East	005	AW Cambridge	2	2	2010-12-02 20:28:29.067
17	2011_Stores	2	NULL	Store Reporting	HO	Head Office	032	AW Campbellsville	6	1	2010-12-02 20:28:29.067
18	2011_Stores	2	NULL	Store Reporting	N	North	035	AW Casper	8	2	2010-12-02 20:28:29.067

Notice that each member contains not only its own attributes (**ChildCode** and **ChildName**), but also a pointer to its parent in the **ParentCode** column, as well as the Parent's Name in the **ParentName** column.

Extracting collections

Collections can also be extracted by using the Subscription Views, by using one of two formats. The *Collections* format provides an extract of the members that exist within the collection, whereas the Collection Attributes format returns the collection level attributes, such as its Name and Code, as well as any custom attributes that have been added to the collection.

We will now create two new Subscription Views to contain the formats for Collections. Repeat the process that we have been through already, entering the following properties for each Subscription View:

	Subscription View 1	Subscription View 2
Name	StoreCollections	StoreCollectionAttributes
Version	2011_Stores	2011_Stores
Entity	Store	Store
Format	Collections	Collection Attributes

We will now take a look at the SQL Server views that have been created. Go into SSMS and locate the new view called **mdm.StoreCollections**. Open the view, which will display the following results:

As we can see from the above screenshot, the view contains the members that we added to our collection in *Chapter 4*. Although not relevant in our situation, the Collections format will actually extract the members from all collections in the model, rather than allowing us to specify which collection we want.

Remaining in SSMS, open the second new view, which will be called **mdm. StoreCollectionAttribtues**, which will display the following results:

The SQL Server view shown includes the attributes of the collection, which may be useful to some downstream applications, in conjunction with the collection members themselves.

Extracting Derived Hierarchies

The final set of Subscription View formats for us to look at are those for Derived Hierarchies, namely *Derived Parent Child* and *Derived Levels*. The Derived Parent Child format will return all the members of a Derived Hierarchy, with each member containing a reference to its parent member. In contrast, the Derived Levels format will return a flattened extract of the hierarchy, adding extra columns to the SQL Server view for each level in the hierarchy. Both of these formats are similar to the formats we encountered when covering Explicit Hierarchies.

We will now create a final set of Subscription Views. Repeat the same process as before, using the settings shown below:

	Subscription View 1	Subscription View 2
Name	StoresByGeographyParentChild	StoresByGeographyLevels
Version	2011_Stores	2011_Stores
Derived Hierarchy	Stores By Geography	Stores By Geography
Format	Derived Parent Child	Derived Levels
Level	N/A	4

Once the new Subscription Views have been created, open the two views as before in SSMS. Examining the **mdm.StoresByGeographyParentChild** view, we will see that we get a result set that includes each member from the derived hierarchy, along with a reference to the member's parent. One point of note is that we are also told the entity that each member belongs to, through the use of the **Child_EntityName** and **Parent_EntityName** columns:

	VersionName	VersionNumber	VersionFlag	Hierarchy	ChildType_ID	Child_ID	ChildCode	ChildName	Child_Entity_ID	Child_EntityName	ParentType_ID	Parent_ID
1	2011_Stores	2	NULL	Stores By Geography	1	1205	AU	Australia	69	Country	2	0
2	2011_Stores	2	NULL	Stores By Geography	1	1206	CA	Canada	69	Country	2	0
3	2011_Stores	2	NULL	Stores By Geography	1	1207	FR	France	69	Country	2	0
4	2011_Stores	2	NULL	Stores By Geography	1	1208	DE	Germany	69	Country	2	0
5	2011_Stores	2	NULL	Stores By Geography	1	1209	IT	Italy	69	Country	2	0
6	2011_Stores	2	NULL	Stores By Geography	1	1210	GB	United Kingdom	69	Country	2	0
7	2011_Stores	2	NULL	Stores By Geography	1	1211	US	United States	69	Country	2	0
8	2011_Stores	2	NULL	Stores By Geography	1	657	NSW	New South Wales	68	State	1	1205
9	2011_Stores	2	NULL	Stores By Geography	1	663	QLD	Queensland	68	State	1	1205
10	2011_Stores	2	NULL	Stores By Geography	1	665	SA	South Australia	68	State	1	1205
11	2011_Stores	2	NULL	Stores By Geography	1	667	TAS	Tasmania	68	State	1	1205

Remaining in SSMS, examine the view called **mdm.StoresByGeographyLevels**, which is shown below:

	VersionName	VersionNumber	VersionFlag	Hierarchy	ROOT	Country_ID	Country_Code	Country_Name	State_ID	State_Code	State_Name	City_ID	City_Code	City_Name
1	2011_Stores	2	NULL	Stores By Geography	ROOT	1205	AU	Australia	657	NSW	New South Wales	3673	291	Alexandria
2	2011_Stores	2	NULL	Stores By Geography	ROOT	1205	AU	Australia	657	NSW	New South Wales	3731	292	Coffs Harbour
3	2011_Stores	2	NULL	Stores By Geography	ROOT	1205	AU	Australia	657	NSW	New South Wales	3737	293	Darlinghurst
4	2011_Stores	2	NULL	Stores By Geography	ROOT	1205	AU	Australia	657	NSW	New South Wales	3757	294	Goulburn
5	2011_Stores	2	NULL	Stores By Geography	ROOT	1205	AU	Australia	657	NSW	New South Wales	3772	295	Lane Cove
6	2011_Stores	2	NULL	Stores By Geography	ROOT	1205	AU	Australia	657	NSW	New South Wales	3775	296	Lavender Bay
7	2011_Stores	2	NULL	Stores By Geography	ROOT	1205	AU	Australia	657	NSW	New South Wales	3777	297	Malabar
8	2011_Stores	2	NULL	Stores By Geography	ROOT	1205	AU	Australia	657	NSW	New South Wales	3778	298	Matraville
9	2011_Stores	2	NULL	Stores By Geography	ROOT	1205	AU	Australia	657	NSW	New South Wales	3783	299	Milsons Point
10	2011_Stores	2	NULL	Stores By Geography	ROOT	1205	AU	Australia	657	NSW	New South Wales	3795	300	Newcastle
11	2011_Stores	2	NULL	Stores By Geography	ROOT	1205	AU	Australia	657	NSW	New South Wales	3797	301	North Ryde
12	2011_Stores	2	NULL	Stores By Geography	ROOT	1205	AU	Australia	657	NSW	New South Wales	3798	302	North Sydney

As the Subscription View was created using the Derived Levels format, we get a flattened representation of the Derived Hierarchy, which is very similar to the Explicit Levels format that we covered when covering Explicit Hierarchies.

Subscription View maintenance

Existing Subscription Views do not get updated automatically if an object they are referencing (for example, an Entity) gets updated.

As an example, if an entity is associated with a Subscription View, and an additional attribute is added to the entity, then the following message will be shown when editing the entity:

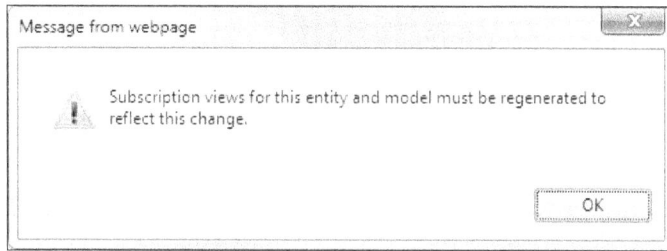

The problem is easily rectified by editing the Subscription View from the same Subscription Views page that we have been using in this chapter. When the Subscription View is saved during the editing process, this will cause the underlying SQL Server view to be dropped and re-created.

Delivering master data using BizTalk

Now that we have created our Subscription Views we will see how BizTalk can be used to synchronize our changes to a subscribing system.

As mentioned at the beginning of the chapter, one of the main reasons to use BizTalk is its ability to transfer data in near real time. Other advantages of BizTalk that can be useful in an MDM scenario are:

- Once master data has been delivered to one target system, less effort is required to deliver data to additional systems, versus a tool such as SSIS

- Data transfer can be configured to automatically retry sending if a failure occurs

- A wide range of out-of-the-box and third party connectors are available to products like SAP, Oracle, PeopleSoft, and Salesforce.com, for example

The examples that we will go through are entirely optional, given that not everyone will have a BizTalk server available.

The pre-requisites for this exercise are:

- Visual Studio 2010 Professional or higher installed
- BizTalk Server 2010 Standard Edition installed and configured

Example scenario background

The example scenario that we will be using is that we have a stock control system that needs to hold stock levels for our stores for various products.

As a new store is created in MDS, we will transfer the new store to the stock control database and insert into one of its tables. We will also cater for updates that may occur to our store data, such as a telephone number change.

Managing deletes and de-duplication will be out of scope, as this is just an example, but these may be areas that you would need to consider in a production scenario.

An overview of how the BizTalk application will work is shown below:

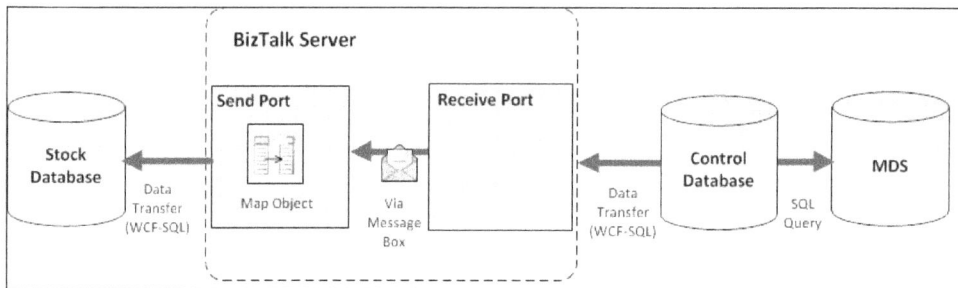

A control database will be created for BizTalk that contains the last time data was successfully transferred to BizTalk via the Windows Communication Foundation (WCF) *SQL adaptor*. BizTalk adaptors are the components that physically transport data, known as *messages*, from a data source into BizTalk.

Receive ports are the BizTalk components that accept a message from an adaptor, and then ultimately write data to the BizTalk *Message Box*, which is the central storage engine for any message that resides in BizTalk. They therefore handle the transport of the messages by using the adaptors as the actual transport mechanism.

In our example, the receive port will poll the control database for changes, and if changes are detected they will be gathered by the receive port via the WCF-SQL adaptor.

The *send port* works in a similar way to the receive port. It handles the delivery of a message to a target system, also by using adaptors as the method of transport.

As the messages are picked up by the send port, they can be transformed to a structure that is required by the target schema, which is carried out by using a BizTalk *map*.

Creating the sample databases

The example BizTalk application requires two sample databases, namely:

- MDSControl—A SQL Server database that holds the last time that MDS changes were synchronized to the target system
- AWStock—The target database that will receive the store data

Carry out the following steps in order to create the MDSControl database:

1. Open the file called `0509_08_CreateControlDatabase.sql` in SQL Server Management Studio (SSMS).

2. At the top of the SQL script, alter the two FILENAME arguments of the CREATE DATABASE statement in order to place the two database files in your preferred location.

3. Scroll to the very bottom of the script. The stored procedure called `dbo.GetMDSStoreChanges` references the Master Data Services database. Alter the part of the script below to ensure that the database reference points to your own Master Data Services database:

```
FROM          MDS.mdm.StoreLeafAttributes      S
INNER JOIN    MDSControl.dbo.MDSLastPoll              MLP
              ON S.LastChgDateTime >= MLP.LastPoll
WHERE         MLP.MDSModel = 'Store'
AND           MLP.MDSEntity = 'Store'
AND           S.ValidationStatus = 'Validation Succeeded'
```

4. Execute the SQL script to create the MDSControl database.

Carry out the following steps in order to create the AWStock database:

1. Open the file called `0509_08_CreateStoreStockDatabase.sql` in SSMS.

2. At the top of the SQL script, alter the two FILENAME arguments of the CREATE DATABASE statement in order to place the two database files in your preferred location.

3. Execute the SQL script in order to create the AWStock database.

Creating the BizTalk project

We will now use Visual Studio 2010 in order to create our BizTalk project. Carry out the following instructions to create the project:

1. Open Visual Studio 2010.

2. Click on **New Project** and then choose **BizTalk Projects** from the resulting pop-up window, as shown below:

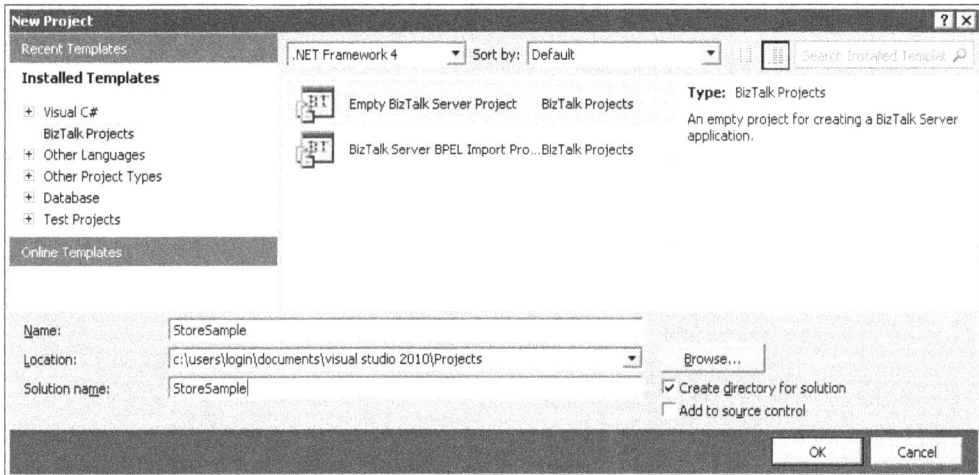

3. Ensure that **Empty BizTalk Server Project** is selected.

4. Enter the **Name** and the **Solution Name** as **StoreSample**, and then pick a suitable location to store the solution files by clicking on the **Browse** button.

5. Click **OK** to create the solution.

We now need to carry out some configuration changes at the project level. In order to do this, carry out the following steps:

1. Right-click on the **StoreSample** project node and choose **Properties**.

2. In the window that will now have appeared, click on the **Signing** tab.

3. Check the checkbox called **Sign the assembly**.

4. Click on **<New>** in the drop-down below.

5. In the pop-up window that will appear, enter a **Key File Name** of MDSSample.

6. Enter a password of your choice, then enter it again, and then finally click on **OK**. The main screen should now look as follows:

While we are in the **Properties** window, we also need to configure the **Deployment** options correctly. In order to do this, carry out the following steps:

1. Click on the **Deployment** tab.

2. Set the **Application Name** to be **StoreSample**.

3. Set the **Server** to be the name of your BizTalk server, if it is not set already.

4. Set the **Configuration Database** to be the name of your configuration database, if it is not set already.

5. Click on the **Save** icon to save the properties.

Building the receive schema and port

Now that we have created a blank BizTalk solution, our first task is to create and configure a schema that will describe the message that we will be receiving. This process will also build a receive port, which will determine whether or not any stores have been added or changed, and if so will transfer them to the BizTalk message box.

Carry out the following steps in order to create the schema and port:

1. Right-click on the **StoreSample** project node and choose **Add**, then **Add Generated Items**, as shown below:

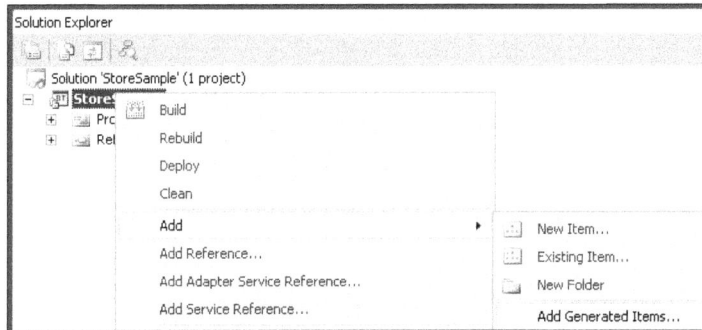

2. In the pop-up window that will appear, choose click on **Consume Adaptor Service** on the left hand side. This will generate a schema file for us that will tell BizTalk about the structure of the MDS data we are importing.

3. Click on the **Add** button. This will bring up the **Consume Adaptor Service** window, as shown below:

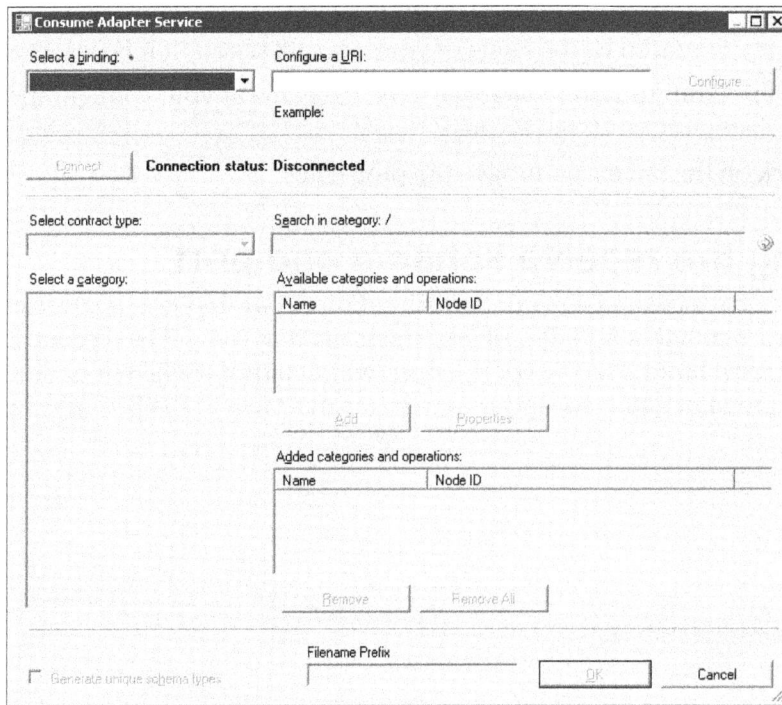

4. In the drop-down underneath **Select a binding**, choose **sqlBinding**.

5. Click on the **Configure** button, on the right-hand side of the screen.

6. In the window that will pop-up, click on the **URI Properties** tab. Within this tab, configure the following properties:

   ◦ **InboundId**—Set this to **GetStoreChanges**.

   ◦ **InititalCatalog**—This is the name of the database that BizTalk will check for changes. Set this to **MDSControl**.

   ◦ **InstanceName**—Set this to the SQL Server instance name where you have deployed the MDSControl database. Leave this option blank if you are using the default SQL Server instance.

   ◦ **Server**—Set this to the SQL Server name where you have deployed the MDSControl database. The completed window should be as follows:

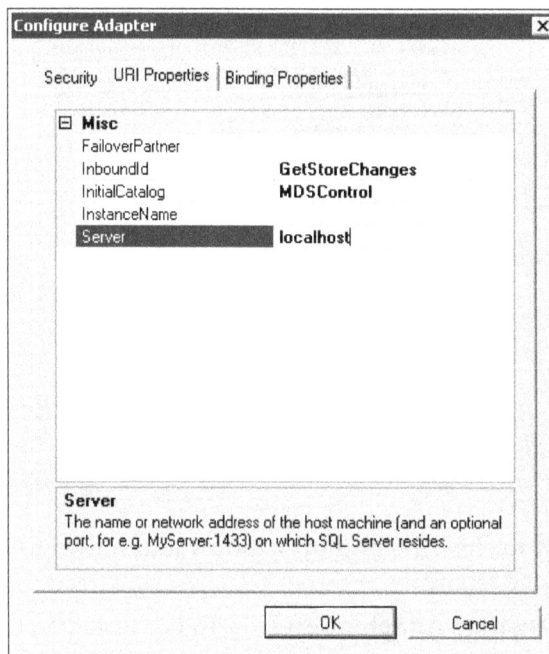

```
┌─────────────────────────────────────────────────────────────┐
│ Configure Adapter                                      [X]   │
│                                                              │
│   Security   URI Properties │ Binding Properties │           │
│                                                              │
│   ⊟ Misc                                                     │
│      FailoverPartner                                         │
│      InboundId                    GetStoreChanges            │
│      InitialCatalog               MDSControl                 │
│      InstanceName                                            │
│      Server                       localhost│                 │
│                                                              │
│                                                              │
│                                                              │
│                                                              │
│                                                              │
│                                                              │
│                                                              │
│                                                              │
│      Server                                                  │
│      The name or network address of the host machine (and   │
│      an optional port, for e.g. MyServer:1433) on which SQL  │
│      Server resides.                                         │
│                                                              │
│                    ┌──────────┐        ┌──────────┐          │
│                    │    OK    │        │  Cancel  │          │
│                    └──────────┘        └──────────┘          │
└─────────────────────────────────────────────────────────────┘
```

7. Click on the **Binding Properties** tab. Within this tab, configure the following properties:

   ° **InboundOperationType** — Set this to **TypedPolling**.

   ° **PolledDataAvailableStatement** — As this statement is quite large, set it to the contents of the file `0509_08_PolledDataAvailableStatement.sql`. As before, ensure that the correct Master Data Services database is specified within the SQL script.

   ° **PollingStatement** — Set this to be `EXEC dbo.GetMDSStoreChanges; EXEC dbo.UpdateMDSLastPoll 'Store', 'Store';`. The completed **Binding Properties** tab should be as follows:

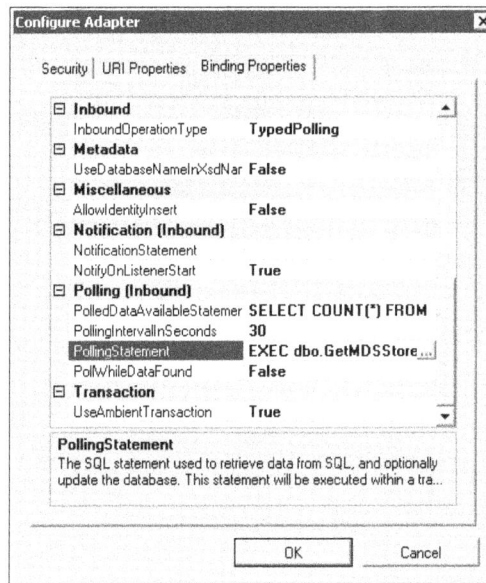

8. Now click **OK** to close the pop-up window and return to the main **Consume Adaptor Service** window.

9. Within the **Consume Adaptor Service** window, click on the **Connect** button.

10. Select **Service (Inbound Operations)** from the **Contract Type** drop-down.

11. Click on the forward slash in the list box below, which will cause the **Available categories and operations** list box to be populated.

12. Click on **TypedPolling** and then click on the **Add** button.

13. Enter **GetStoreChanges** in the **Filename Prefix** textbox. The completed screen should look as follows:

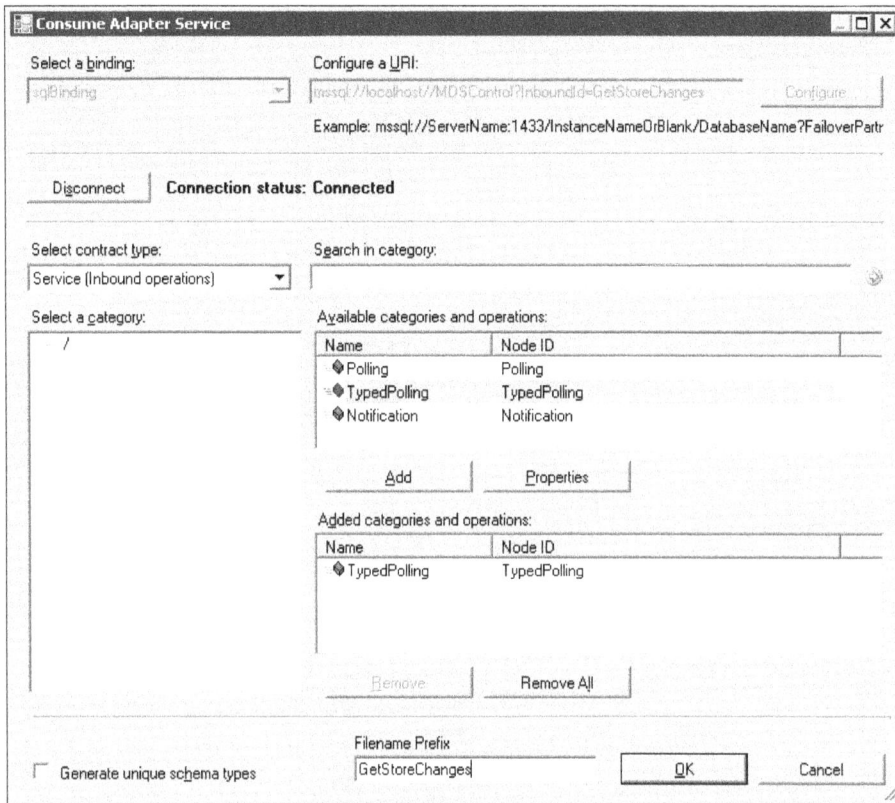

14. Finally, click on the **OK** button, which will generate a `*.xsd` file and a `*.xml` file.

We now need to make a few changes to the schema file that Visual Studio has generated for us. Specifically, we need to alter the schema so that the MDS store records are received as individual elements, rather than one large message. The properties of the schema that we have change are:

- **Envelope**
- **Body Xpath**
- **Min** and **Max Occurs**

Carry out the following steps in order to make the changes outlined above:

1. Using **Solution Explorer**, double-click on the schema called `GetStoreChangesTypedPolling.GetStoreChanges.xsd`.

2. On the left-hand side of the window that opens, click on the node called `<Schema>`.

3. Using the properties of the selected node, set its **Envelope** property to **Yes**, as shown below:

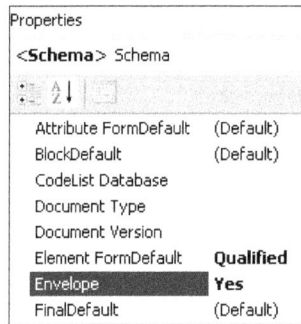

4. Remaining in the current window, use the tree view structure on the left-hand side to select the **TypedPolling** node:

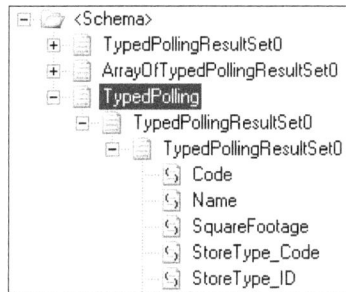

5. Using the properties of the selected node, click the ellipsis icon of the **Body XPath** property. Select the node directly below the current node, as shown:

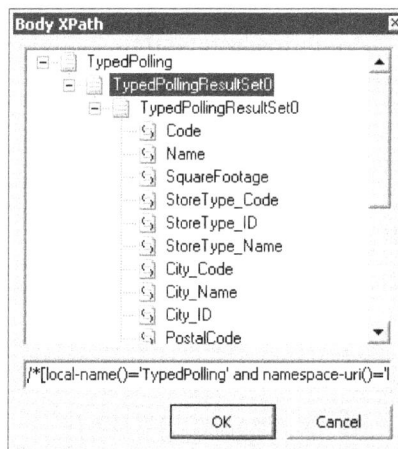

6. Click **OK** to close the **Body XPath** window.

7. Finally, use the tree view structure on the left-hand side of the screen to the leaf level node called **TypedPollingResultSet0**.

8. Using the properties window, set the **Max Occurs** property to **1**, as shown below:

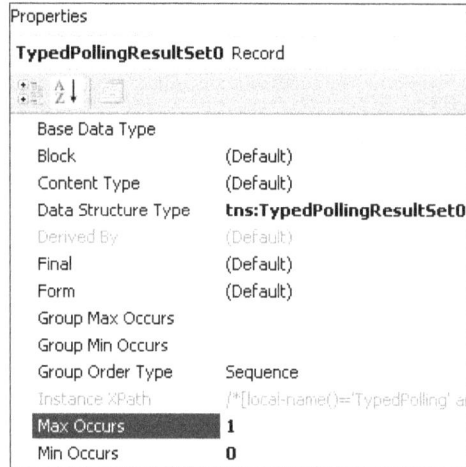

Properties	
TypedPollingResultSet0 Record	
Base Data Type	
Block	(Default)
Content Type	(Default)
Data Structure Type	**tns:TypedPollingResultSet0**
Derived By	(Default)
Final	(Default)
Form	(Default)
Group Max Occurs	
Group Min Occurs	
Group Order Type	Sequence
Instance XPath	/*[local-name()='TypedPolling' a
Max Occurs	1
Min Occurs	0

9. Click on the save icon to save the changes to the schema.

Building the destination schema

We're now ready to create the destination message schema. This will describe the structure of the message that the send port must deliver to the target, as well as saying what the target action is, which in this case is a stored procedure. We will generate the schema by connecting to the stored procedure that we want the send port to fire, which exists in the AWStock database.

Carry out the following steps in order to create the destination schema:

1. Using **Solution Explorer**, right-click on the **StoreSample** project node and choose **Add**, then choose **Add Generated Items**.

2. As we did with the receive adaptor, select **Consume Adaptor Service** from the templates on the left-hand side, and click on the **Add** button. This will cause the **Consume Adaptor Service** window to appear again.

3. The window remembers the binding that we used before as **sqlBinding**, which is what we need again, so there is no need to change it. Instead, click on the **Configure** button.

4. Click on the **URI Properties** tab. Note that the properties that we entered before are remembered by Visual Studio.

5. The **URI Properties** must be configured to connect to the **AWStock** database. Set the properties as shown below, but entering the **Server** and **InstanceName** properties for your own environment:

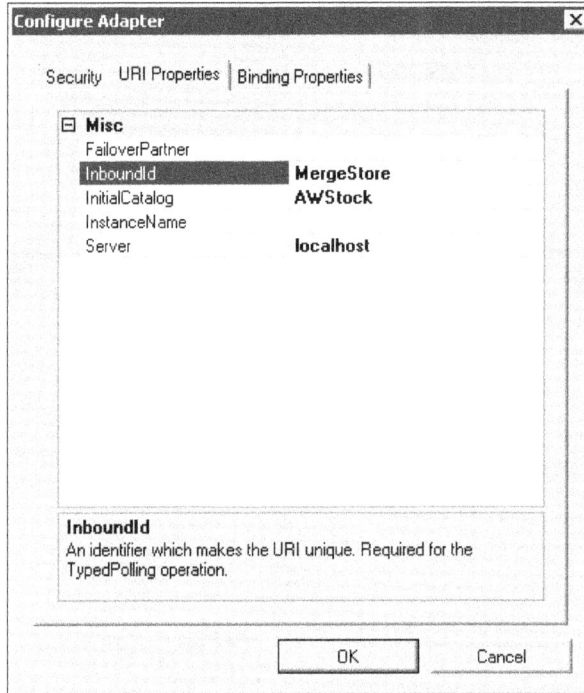

6. Click on the **Binding Properties** tab.

7. As before, the changes we made for the receive schema have been retained. Make the following changes to the **Binding Properties** window:

   ◦ **InboundOperationType** — Polling.

   ◦ **PolledDataAvailableStatement** — Clear the value for this property.

   ◦ **PollingStatement** — Clear the value for this property. The window should now appear as follows:

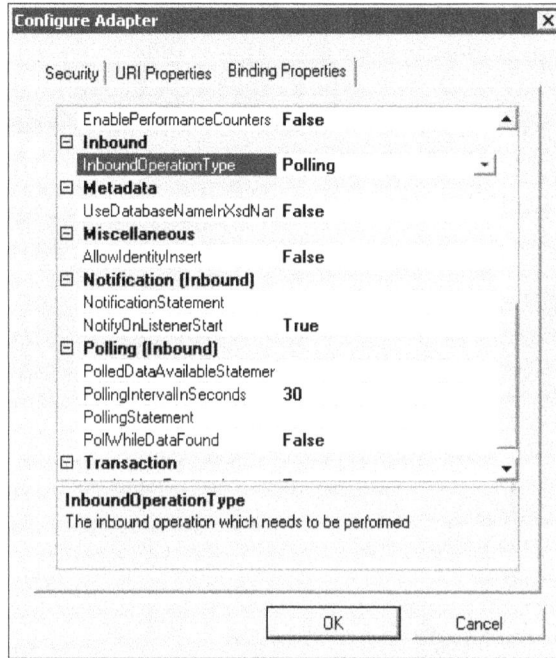

8. Click **OK** to confirm the changes and return to the **Consume Adaptor Service** window.

9. Click **Connect** on the **Consume Adaptor Service** window.

10. Change the **Select contract type** drop-down to be **Client (Outbound operations)**.

11. Using the tree view below, click on the **Procedures** node. In the adjacent list box, select **[dbo].[MergeStore]** and then click on the **Add** button.

12. Enter **MergeStore** as the **Filename Prefix**. The completed screen should look as follows:

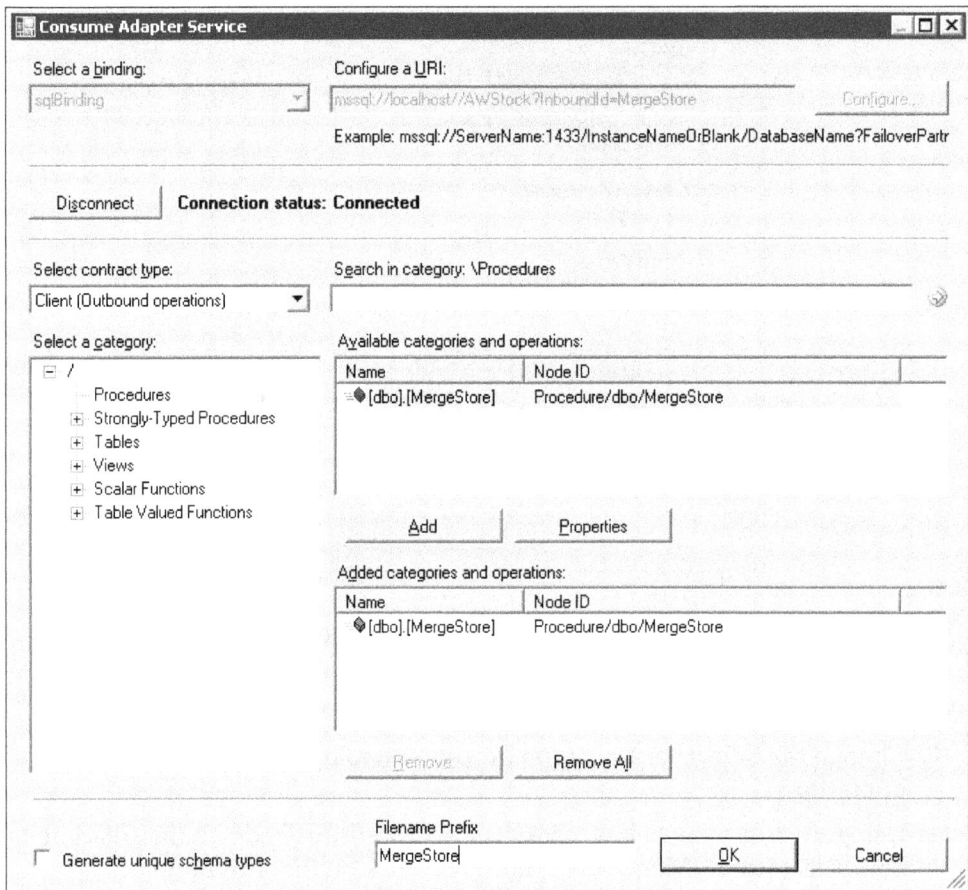

13. Click on **OK** in order to create the schema.

Two files were created as part of the above process, namely the schema file and an XML file with the send port bindings. This will create a send port that will send the message to the destination, but then also send a response back. Although this is useful for some scenarios, we don't want to handle the response for this example, as we're creating a pure messaging solution. Therefore, right-click on the file called **WcfSendPort_SqlAdapterBinding_Custom.bindinginfo.xml** and select **Delete**.

Building the map

We're now in a position where we have successfully created a source and destination schema. We now need to define a BizTalk Map, which will map and transform data that comes from our source MDS schema into our target.

The transforming that we need to do between the two schemas is minimal. The only change that we will actually have to make is to trim our data types, but it will give you an idea of the kind of transformations that you can do with BizTalk.

Carry out the following steps in order to build the map:

1. Using **Solution Explorer**, right-click on the **StoreSample** project and choose **Add**, then **New Items**.

2. Pick the **Map** item from the list.

3   Set the **Name** to be **MDSStoreToStock.btm** and then click on the **Add** button.

4. On the resulting screen that will appear, click the link marked **Open Source Schema**, which will cause the BizTalk Type Picker window to appear.

5. Expand the **StoreSample** node, and then the **Schemas** node, and then pick the **StoreSample.GetStoreChangesTypedPolling_GetStoreChanges** node, as shown below:

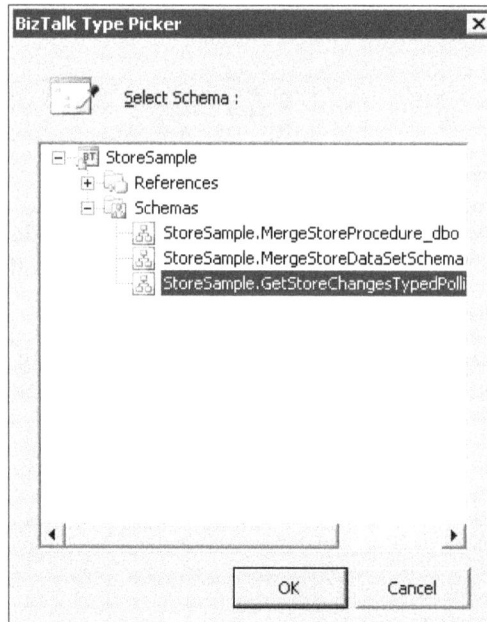

6. Click **OK** to select the schema. This will cause the **Select Root Node** window to appear. Select **TypedPollingResultSet0** from the available options and then click OK, which will populate the left-hand side of the map window.

7. We now need to repeat the same process with the Destination Schema. Click on the **Destination Schema** link, which will again cause the **BizTalk Type Picker** window to appear.

8. Expand the **StoreSample** node, and then the **Schemas** node, and then pick the **StoreSample.MergeStoreProcedure_dbo** node, as shown below:

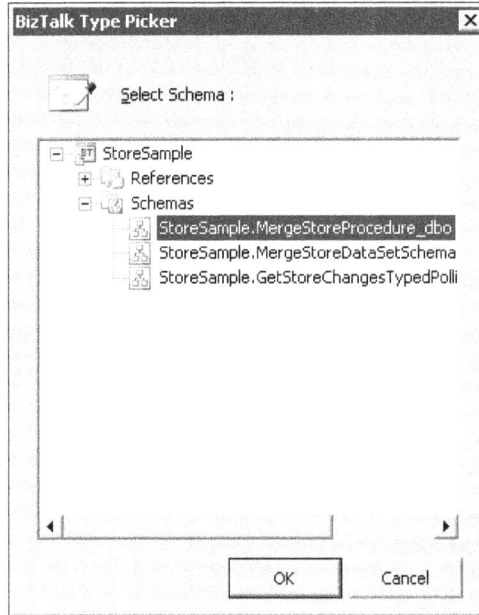

9. Click **OK** to select the schema. In the **Select Root Node** window that will appear, pick the **MergeStore** node and then click on **OK**.

10. Expand the nodes on both sides of the map.

11. Click on the **Code** node of the source schema and drag it to the **StoreCode** of the destination schema. The screen should now look as follows:

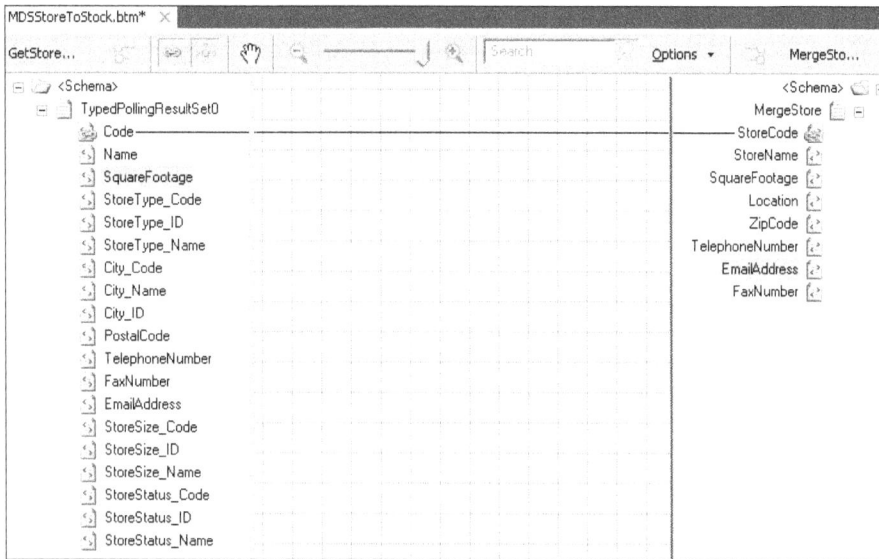

12. Strictly speaking, we should have dealt with the fact that the Code column in the source schema is a character data type, but this will be ok for the purposes of the example. What we will now see is how to handle data type issues on some of the other columns. Open the Visual Studio toolbox and expand the category called **String Functiods**. Drag the **String Left functiod** into the middle of the canvas, in line with the **Name** and **StoreName** nodes.

13. Click on the **Name** source node and drag it to the functiod. The screen should now appear as follows:

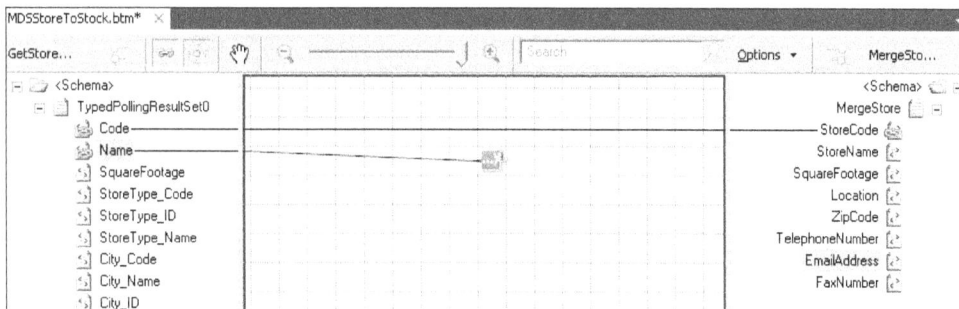

14. Double-click on the functiod, which will open a pop-up window. Enter 100 for the **Index** property and then click **OK**. This will configure the functiod to take the left most 100 characters from the input string.

15. Click on the **StoreName** destination node and drag it to the functiod in the middle of the screen. The warning symbol should disappear from the functiod and the screen should now appear as follows:

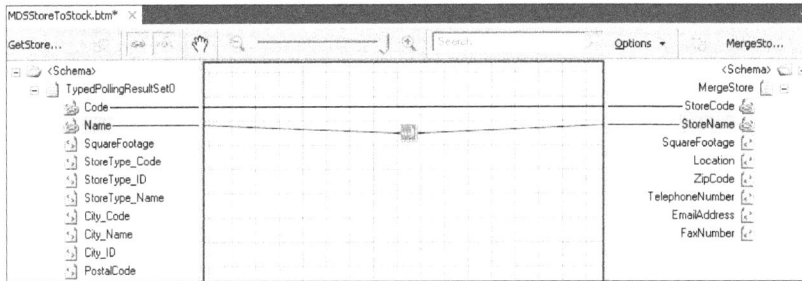

16. Now map the remaining columns, using the following table for guidance:

Source	Destination	Transformation Type	Transformation Options
SquareFootage	SquareFootage	None	N/A
City_Name	Location	String Left	Index = 100
PostalCode	ZipCode	String Left	Index = 20
TelephoneNumber	TelephoneNumber	String Left	Index = 25
FaxNumber	FaxNumber	String Left	Index = 25
EmailAddress	EmailAddress	String Left	Index = 50

17. The completed map should look as follows:

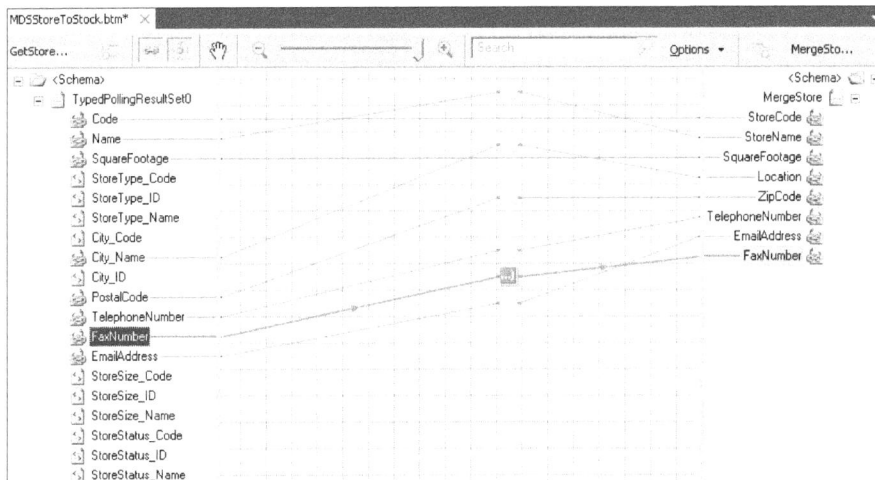

18. Click the save icon complete building the map.

Deploying the BizTalk solution

We're now ready to deploy our new solution to the BizTalk Server. Carry out the following steps in order to deploy the solution:

1. Using **Solution Explorer**, right-click on the solution called **StoreSample** and select **Build Solution**.

2. Verify that **Build Succeeded** is returned on the status bar; in the bottom left-hand of the screen.

3. If there are no errors, right-click on the solution called **StoreSample** and select **Deploy**, which will deploy the assemblies of our solution to the BizTalk server.

4. Verify that **Deploy Succeeded** is returned on the status bar, in the bottom left-hand of the screen.

As the deploy action just deploys the project assemblies, we must now set up our send and receive ports before we're able to use the solution.

Receive port

Carry out the following steps in order to set up the receive port:

1. Using the Windows **Start** menu, open **BizTalk Server Administration**.

2. Expand the tree view on the left-hand side until you reach the **Applications** node. Expand **Applications** and you should see the **StoreSample** application.

3. Right click on **StoreSample** and choose **Import**, and then **Bindings**.

4. In the pop-up window that will appear, navigate where you have stored the Visual Studio solution, and drill down to the `StoreSample\StoreSample` directory. Select the file called `WcfReceivePort_SqlAdapterBinding_Custom.bindinginfo` and then click **Open**, as shown below:

5. Click on the **Receive Ports** node underneath the **StoreSample** application and verify that a receive port now exists.

Send port

The sending part of the solution requires a little bit more effort, as we will be creating the send port manually.

Carry out the following tasks in order to create the send port:

1. Remaining in **BizTalk Server Administration**, right-click on **Send Ports** and choose **New** and then **Static One-way Send Port**.

2. Enter **SendStoreChanges** as the name.

3. Pick **WCF-SQL** from the **Type** drop-down.

4. Click the adjacent **Configure** button, which will open the **WCF-SQL Transport Properties** window.

5. Click on the **Configure** button.

6. Enter the properties as shown below, but enter your own **Instance** and **Server** name:

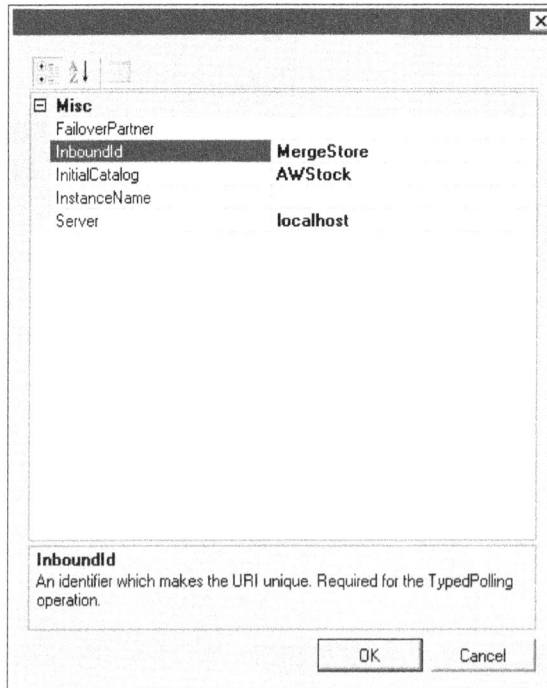

7. Click **OK** to return to the main window.

8. Enter **Procedure/dbo/MergeStore** as the **SOAP Action Header**. The completed screen should look as follows:

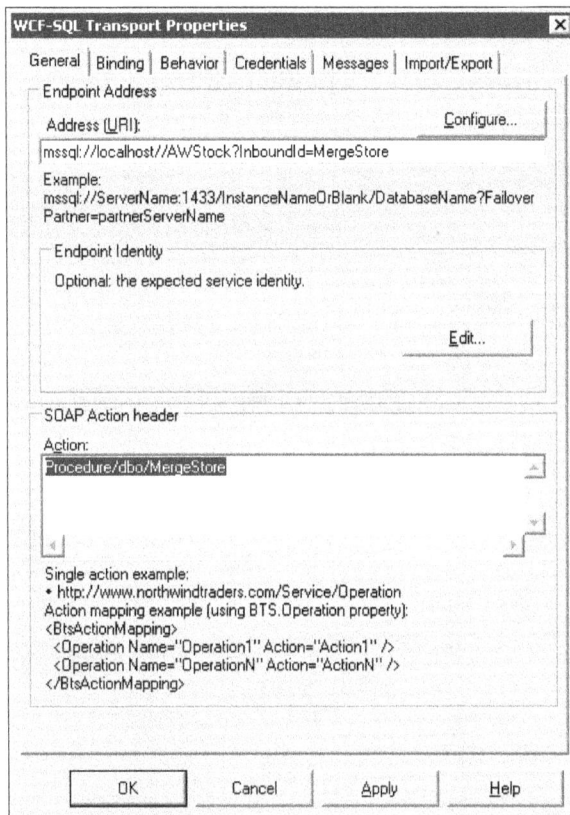

9. Click **OK** to close the window.

10. Alter the **Send Pipeline** drop-down to **XML Transmit**.

11. Click on the **Outbound Maps** item on the left-hand side of the window. Here we can transform the incoming message, to the target message schema. The transformation will be carried out by the map that we created earlier.

12. Pick the following values for the three columns in the **Outbound Maps** window:

- ◦ **Source Document — GetStoreChangesTypedPolling_ GetStoreChanges**

- ◦ **Map — MDSStoreToStock**

- ◦ **Target Document — MergeStoredProcedure_dbo**. The completed window should look as follows:

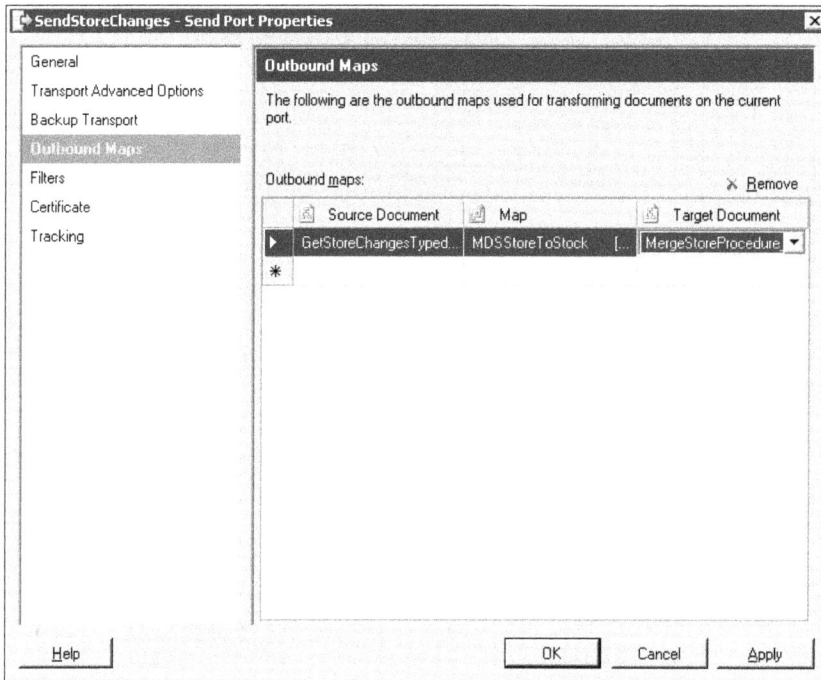

13. Finally, click on the **Filters** item on the left-hand side. Here we want to filter the types of messages that are allowed to our send port.

14. Enter the following filter:

- ◦ **Property — BTS.MessageType**

- ◦ **Operator — ==**

- ◦ **Value — http://schemas.microsoft.com/Sql/2008/05/TypedPolling/ GetStoreChanges#TypedPollingResultSet0.** The screen should look as follows:

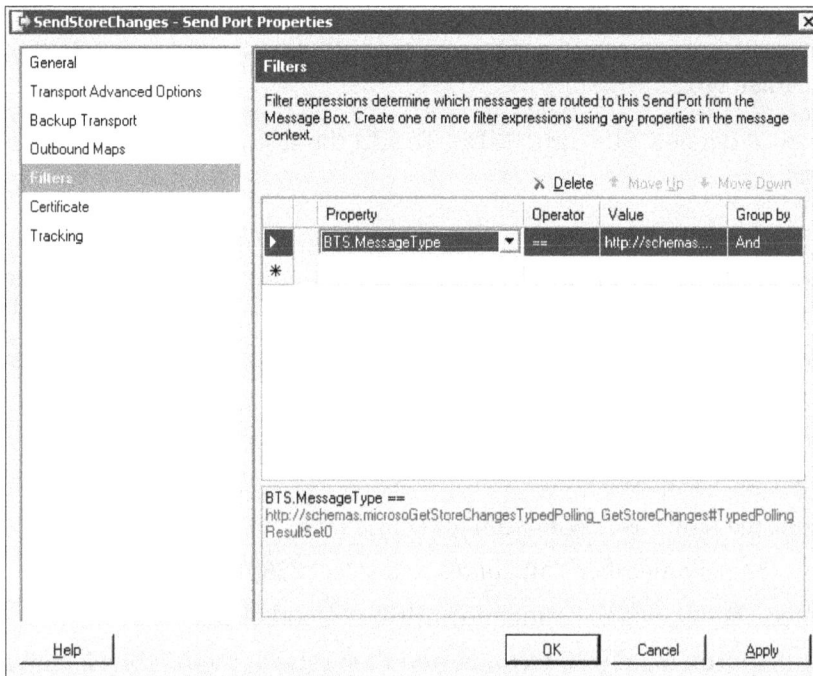

15. Click **OK** to complete creating the send port.

Testing the BizTalk solution

Now that our send and receive ports are created, we are in a position to start our BizTalk solution, which will synchronize our all of the existing stores to the stock database. We will then add a new store to MDS, and verify that it also arrives in the stock database.

Carry out the following steps in order to synchronize the existing stores:

1. Remaining in **BizTalk Server Administration**, right-click on the **StoreSample** application, and select **Start**.

2. Wait approximately 30 seconds, and then connect to the **AWStock** database, using **SSMS**.

3. Right click on the **dbo.Store** table and choose **Select Top 1000 Rows.**

4. Verify that all the MDS stores are now shown.

5. Remaining in SSMS, connect to the **MDSControl** database.

6. Right-click on the **dbo.MDSLastPoll** table and choose **Select Top 1000 Rows**.

7. Verify that the **LastPoll** column holds today's date and a recent time. This shows that the receive port has successfully transferred data into the BizTalk message box.

We will now add a new Store into MDS. To add the store, carry out the following instructions:

1. Open Master Data Manager.

2. Ensure that **Store** is the currently selected model and that **2011_Stores** is the currently selected version.

3. Click on the **Explorer** function.

4. Click the green plus icon to add a new member, and choose **Add Leaf** from the drop-down that will appear.

5. Enter the **Code** as **055.**

6. Enter the name as **AW Boston** and click save.

7. Edit the new member's attributes and select **226{Boston}** as the **City**.

8. Enter test data for the remaining attributes and click save.

9. Wait approximately 30 seconds, and then refresh the **AWStock** stores query in SSMS. The new Boston store should now have arrived, as shown below:

	StoreId	StoreName	Location	ZipCode	TelephoneNumber	FaxNumber	EmailAddress	SquareFootage
45	46	AW Branch	Branch	55056	723-555-0187	723-555-0188	branch@adventureworks.com	6000
46	47	AW Chandler	Chandler	85225	565-555-0112	565-555-0113	chandler@adventureworks.com	6000
47	48	AW Billings	Billings	59101	822-555-0184	822-555-0185	billings@adventureworks.com	6000
48	49	AW Chicago	Chicago	60610	430-555-0120	430-555-0121	chicago@adventureworks.com	6000
49	50	AW Bellevue	Bellevue	98004	230-555-0144	230-555-0145	bellevue@adventureworks.com	6000
50	51	AW Houston	Houston	77999	NULL	NULL	houston@adventureworks.com	3000
51	52	AW Denver	Denver	14223	789-999-9999	NULL	denver@adventureworks.com	2000
52	54	AW Seattle	Seattle	56789	NULL	NULL	seattle@adventureworks.com	4000
53	55	AW Boston	Boston	88888	617-123-4567	NULL	boston@adventureworks.com	3000

Query executed successfully.

Although this is just an example, we have successfully transferred data from MDS to another system via BizTalk. As mentioned, the architecture of BizTalk is such that we would just need to add further send ports and maps to extend this solution to output data to other systems if needed, which makes it an attractive option for this kind of integration.

Summary

In this chapter, we have covered the methods available for extracting data from Master Data Services. In particular, we have learnt:

- BizTalk and SSIS can be used to deliver master data to downstream systems
- Subscription Views result in a physical SQL Server view being created in the MDS database
- Leaf and Consolidated Members, Collections, Explicit Hierarchies, and Derived Hierarchies can all be extracted from MDS using Subscription Views
- Existing Subscription Views do not get updated automatically if a referenced object, such as an entity, has changed

Looking ahead to the next chapter, we will see how the MDS API can be used to extract and update data in MDS.

9

Application Programming Interface

In addition to the Master Data Manager web application discussed so far, Microsoft SQL Server 2008 R2 MDS provides an Application Programming Interface (API) that can perform all functions that the Master Data Manager can, while adding some additional functionality that is only available through the API. To use the Microsoft SQL Server 2008 R2 MDS API you must be comfortable developing software using Microsoft Visual Studio. The code examples within this chapter are written in C#, using Visual Studio 2010.

The example solution worked through in previous chapters will be extended further to cover read and write integration with SharePoint 2010 workflow. We will also look at creating a small SharePoint 2010 web part, using the API to display entity data.

In this chapter, we will cover the following topics:

- Introduction to the MDS API
- Getting started with Web Service API
- MDS assemblies
- Creating a simple Microsoft SharePoint Web Part
- Microsoft SharePoint workflow integration

Introduction to the MDS API

The API provides a standard and consistent way in which to interact with MDS programmatically. The practice of creating and using an API allows an open architecture for sharing content and data between applications. The API in MDS can be used to embed MDS functionality in any application without the need to understand the underlying database structure, whilst ensuring that the integrity of the data is not compromised.

All functionality, and more, that is available in the Master Data Manager web application is also available in the Web Service API. There is only one available exposed service which is exposed as a Windows Communication Foundation (WCF) service. The WCF service API provides a dynamic, strongly-typed development reference that provides a robust and reliable application development experience.

The WCF service is not the only way to access MDS; Microsoft also offers the following assemblies that you can use to interact with MDS, as well as aiding with deployment:

- `Microsoft.MasterDataServices.Core.dll`
- `Microsoft.MasterDataServices.Deployment.dll`
- `Microsoft.MasterDataServices.Services.dll`

The use of WCF services is preferable in most cases, and as such we only cover the use of the assemblies briefly, in a "hello world" example.

To progress with this chapter, there are the following pre-requisites:

- Microsoft SQL Server 2008 R2 with MDS
- Microsoft SharePoint Foundation 2010 or Microsoft SharePoint Server 2010
- Microsoft Visual Studio 2010

What is a WCF service?

WCF (Windows Communication Foundation) is Microsoft's framework for building Service-Oriented Applications and allows asynchronous communication between endpoints. Endpoints are defined as continuously available services that can be hosted by IIS, Windows itself, or any other application. Messages that are exchanged through WCF can be anything from a character to a binary object.

For more information on WCF, please see MSDN online.

Getting started with the Web Services API

Prior to using the methods and logic available in MDS, we must configure the MDS WCF service to allow us to generate a proxy class. In order to do this we need to expose the WSDL by making a change to the web.config of the MDS Web Application. Please note that making this change will recycle the IIS application cache.

1. Open the `Web.config` usually found in `C:\Program Files\Microsoft SQL Server\Master Data Services\WebApplication\web.config`.

2. Find the `<ServiceMetaData>` section.

3. Change `httpGetEnabled` to `True`. If you have MDS set up using SSL, set `httpsGetEnabled` to `True` instead.

Now we have configured MDS we can get started with the MDS WCF Service. We will begin by creating a new console application in Visual Studio by adding the WCF service API reference to our project.

MDS WCF Service Endpoint: `http://<MDSSERVER>/Service/Service.svc`.

This service endpoint can be checked by simply entering the URL into a browser window and ensuring that you get a screen as follows:

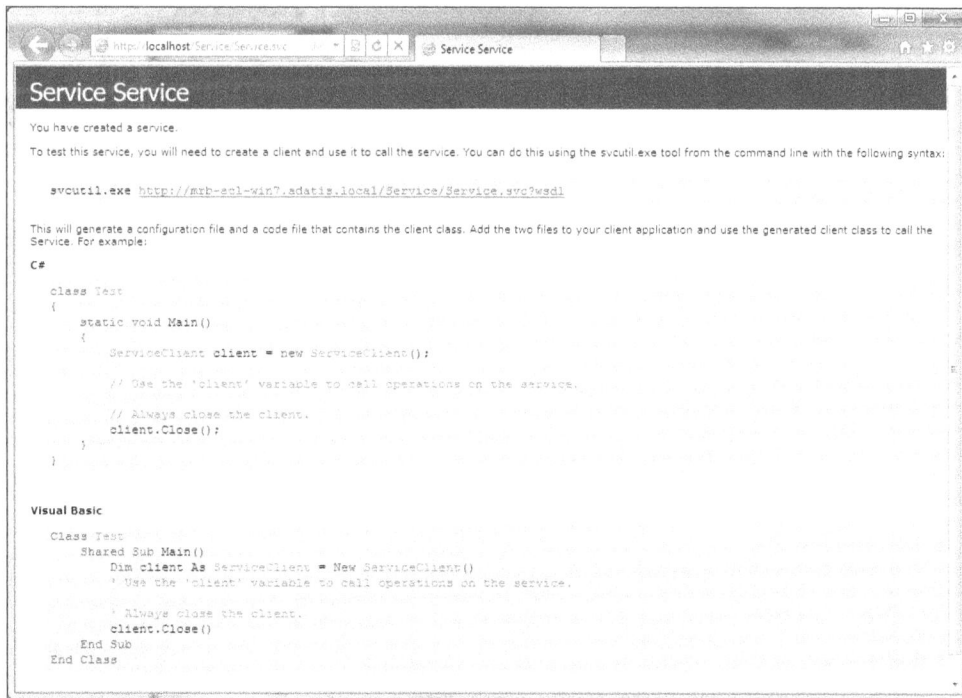

If this screen does not appear ensure that you have enabled the Web Service in the configuration manager (See *Chapter 3, Installing and Configuring Master Data Services,* section Web configuration).

Creating a Web Services project

To get started, we will create a simple project, add a reference to the WCF service, and explore some of the key methods within the service:

1. Open Microsoft Visual Studio, and navigate to **File | New | Project**.

2. Create a new Console Application, and name it "HelloMDS".

3. Right-click on the project in the **Solution Explorer**, right-click and select **Add Service Reference**:

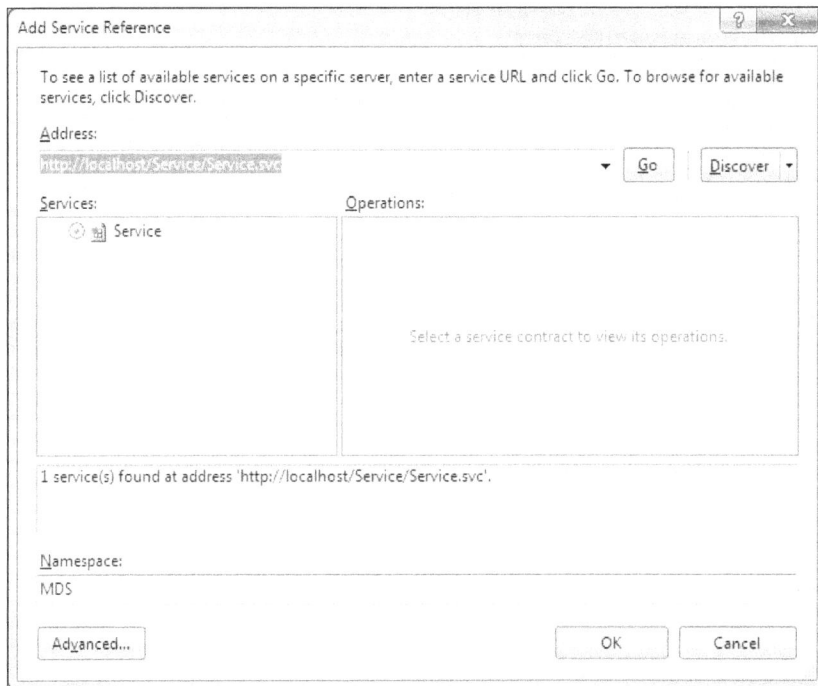

4   Enter the **Address** of the WCF service endpoint then click on **Go**. Once the Service is displayed, change the **Namespace** to something appropriate, in this example we have used **MDS**.

5. Click on **OK**.

6. This will add an App.Config file to your project, as well as a Service Reference with the name specified in step 4.

We have now successfully added the MDS WCF endpoint as a Service Reference to our project. We can now explore the basics of the service. As we will discover, the WCF service employs the Request/Response development pattern (See MSDN for further information). The following elements are surfaced through Request / Response methods:

- Annotations
- Business rules
- Entity members
- Metadata
- Security
- Transactions
- User preferences
- Validation

In this chapter, we will focus on the `Metadata` and `EntityMembers` objects. A full list of the classes, enumerations and interfaces are available at: `http://msdn.microsoft.com/en-us/library/microsoft.masterdataservices.aspx`.

Further details on the underlying methods can be found here: `http://msdn.microsoft.com/en-us/library/microsoft.masterdataservices.services.service.aspx`.

Exploring MDS Metadata

The Metadata is the first step to getting access to the data in MDS. To get information on models, versions, or entities, we need to explore the Metadata objects exposed within the Service Reference. To simply show this, we will create a method call that returns all the models in your MDS system. We will continue with the project created before.

The project and source code is available in the file called `0509_09_HelloMDS.csproj`, if you prefer to open the completed project:

1. Open the project created earlier called `HelloMDS`.
2. Create a new placeholder method that will eventually return a list of all the Models in the MDS database:

```
/// <summary>
/// Simple "Hello World" Implementation that returns a
/// list of all available models in the MDS database.
/// </summary>
```

```
        private static string ObtainModels()
          {
            StringBuilder sb = new StringBuilder();
            //Return Data from service here
            sb.Append("IMPLEMENT METHOD ObtainModels()");
            return sb.ToString();
          }
```

3. Add a call to the method from the `Main` method that fires when the console application runs. We will also add some user waits so the application remains open:

```
/// <summary>
/// Runs HellMDS Console Application
/// </summary>
/// <param name="args"></param>
static void Main(string[] args)
{
//Confirm if user wants to return a list of
//available Models
    Console.WriteLine("Show All Models in MDS Database (Y/N)?");
    //Read the Response from the user
     string result = Console.ReadLine();
    //If the user has responded with a Y,
    //then call ObtainModels
    if (result =="y")
    {
            //return the output of the method "Obtain Models"
            //to the console.
            Console.WriteLine(ObtainModels());
    }
    //Pause the application so the output can be seen
    Console.WriteLine("Press any key to close");
    Console.ReadLine();
}
```

4. Compile and run the application. The output should be as follows:

5. Now write the `ObtainModels` method as follows:

```
/// <summary>
/// Simple "Hello World" implementation that returns a list
/// of all available models in the MDS database.
/// </summary>
private static string ObtainModels()
{
StringBuilder sb = new StringBuilder();
    //Return data from service here
    //instantiate the objects required for the
    //Metadata Service Call
    MDS.ServiceClient service = new MDS.ServiceClient();
    MDS.MetadataResultOptions metadataResultOptions = new MDS.
MetadataResultOptions();
    MDS.MetadataSearchCriteria metadataSearchCriteria = new MDS.
MetadataSearchCriteria();
    MDS.OperationResult operationResult = new MDS.
OperationResult();
    MDS.International international = new MDS.International();
    MDS.Metadata metadata = new MDS.Metadata();

    //Define result options
    //Tell the Service we would like Metadata
    //for both user and system object
    metadataSearchCriteria.SearchOption = MDS.SearchOption.
BothUserDefinedAndSystemObjects;
    //Tell the system that in the results we only
    //require the identifiers
    metadataResultOptions.Models = MDS.ResultType.Identifiers;

    //Make the call to the service, which returns the
    //Metadata object.
    metadata = service.MetadataGet(international,
metadataResultOptions, metadataSearchCriteria, out
operationResult);

    //Convert the Models names into strings for simple output
    foreach (MDS.Model model in metadata.Models)
    {
        sb.Append(" (");
        sb.Append(model.Identifier.Id.ToString());
        sb.Append(") ");
        sb.Append(model.Identifier.Name);
        sb.Append("\r\n");
    }
//Return the string of models
return sb.ToString();
        }
```

6. This will return a list of Models in the console application, including the system model(s). In this example we simply have the Metadata System Model and the Store Model:

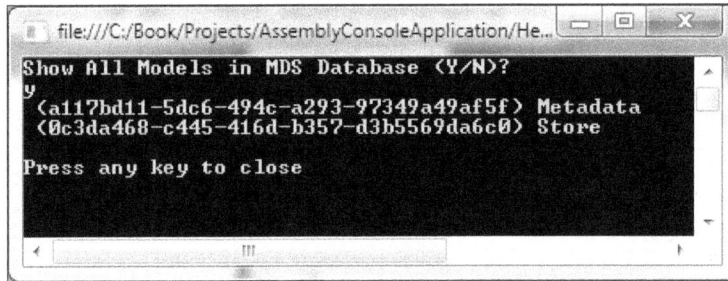

This example has demonstrated the use of the WCF service to return data from MDS in a single method. Although we have consumed this within a console application, the WCF service can be used in many different application types, from a smart phone application to a SharePoint Web Part. We will discuss the creation of a SharePoint Web Part to return a list of entity members later in this chapter.

We can explore the objects used in this example further.

`MetadataResultOptions`: Used to specify what is returned in the Metadata result. By default, nothing will be returned. In the previous example, we specified that we required Models by using the following command:

```
metadataResultOptions.Models = MDS.ResultType.Identifiers;
```

The result type is set to either Identifiers, Details, or None. Identifiers simply return the information required to identify the Model. Details returns the entire model object, and None specifies that nothing is to be returned for Models metadata. The same concept is used in other objects as well as the metadata object.

`MetadataSearchCriteria`: Used to specify single or a multiple elements to be returned. For example, if we wanted all Entities to be returned for a given Model, we would pass the Model Identifier into the search criteria and alter the Metadata result options as follows:

```
MDS.Identifier[] modelCollection = new MDS.Identifier[1];
modelCollection[0] = [[SPECIFIC MODEL]]
metadataResultOptions.Versions = MDS.ResultType.Identifiers;
metadataSearchCriteria.Models = modelCollection;
```

In the Metadata returned for versions, we will only return the versions that are in the specific Model. The `MetadataSearchCriteria` can be applied to any of the Metadata items.

`OperationResult`: This is a generic object that is used in all operations. It can be interrogated after a service call has been made and contains error information and any request information that may be useful for tracking and debugging.

The method to retrieve Metadata from the web service is called `MetadataGet`. This method requires the aforementioned objects to be passed for the method to return a Metadata object. This is the only call to the service required to get all Metadata from MDS. The same principle applies when retrieving Entity data.

The MDS WCF service is a very simple mechanism to retrieve MDS data. The same principles in the previously mentioned example can be applied to retrieving any data from the WCF service, albeit using different methods and objects. We have only shown a simple example of how to use the WCF service; in reality the service could be wrapped with an adapter class that would reduce the number of calls made to the service, and expose more specific methods, such as `ObtainModel`, `CreateModel`, `EntityMemberList`, and so on.

MDS assemblies

As discussed previously, the WCF service is not the only way to access MDS programmatically. Using the MDS Assemblies requires the DLLs to be available to the machine that is executing the code. This needs to be taken into consideration when building distributed applications. Direct use of the assemblies is predominantly used for administrative processes, such as:

- Cloning models
- Creating model deployment packages
- Creating model update packages
- Deploying packages
- Deploying update packages
- Deleting models

For this example, we will be creating a simple console application to demonstrate how to retrieve a list of Models from our MDS database. The project and source code for the following example is available in the file called `0509_09_HelloMDSAssemblies.csproj`, if you prefer to open the completed project.

Creating an MDS Assemblies project

Carry out the following steps in order to create a new console project that will be the basis for the simple example that utilizes the MDS Assemblies.

1. Create a new Console Project in Visual Studio, calling this `HelloMDSAssemblies`. Ensure that you create a .NET 3.5 project.

2. Right-click the **Project** and then click on **Add Reference**.

3. On the **.NET** tab, add the following assemblies:

   ° `Microsoft.MasterDataServices.Services.dll`

   ° `Microsoft.MasterDataServices.Core.dll`

   ° `Microsoft.MasterDataServices.Deployment.dll`

> If not visible on the **.NET** tab, add the assemblies from the directory `C:\Windows\assembly\GAC_MSIL\`.

4. Click on **OK**.

5. Your **References** should appear as shown below:

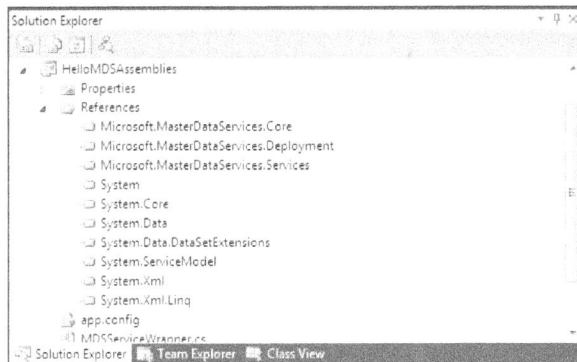

Now that we have created the references to the MDS DLL's, we can create a connection to the MDS configuration database, and retrieve data.

Setting up an MDS connection

The following steps configure a connection to the MDS database that will be used by the assemblies to connect to MDS.

1   Right-click the **Project** and click on **Properties**.

2. Click on the **Settings** tab.

3. Click on **This project does not contain a default settings file. Click here to create one**.

4. Change **Scope** from **User** to **Application**.

5. Change **Type** to (**Connection String**).

6   Change **Name** to **defaultMdsConnection**.

7. In the **Value** textbox, click the ellipsis (**...**).

8. Configure the connection to your MDS configuration server:

    ° Select **Microsoft SQL Server** and click on **Continue**

    ° Enter or select the Server name on which the MDS database resides

    ° Select the MDS database name from the drop-down list

    ° Test the connection to ensure you have configured it correctly

    ° Click on **OK** to close the **Connection Properties** dialog

9. Check the newly created `app.config` file and ensure that the following entry exists:

```
<connectionStrings>
    <add name="defaultMdsConnection"
      connectionString="Data Source=[SERVER];
          Initial Catalog=[DATABASE];
              Integrated Security=True"
          providerName="System.Data.SqlClient" />
</connectionStrings>
```

You have now configured a connection to the MDS configuration server, which the DLLs will pick up and use with any methods that are invoked. The following exercise will demonstrate how to get a list of Models from the MDS configuration server:

1. Add the following to the top of `Program.cs`:

```
using System.Collections.ObjectModel;
using Microsoft.MasterDataServices.Deployment;
using Microsoft.MasterDataServices.Services.DataContracts;
```

2. Add the method called `ListModels` to the `Program.cs` class:

```
/// <summary>
/// Displays a list of the models in the system.
/// </summary>
private static void ListModels()
{
    //Reads a model's metadata, business rules, and master data
    ModelReader reader = new ModelReader();
```

```
//Write out the Current User Name
Console.WriteLine(reader.CurrentUser.DisplayName);

Console.WriteLine("Models:");
Collection<Identifier> models = reader.GetModels();
foreach (Identifier modelId in models)
{
    Console.WriteLine(modelId.Name);
}
}
```

3. Add the following to the Main method of the program class:

```
ListModels();
Console.WriteLine(string.Empty);
Console.WriteLine("Press Enter to continue...");
Console.ReadLine();
```

4. This will call the ListModels method on the application load and display all the Models that exist in the MDS database selected earlier.

5. Compile and run the project. Check if the output displays your user name and a list of Models in your MDS database.

In this example, we have used the method available in the Master Data Services deployment class. As discussed previously, this class is primarily used for packaging and deploying, copying, and deleting models. As we have seen, this is more simplistic to use than the WCF service. However, there are fewer methods exposed in this simple manner. It is possible to use all the methods exposed in the WCF service by using the assemblies directly. The following example will show that we can use the assemblies to create a model, using the Microsoft.MasterDataServices. Services assembly. To create this we will introduce the lightweight service wrapper that we can utilize later on in this chapter:

1. Using the same project as before, add a new class called MDSServiceWrapper.

2. Add the following to the beginning of the class:

```
using System.Collections.ObjectModel;
using Microsoft.MasterDataServices.Deployment;
using Microsoft.MasterDataServices.Services.DataContracts;
using Microsoft.MasterDataServices.Services;
using Microsoft.MasterDataServices.Services.MessageContracts;
```

3. Add a private object reference to MDS Service, within the MDSServiceWrapper class.

```
private Service service = new Service();
```

4. We need to create a Model, so add a new public method called `CreateModel`:

```
/// <summary>
/// Creates a new MDS Model
/// </summary>
/// <param name="modelName"></param>
public void CreateModel(string modelName)
{

}
```

5. As we learnt earlier in this chapter, a Model is simply Metadata, therefore we need to create new Metadata and send this back to the API. Add the following to the `CreateModel` method:

```
//Create New Metadata object
Metadata metadata = new Metadata();
//Create New Model Object
Model model = new Model();

//Give the new Model an Identifier and Name
model.Identifier = new Identifier();
model.Identifier.Name = modelName;

//Add the new Model to the Metadata
metadata.Models.Add(model);
```

6. Now we have created the `Metadata` object, we need to send it to be created in the MDS database. To do this we will implement another method to create Metadata, so we can reuse it for other Metadata creation objects:

```
/// <summary>
/// Create Metadata
/// </summary>
/// <param name="metadataToCreate"></param>
/// <returns></returns>
internal Metadata CreateMetadata(Metadata metadataToCreate)
{
//Create Object references
MetadataCreateResponse response = null;
MetadataCreateRequest request = new MetadataCreateRequest();
    MessageResponse mesageResponse = new MessageResponse();

    //Add items to the request
    request.ReturnCreatedIdentifiers = true;
    request.Metadata = metadataToCreate;
```

```
//Call the service
response = service.MetadataCreate(request);

//Return the Metadata
    return response.MetadataCreated;
}
```

7. Add the `CreateMetadata` method call to the `CreateModel` method:

    ```
    CreateMetadata(metadata);
    ```

8. Update the `Main` method call that resides in the class `Program.cs`.

    ```
    static void Main(string[] args)
    {
    //Return all the Current Models
        ListModels();
        Console.WriteLine(string.Empty);
        Console.WriteLine("Create a New Model?");
        ConsoleKeyInfo a = Console.ReadKey();

        //Check if the user has pressed Y
        if (a.Key == ConsoleKey.Y)
        {
            Console.WriteLine("Enter New model name");
            string modelName = Console.ReadLine();
            //Create a new reference to the MDSServiceWrapper
            MDSServiceWrapper sr = new MDSServiceWrapper();
            //Create the model
            sr.CreateModel(modelName);
            //Re Display the models
            ListModels();
        }
    Console.WriteLine("Press Enter to continue...");
    Console.ReadLine();
    }
    ```

9. Add another project reference to the DLL `System.ServiceModel`.

10. Compile and run the project.

This example has demonstrated how to create a Model using the assemblies. In the subsequent sections of this chapter, we will use the same concept of using a service wrapper, however, we will build this on top of the provided WCF Service, as opposed to the assemblies. The primary restriction to using the assemblies, as opposed to a service endpoint, is the need for the DLLs to be available on the machine the code is running on. Using the service allows the distribution of application with greater ease and there is no need to have the DLLs installed on the host server.

Creating an MDS SharePoint Web Part

In this example, we will examine how we can integrate MDS into SharePoint 2010. The theory applied here could be used to build applications that seamlessly integrate MDS into any software. The example will walk you through creating a SharePoint 2010 web part that will allow you to select a Model, a Version, and the Members within the Entities. This example is built using Visual Studio 2010 and SharePoint 2010.

Setup

For us to develop a SharePoint 2010 web part to retrieve data from MDS, we need to install two additional products, namely:

- SharePoint 2010 Foundation or SharePoint Server 2010
- Microsoft Visual Studio 2010 Professional

Installing both SharePoint and Visual Studio are outside the scope of this book. There are, however, useful guides available for both:

- SharePoint—`http://msdn.microsoft.com/en-us/library/ ee554869(office.14).aspx`
- Visual Studio—`http://msdn.microsoft.com/en-us/library/e2h7fzkw. aspx`

We also need to ensure that a site is available on a different port to the MDS service, to allow us to debug the Web Part.

Creating the Web Part

1. Open Visual Studio 2010. Create a new project of the type SharePoint 2010 Visual Web Part, and call the project **MDSEntities**:

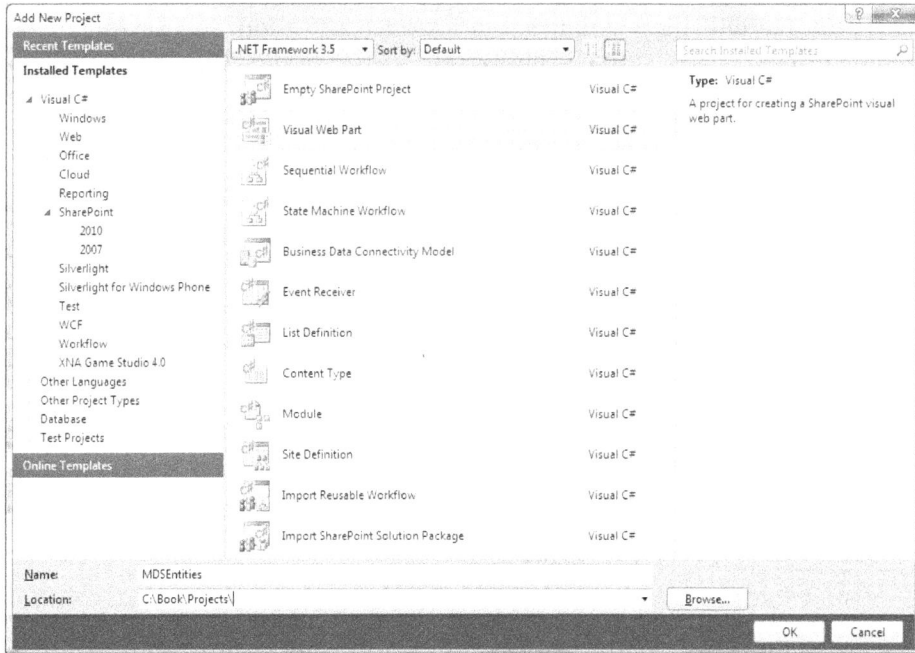

2. Select an appropriate installation of SharePoint 2010 for debugging purposes on the SharePoint Customization Wizard screen that will appear.

3. Add a new class to the project called MDSServiceWrapper.cs.

4. Add the Service Reference to the project, and ensure you Namespace it as MDS (see *Getting started with Web Service API*).

5. Add the following controls to the UserControl called VisualWebPart1UserControl.ascx:

```
Pick a Model:
<asp:DropDownList ID="ddlModel" runat="server"
DataTextField="value" DataValueField="key" AutoPostBack="True"></
asp:DropDownList>
<BR />


Pick a Version:
<asp:DropDownList ID="ddlVersion" runat="server"
DataTextField="value" DataValueField="key" AutoPostBack="True"></
asp:DropDownList>
```

```
<BR />

Pick an Entity:
<asp:ListBox ID="lsbEntity" runat="server" DataTextField="value"
DataValueField="key" Width="400"></asp:ListBox>
<BR />

Entity Members:
<asp:GridView ID="grdMembers" runat="server"
AutoGenerateEditButton="True" AutoGenerateDeleteButton="True"></
asp:GridView>
```

Deploying the Web Part

Although we have only just got started with the Web Part, we can deploy the solution to see what we will be populating with data from MDS:

1. Remaining within Visual Studio, click on the **Build** menu, and choose **Build Solution**.

2. Verify that **Build Succeeded** is shown in the bottom-left hand corner, or address any errors that are shown in the **Error List**.

3. Click on the **Build** menu again and choose the **Deploy Solution** option to deploy to SharePoint.

4. You will need to add our new Web Part to a page. Navigate to your SharePoint site, and select a page you want your Web Part to appear on. You may need to create a Web Part page on your site.

5. On a Web Part page navigate to **Site Actions** and select **Edit Page**.

6. Select **Add a Web Part** in the zone where you wish your web part to appear.

7. From the **Categories** window, select **Custom**.

8. Select **VisualWebpart1**. Press **Add** and select **Stop Editing**.

9. Verify that you can see the **VisualWebPart1** with three visible controls as shown:

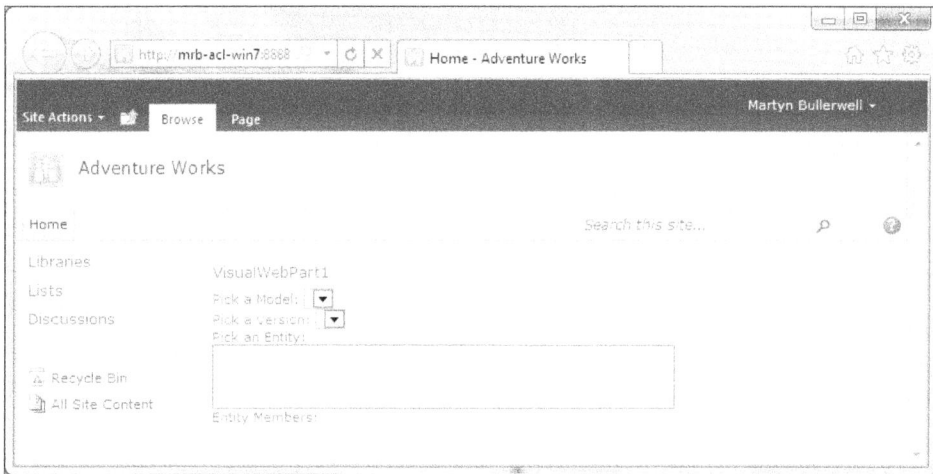

Retrieving data from MDS

We have now created a simple Web Part, and a framework to populate data from MDS. In the following example, we will use this template, and build a simple class wrapper that will allow us to get a list of Models, Versions, Entities, and Members. We will now create a simple wrapper with methods to retrieve the required data:

1. Add the following code to the `MDSServiceWrapper.cs` in the MDSEntities web part project:

```
using System;
using System.Linq;
Using System.Data;
using System.Collections.Generic;
using MDSEntities.MDS;
namespace MDSEntities
{
    class MDSServiceWrapper
    {
        private ServiceClient service = new ServiceClient();

        /// <summary>
        /// Method to Return Metadata based on Search
        ///Criteria, and Result options passed
        /// </summary>
        /// <param name="search"> MetaDataSearchCriteria
        ///</param>
        /// <param name="result">MetadataResultOptions</param>
```

```
/// <returns>Metadata</returns>
private Metadata ObtainMetadata(
                MDS.MetadataSearchCriteria search,
                MDS.MetadataResultOptions result)
{
    try
    {
        OperationResult operationResult
                            = new OperationResult();
        International international
                            = new International();
      //use the service to retrieve the requested data
        return service.MetadataGet(
                        international, result, search,
                        out operationResult);
    }
    catch
    {
        return null;
    }
}
}
}
```

2. Create a method to retrieve a list of Models.

```
/// <summary>
/// Return a generic dictionary object of all Models within the
MDS Database
        /// </summary>
        /// <returns>Dictionary Collection of Models</returns>
    public Dictionary<int, string> ObtainModelList()
    {
        //Create simple dictionary that will be returned
        Dictionary<int, string> models = new
Dictionary<int,string>();

        //Create Object required to retrieve the metadata
        MetadataSearchCriteria metadataSearchCriteria = new
MetadataSearchCriteria();
        MetadataResultOptions metadataResultOptions = new
MetadataResultOptions();

        //Return only objects created by users of MDS
```

```
         metadataSearchCriteria.SearchOption = MDS.
SearchOption.UserDefinedObjectsOnly;
         //Simply return identifier information on the models
         metadataResultOptions.Models = MDS.ResultType.
Identifiers;

         //Obtain the metadata from MDS
         MDS.Metadata metadata = ObtainMetadata(metadataSearchC
riteria, metadataResultOptions);

         //Add each model into the dictionary
         foreach (MDS.Model model in metadata.Models)
         {
             //Add the internal ID and the Model Name to the
dictionary to display.
             models.Add(model.Identifier.InternalId, model.
Identifier.Name);
         }

         //Return the dictionary of models
         return models;
     }
```

3. Create an internal class method that will return a single Model identifier. This will allow us to pick a single Model, and use the identifier in the `SearchCriteria` object:

```
/// <summary>
         /// Returns a single Model based on the internal
identifier
         /// </summary>
         /// <param name="internalModelId">Internal identifier of a
Model</param>
         /// <returns>Model (Identifier)</returns>
         private Model[] ObtainModel(int internalId)
         {

             //Create Object required to retrive meta data
             MetadataSearchCriteria metadataSearchCriteria = new
MetadataSearchCriteria();
             MetadataResultOptions metadataResultOptions = new
MetadataResultOptions();

             //Specify what to return
             metadataResultOptions.Models = MDS.ResultType.
Identifiers;
```

```
        //get the metadata back
        Metadata metadata = this.ObtainMetadata(metadataSearch
Criteria, metadataResultOptions);


        //Use Linq to find the object we are after based on
the internal model Id
        Model[] list = metadata.Models.Where(model => model.
Identifier.InternalId == internalId).ToArray<Model>();


        //Return the Model, if there is a model matching the
InternalId.
        return list;


}
```

4. We can now create similar methods to enable the picking up of Versions that relate to a chosen Model. For this we require two methods:

```
/// <summary>
/// Returns a dictionary of Versions within a given model
/// </summary>
/// <param name="internalModelId"></param>
/// <returns></returns>

public Dictionary<int, string> ObtainVersionList(int
internalModelId)
{
//Create simple dictionary that will be returned
    Dictionary<int, string> versions =
                    new Dictionary<int, string>();

    //Create Object required to retrieve meta data
    MetadataSearchCriteria metadataSearchCriteria =
                    new MetadataSearchCriteria();
    MetadataResultOptions metadataResultOptions =
                    new MetadataResultOptions();

    //Return only objects created by users of MDS
    metadataSearchCriteria.SearchOption =
        SearchOption.UserDefinedObjectsOnly;
    //Return versions for just the model we are interested in
    Identifier[] identifier = new Identifier[1];
    Model[] model = ObtainModel(internalModelId);
    identifier[0] = ObtainModel(internalModelId)[0].Identifier;
    metadataSearchCriteria.Models = identifier;
```

```
  //Simply return identifier information on the models
  metadataResultOptions.Versions = ResultType.Identifiers;



  //Obtain the metadata from MDS
  Metadata metadata = ObtainMetadata(metadataSearchCriteria,
      metadataResultOptions);

  //Add each version into the dictionary
  foreach (MDS.Version version in metadata.Versions)
  {
    //Add the internal ID and the Version Name to the dictionary
    //to display.
        versions.Add(version.Identifier.InternalId,
  version.Identifier.Name);
  }

  //Return the dictionary of versions
  return versions;
}

/// <summary>
/// Returns a single Version based on the internal identifier
/// </summary>
/// <param name="internalModelId">Internal identifier of a
Version</param>
/// <returns>Version (Identifier)</returns>

private MDS.Version[] ObtainVersion(int internalId)
{
   //Create Object required to retrieve meta data
   MetadataSearchCriteria metadataSearchCriteria = new
                MetadataSearchCriteria();
   MetadataResultOptions metadataResultOptions = new
                   MetadataResultOptions();

   //Specify what to return
   metadataResultOptions.Versions =
                      MDS.ResultType.Identifiers;

   //Get the metadata back
   Metadata metadata =
                this.ObtainMetadata(metadataSearchCriteria,
                metadataResultOptions);
```

```
//Use Linq to find the object we are after based on
//the internal version Id
MDS.Version[] list = metadata.Versions.Where
    (version => version.Identifier.InternalId
    == internalId).ToArray<MDS.Version>();

//Return the Version, if there is a Version matching the
//Internal Id.
return list;
}
```

5. We can now use these methods to return the data to the Web Part. Add the following to the code behind (`VisualWebPart1UserControl.ascx.cs`) of the user control:

```
public partial class VisualWebPart1UserControl : UserControl
{
    // Create the Service Wrapper object.
    MDSServiceWrapper mdsServiceWrapper =
                            new MDSServiceWrapper();

    protected void Page_Load(object sender, EventArgs e)
    {
        //We only need to populate the Dropdown if
        //this is not a postback
        if (!Page.IsPostBack)
        {
        //Set the source of the data to the service
        //wrappers Model Dictionary
            ddlModel.DataSource =
                mdsServiceWrapper.ObtainModelList();
                //Bind the drop down.
                ddlModel.DataBind();
        }
    }
}
```

6. We need to wire up an event, so when the **Model** drop-down is selected, we get a list of related Versions. To do this amend the HTML in the user control (`VisualWebPart1UserControl.ascx`) as follows:

```
<asp:DropDownList ID="ddlModel" runat="server"
DataTextField="value" DataValueField="key" AutoPostBack="True"
OnSelectedIndexChanged="ddlModel_SelectedIndexChanged"></
asp:DropDownList>
```

7. Add the new method to to the code behind (`VisualWebPart1UserControl.ascx.cs`) of the user control in order to handle the event when the **Model** drop-down list is changed:

```
/// <summary>
/// Fires when a different model is selected.
/// </summary>
/// <param name="sender"></param>
/// <param name="e"></param>

protected void ddlModel_SelectedIndexChanged(object sender,
EventArgs e)
{
    //Set the source of the data to the Service Wrappers
    //Version Dictionary
    ddlVersion.DataSource = mdsServiceWrapper.ObtainVersionList
                       (Convert.ToInt32(ddlModel.SelectedValue));
    //Bind the drop down
    ddlVersion.DataBind();
}
```

8. Build the project and ensure that there are no errors.

9. Add the service endpoint to the SharePoint web.config.

   a. Navigate to the SharePoint web directory (normally located here: `C:\inetpub\wwwroot\wss\VirtualDirectories\[SITE PORT]`)

   b. Open the `web.config` in an editor

   c. Under the `<system.serviceModel>` node add the service endpoint node from the `app.config` in your web part project

```
<bindings>
 <wsHttpBinding>

  <binding name="WSHttpBinding_IService" closeTimeout =
"00:01:00" openTimeout ="00:01:00" receiveTimeout ="00:10:00"
sendTimeout ="00:01:00" bypassProxyOnLocal="false"
transactionFlow="false" hostNameComparisonMode= "StrongWildcard"
maxBufferPoolSize="524288" maxReceivedMessageSize="65536"
messageEncoding="Text" textEncoding="utf-8"
useDefaultWebProxy="true"
allowCookies="false">

  <readerQuotas maxDepth="32" maxStringContentLength="8192"
maxArrayLength="16384" maxBytesPerRead="4096"
maxNameTableCharCount="16384" />
```

```
  <reliableSession ordered="true" inactivityTimeout="00:10:00"
enabled="false" />

  <security mode="Message">

    <transport clientCredentialType="Windows"
proxyCredentialType="None" realm="" />

    <message clientCredentialType="Windows" negotiateServiceCreden
tial="true"                          algorithmSuite="Default" />
    </security>
   </binding>
  <wsHttpBinding>
 </bindings>
 <client>
   <endpoint address="http://localhost/MDS/Service/Service.svc"
Binding ="wsHttpBinding" bindingConfiguration ="WSHttpBinding_
IService" contract="MDS.IService" name="WSHttpBinding_IService">
    <identity>
     <userPrincipalName value="SERVERNAME\USERNAME" />
    </identity>
   </endpoint>
  </client>
 </client>
```

10. Deploy the project to SharePoint and navigate to your SharePoint page where you added the web part earlier. You will see a basic web page with two drop down boxes, one that allows you to select a Model and a second that allows the Version selection.

We now should have a web part that allows us to pick a Model, and a Version that belongs to that Model. We now need to return the Entities and the Members within a given Entity. The Entities are also considered as Metadata and therefore we use the same objects as before. To get a list of entities we need to know which Model and Version we are interested in. The following example will take you through returning Entities and their corresponding Members. Entity Members are not accessed using the metadata object; they are returned using a specific object for Entity Members. The next example will guide you through the use of the `EntityMembers` object:

1. Continue from the example project from before and add the following method to the `MDSServiceWrapper` class:

    ```
    /// <summary>
    /// Return a generic dictionary object of all Entities
    /// within a given Model and version
    ```

```
/// </summary>
/// <param name="internalModelId">Model Id</param>
/// <param name="intenalVersionId">Version Id</param>
/// <returns></returns>
public Dictionary<int, string> ObtainEntityList(int
internalModelId, int intenalVersionId)
{
//Create the Object to be returned
   Dictionary<int, string> entities =
                          new Dictionary<int, string>();
   //Create Object required to retrieve meta data
   MetadataSearchCriteria metadataSearchCriteria =
                          new MetadataSearchCriteria();
   MetadataResultOptions metadataResultOptions =
                       new MetadataResultOptions();

   //Create the Identifier collection objects
   Identifier[] modelCollection =   new Identifier[1];
   Identifier[] versionCollection = new Identifier[1];

   //Add the Identifiers to the collection objects.
   modelCollection[0] =
           ObtainModel(internalModelId)[0].Identifier;
   versionCollection[0] =
           ObtainVersion(intenalVersionId)[0].Identifier;

   //Add the Identifier Collections to the
   //Search Criteria Object
   metadataSearchCriteria.Models = modelCollection;
   metadataSearchCriteria.Versions = versionCollection;

   //Return just the entity identifiers
   metadataResultOptions.Entities =
                          MDS.ResultType.Identifiers;

   //Obtain the metadata from MDS
   MDS.Metadata metadata =
                this.ObtainMetadata(metadataSearchCriteria,
                metadataResultOptions);

   //Add each model into the dictionary
   foreach (MDS.Entity entity in metadata.Entities)
   {
       //Add the internal ID and the Entity Name to the
```

```
                      //dictionary to display.
          entities.Add(entity.Identifier.InternalId,

entity.Identifier.Name);
    }
//Return the dictionary of Identities
return entities;
}
```

2. Create a method to retrieve the entity dictionary from the
   MDSServiceWrapper, by adding the following to the code of VisualWebPart:

```
/// <summary>
/// Fires when a different version is selected.
/// </summary>
/// <param name="sender"></param>
/// <param name="e"></param>

protected void ddlVersion_SelectedIndexChanged(object sender,
EventArgs e)
{
//Get the Internal Id's of the Model and Version
   int internalModelID =
             Convert.ToInt32(ddlModel.SelectedValue);
   int internalVersionID =
               Convert.ToInt32(ddlVersion.SelectedValue);
   //Set the source of the data to the Service
   //Wrappers Version Dictionary
   lsbEntity.DataSource = mdsServiceWrapper.ObtainEntityList
                         (internalVersionID, internalModelID);
   //Bind the drop down
   lsbEntity.DataBind();
}
```

3. Wire up the event on the Version drop-down to populate the entity list box.
   Add the following to the ddlVersion drop-down list in the User Control:

   `OnSelectedIndexChanged="ddlVersion_SelectedIndexChanged"`

4. Compile and run the project; test that a list of Versions are returned as
   follows:

5. Create a method to return a single Entity identifier in the
   `MDSServiceWrapper` as follows:

```
/// <summary>
/// Returns a single Entity based on the internal identifier
/// </summary>
/// <param name="internalModelId">Internal identifier of an
Entity</param>
/// <returns>Entity (Identifier)</returns>
private MDS.Entity[] ObtainEntity(int internalId)
{
    //Create Object required to retrive meta data
    MetadataSearchCriteria metadataSearchCriteria =
                                new MetadataSearchCriteria();
      MetadataResultOptions metadataResultOptions =
                                new MetadataResultOptions();

    //Specify what to return
    metadataResultOptions.Entities =
                                MDS.ResultType.Identifiers;

    //get the metadata back
    Metadata metadata = this.ObtainMetadata
             (metadataSearchCriteria, metadataResultOptions);

    //Use Linq to find the object we are after based on
    //the internal model Id
    MDS.Entity[] list = metadata.Entities.Where
             (entity => entity.Identifier.InternalId ==
                        internalId).ToArray<MDS.Entity>();

    //Return the Entity List, if there is a model matching the
    //Internal Id.
    return list;
}
```

6. Now we have a method to return a single Entity, we can write a method to get the Members within an Entity. This does not use the MetaData object, but instead the `EntityMember` objects. Add the following method to return the Members from MDS:

```
/// <summary>
        /// Returns an Entity Members object
        /// </summary>
        /// <param name="internalEntityId">Internal Entity Id</
param>
        /// <returns></returns>
        private EntityMembers ObtainEntityMembers(int
internalEntityId, int internalModelId, int internalVersionId)
        {
            //Create an Object required to retrieve Entity Member
Data
            EntityMembersGetCriteria entityMembersGetCriteria =
new EntityMembersGetCriteria();
            Identifier identifier = new Identifier();
            International international = new MDS.International();
            EntityMembersInformation information = new
EntityMembersInformation();
            OperationResult result = new OperationResult();

            //Get the model, version and entity for which we
require the members
            Entity[] entity = ObtainEntity(internalEntityId);
            Model[] model = ObtainModel(internalModelId);
            MDS.Version[] version = ObtainVersion(internalVersion
Id);

            //Set the Object Criteria to only get the members back
for the exact entity
            entityMembersGetCriteria.EntityId = entity[0].
Identifier;
            entityMembersGetCriteria.ModelId = model[0].
Identifier;
            entityMembersGetCriteria.VersionId = version[0].
Identifier;

            //Return Leaf Members
            entityMembersGetCriteria.MemberType = MemberType.Leaf;

            //Set the sort column
            identifier.Name = "Code";
            entityMembersGetCriteria.SortColumnId = identifier;

            ///Return the Entity Members object
            return service.EntityMembersGet(international,
entityMembersGetCriteria, out information, out result);
        }
```

For example purposes we will convert the Entity Members object into a data table. To perform this we have made the code available under the Code Snippets directory. The method is called `ConvertEntityMembersToDataTable`. You will need to copy this method into the class we are currently working in.

7. Create the public method in the `MDSServiceWrapper` to return the data table as follows:

```
/// <summary>
/// Public method to return Entity Members in a data table
/// </summary>
/// <param name="internalEntityId">Internal Entity Id</param>
/// <param name="internalModelId">Internal Model Id</param>
/// <param name="internalVersionId">Internal Version Id ///</
param>
/// <returns>DataTable</returns>

public DataTable ObtainMember(int internalEntityId, int
internalModelId, int internalVersionId )
{
MDS.EntityMembers members =
ObtainEntityMembers(internalEntityId,internalModelId,
                                  internalVersionId);
   return ConvertEntityMembersToDataTable
                             (members, DisplayType.Code);
}
```

8. Now we have to wire up the Select Entity event. In turn this will return the Members within the given Entity. Add the following to the code behind of the User Control:

```
/// <summary>
/// Fires when a different Entity is selected.
/// </summary>
/// <param name="sender"></param>
/// <param name="e"></param>
protected void lsbEntity_SelectedIndexChanged(object sender,
EventArgs e)
{
  //Get the Internal Id's of the Model and Version
  int internalEntityID =
               Convert.ToInt32(lsbEntity.SelectedValue);
  int internalModelID =
               Convert.ToInt32(ddlModel.SelectedValue);
  int internalVersionID =
               Convert.ToInt32(ddlVersion.SelectedValue);
  //Set the source of the data to the Service Wrappers
  //Version Dictionary
  grdMembers.DataSource =
```

```
        mdsServiceWrapper.ObtainMember
      (internalEntityID, internalModelID, internalVersionID);
    //Bind the drop down
    grdMembers.DataBind();
}
```

9. Add the following to the list box control called `lsbEntity`:

```
OnSelectedIndexChanged="lsbEntity_SelectedIndexChanged"
AutoPostBack="True"
```

10. Compile and run the project. You can now see the Members of a selected Entity.

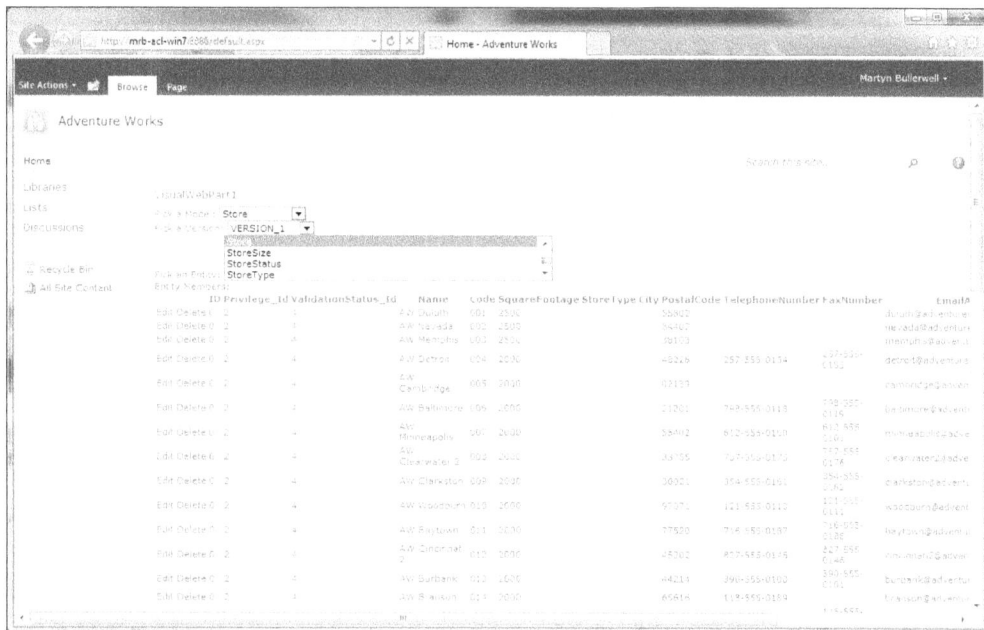

This example has demonstrated how to return Entity data through a SharePoint Web Part. In reality you may wish to further enhance this, to allow adding and editing of entities, members, hierarchies, and so on, which is all possible using the WCF service.

Although very simple, this highlights the possibilities of integrating data in MDS into business applications. For example, if an application required the list of stores it could simply access the WCF service, in the same way we have done here, and return any master data. This would harness the benefits of MDS in distributed systems, negating the requirement to further move data into other systems for consumption.

SharePoint workflow integration

This section looks at extending the SharePoint 2010 workflow created in *Chapter 7, Business Rules and Workflow*, to allow data to be written back to MDS. In this example, we will return the approval status for a new store back to MDS, demonstrating that we can automatically update members in MDS directly from SharePoint. To get started with this example we will need the completed exercises from *Chapter 7*, which we will then extend.

To begin, we must understand the XML that MDS sends to an external workflow. The following shows an example of this structure:

```
<ExternalAction>
  <Type>SPWF</Type>
  <SendData>1</SendData>
  <Server_URL>http://localhost:8888/</Server_URL>
  <Action_ID>StoreApprovalWorkflow</Action_ID>
  <Model_ID>5</Model_ID>
  <Model_Name>Store</Model_Name>
  <Entity_ID>12</Entity_ID>
  <Entity_Name>Store</Entity_Name>
  <Version_ID>5</Version_ID>
  <MemberType_ID>1</MemberType_ID>
  <Member_ID>92</Member_ID>
  <MemberData>
    <ID>92</ID>
    <Version_ID>5</Version_ID>
    <ValidationStatus_ID>2</ValidationStatus_ID>
    <ChangeTrackingMask>0</ChangeTrackingMask>
    <EnterDTM>2011-02-12T18:48:01.143</EnterDTM>
    <EnterUserID>1</EnterUserID>
    <EnterUserName>ADATIS\mrb</EnterUserName>
    <EnterUserMuid>7971F83F-1DB4-4B75-8CA1-9F98A7570828</
EnterUserMuid>
```

```
    <EnterVersionId>5</EnterVersionId>
    <EnterVersionName>VERSION_1</EnterVersionName>
    <EnterVersionMuid>0C0C6FAF-6B8D-47D3-B4B1-06064A3AEDFE</
EnterVersionMuid>
    <LastChgDTM>2011-02-12T18:48:01.357</LastChgDTM>
    <LastChgUserID>1</LastChgUserID>
    <LastChgUserName>ADATIS\mrb</LastChgUserName>
    <LastChgUserMuid>7971F83F-1DB4-4B75-8CA1-9F98A7570828</
LastChgUserMuid>
    <LastChgVersionId>5</LastChgVersionId>
    <LastChgVersionName>VERSION_1</LastChgVersionName>
    <LastChgVersionMuid>0C0C6FAF-6B8D-47D3-B4B1-06064A3AEDFE</
LastChgVersionMuid>
    <Name>AW Farnham</Name>
    <Code>AWS134</Code>
    <StoreSize>Small</StoreSize>
    <StoreSize.ID>1</StoreSize.ID>
    <StoreSize.Code>Small</StoreSize.Code>
    <StoreSize.Name>Small</StoreSize.Name>
  </MemberData>
</ExternalAction>
```

As you can see from the above XML we have all the required information to update MDS. We will now extend the workflow written in *Chapter 7* to capture this information in the task itself:

1. Open your `MDSWorkflow` project that you created in *Chapter 7*.

2. Ensure that your project still compiles and deploys. Also check that when adding a store we still get a new task in the SharePoint task list.

3. Add the following declarations beneath the `storeName` declaration:

   ```
   private int modelId;
   private int versionId;
   private int entityId;
   private string memberCode;
   private int memberId;
   ```

4. This step will get all the required information to write back to MDS. Add the following code to the createTask1_MethodInvoking method:

```
//Store the Id's that distinguish the member
              modelId = Convert.ToInt32(mdsXml.
SelectNodes("ExternalAction/Model_ID")[0].InnerXml);
              versionId = Convert.ToInt32(mdsXml.
SelectNodes("ExternalAction/Version_ID")[0].InnerXml);
              entityId = Convert.ToInt32(mdsXml.
SelectNodes("ExternalAction/Entity_ID")[0].InnerXml);
              memberId = Convert.ToInt32(mdsXml.
SelectNodes("ExternalAction/Member_ID")[0].InnerXml);
              memberCode = mdsXml.SelectNodes("ExternalAction/
MemberData/Code")
[0].InnerXml;
```

5. Once again we need to add the Service Reference in order to access the MDS API from the workflow. This is covered earlier in this chapter. Ensure that you namespace the Service as MDS.

6. Add a new class called MDSServiceWrapper.cs to the project, and copy the class code from the Web Part project completed previously in this chapter.

7. Add the following to the top of the ServiceWrapper.cs:

```
using MDSWorkflow.MDS;
using System.Data;
```

8. We can add the method stub to update a given Member. Add the following method to the ServiceWrapper.cs:

```
/// <summary>
/// Update an Attribute on an entity member
/// </summary>
public bool UpdateEntityMemberAttribute(int internalEntityId, int
internalModelId, int internalVersionId, string memberCode, string
attributeName, string attributeValue)
  {
  //NOT YET IMPLEMENTED
  return false;
}
```

We have now set up the project to begin changing the workflow. We need to make three key changes:

- On rejection of the first stage, we must update the store to be rejected in MDS
- On rejection at the second stage, we must update the store to be rejected in MDS
- On Approval at the second stage, we must update the store to be approved in MDS

To begin with we will get the workflow to handle the rejections:

1. Open up the Workflow Designer for `Workflow 1`:

2. Click on **ifElseBranchActivity2**. Set its condition to be a Declarative Rule Condition and create a new condition called First Task Rejected with the code: **this.firstTaskApprovalStatus == "Rejected"**.

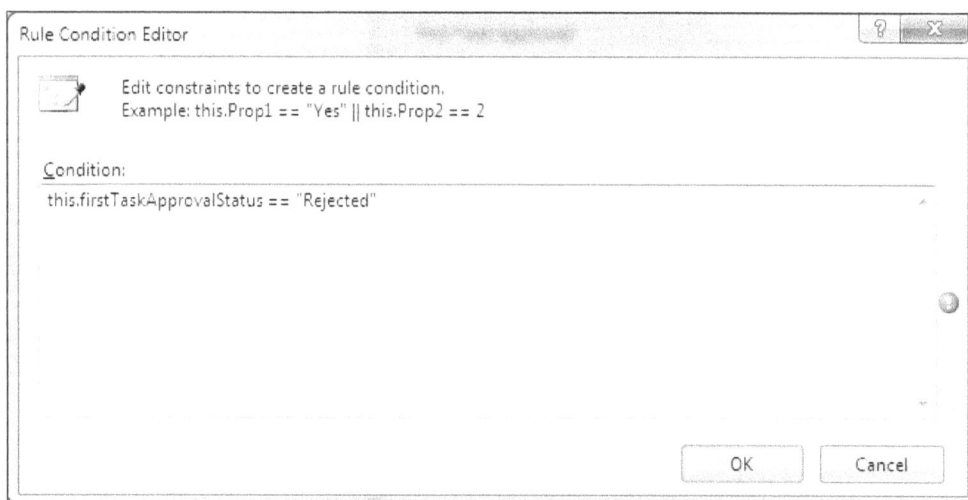

3. Click on **OK**.

4. Go to the SharePoint Workflow section of the toolbox and drag the CompleteTask item onto the designer, inside the **ifElseBranchActivity1** object.

5. Click on **createTask3** and change its **CorrelationToken** property to be firstTask, and ensure that its OwnerActivityName is Workflow1.

6. Click on **TaskId** and click the ellipsis (…). Expand **createTask1**, and select **TaskId**:

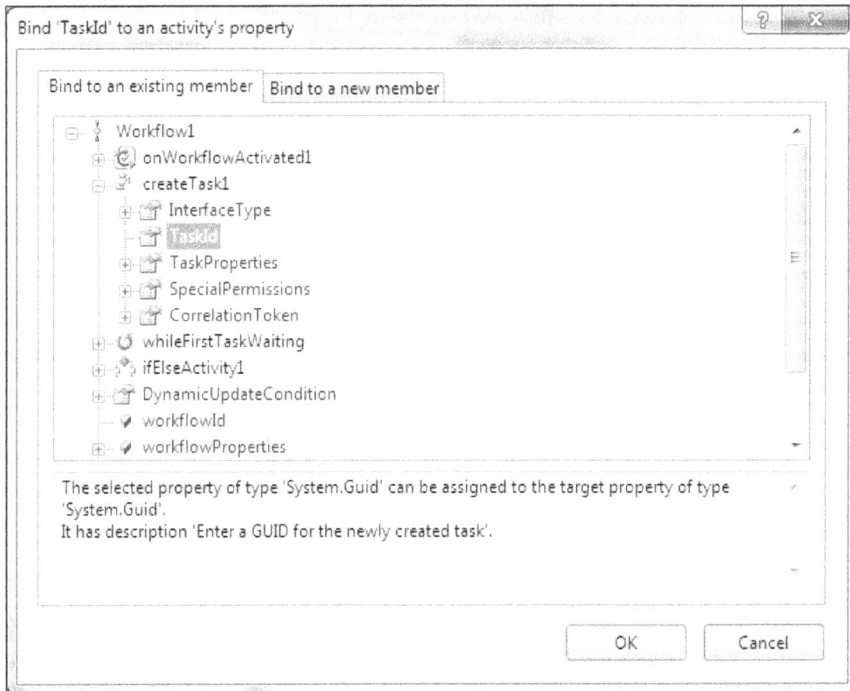

7. Click OK.

8. Double-click **completeTask3** to create the method stub. Within this method, we will update the MDS EntityMember.

9. Click on **ifElseBranchActivity4**. Set its condition to be a **Declarative Rule Condition** and create a new condition called **Second Task Rejected** with the code: this.secondTaskApprovalStatus == "Rejected".

10. Go to the **SharePoint Workflow** section of the toolbox and drag the **CompleteTask** item onto the designer, inside the **ifElseBranchActivity4** object.

11. Double click **completeTask4** to create another method stub.

12. Click on **createTask4** and change its **CorrelationToken** property to be **secondTask**, and ensure that its **OwnerActivityName** is **Workflow1**

13. Click on **TaskId** and click the ellipsis (…). Expand **ifElseFirstTaskApproved**, **IfFirstTaskApproved**, **createTask2** and Select **TaskId**.

14. Click **OK**. Your Workflow should now appear as follows:

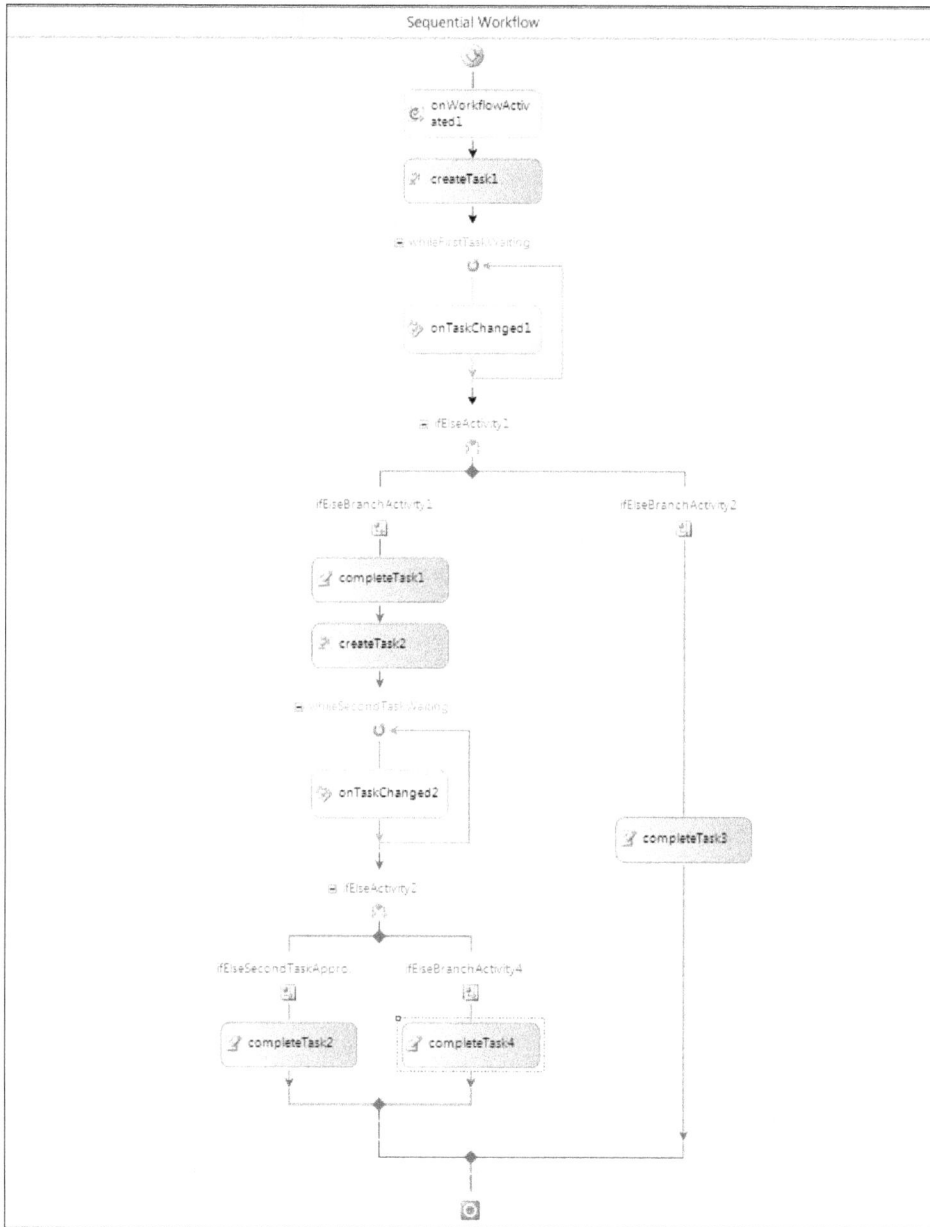

We have now created the workflow, ready to write back to MDS. The following section will see us creating the method to write back to the Member using the WCF service, and wiring the whole workflow together:

1. Open up the `MDSServiceWrapper` class, and add the following code to the method `UpdateEntityMemberAttribute`:

```
OperationResult operationResult = new OperationResult();
International international = new International();
//Get the Version, Model and Entity identifiers
MDS.Version[] version = this.ObtainVersion(internalVersionId);
Entity[] entity = this.ObtainEntity(internalEntityId);
Model[] model = ObtainModel(internalModelId);
string searchTerm = string.Format("{0} = '{1}'", new object[] {
"Code", memberCode });

EntityMembers entityMembers =
      ObtainEntityMembers(internalEntityId, internalModelId,
      internalVersionId, searchTerm);

//Get the Entity we are interested in N.B this could be more
//efficient by using the Search Criteria, however it out of
//the scope of this book.
MDS.Member[] list = entityMembers.Members.Where(member =>
  member.MemberId.Code == memberCode).ToArray<MDS.Member>();

//Update the entity attributes
Member entityMember = list[0];
entityMember.Attributes = new MDS.Attribute[] { new MDS.
Attribute() { Identifier = new Identifier() { Name = attributeName
}, Value = attributeValue } };

//Create an Entity Members object to return to the service //with
all the updates
//We could do bulk updates here
entityMembers = new EntityMembers();
entityMembers.VersionId = version[0].Identifier;
entityMembers.ModelId = model[0].Identifier;
entityMembers.EntityId = entity[0].Identifier;
entityMembers.MemberType = new
    MemberType?(entityMember.MemberId.MemberType);
```

```
entityMembers.Members = list;

//use the service to update the members
operationResult = service.EntityMembersUpdate(international,
        entityMembers);

//Check if we had any errors
if (operationResult.Errors.Length > 0) {return false;}
else {return true;}
```

2. We need to update the method we created previously that returns the Entity Member list. This is because we just wish to update one entity at a time. Update the ObtainEntityMembers method signature as follows:

```
private EntityMembers ObtainEntityMembers(int internalEntityId,
int internalModelId, int internalVersionId, string searchTerm)
```

3. Add the following code to the ObtainEntityMembers method beneath where we set the member type of the GetCriteria object:

```
if (searchTerm.Length > 0) entityMembersGetCriteria.SearchTerm =
searchTerm;
```

4. For the code to compile, we also need to update the ObtainMember method as follows:

```
    public DataTable ObtainMember(int internalEntityId, int
internalModelId, int internalVersionId)
        {
            MDS.EntityMembers members = ObtainEntityMembers(intern
alEntityId, internalModelId, internalVersionId, string.Empty);
            return ConvertEntityMembersToDataTable(members,
DisplayType.Code);
        }
```

5. We can now wire up the complete task events from the workflow. Navigate to the code behind of the workflow. We will create two methods: one that sets the Store Status to "approved" and one that sets the Store Status to "rejected".

```
/// <summary>
/// Sets the Store Status to Rejected for a given Member
/// </summary>
private void RejectStore()
{
MDSServiceWrapper sr = new MDSServiceWrapper();
    sr.UpdateEntityMemberAttribute(entityId, modelId,
    versionId, memberCode, "StoreStatus", "Rejected");
}
```

```
/// <summary>
/// Sets the Store Status to Approved for a given Member
/// </summary>
private void ApproveStore()
{
  MDSServiceWrapper sr = new MDSServiceWrapper();
  sr.UpdateEntityMemberAttribute(entityId, modelId, versionId,
      memberCode, "StoreStatus", "Approved");
}
```

6. Remember that **completeTask3** and **completeTask4** were rejections, so for both of these, we call the `RejectStore` method as follows:

```
private void completeTask3_MethodInvoking(object sender, EventArgs
e)
    {
        RejectStore();
    }


private void completeTask4_MethodInvoking(object sender, EventArgs
e)
    {
        RejectStore();
    }
```

7. Finally, we need to approve the store if the second approver approves the tasks. **completeTask2** is the task that can be wired up to approve the new Store. Go to the workflow designer, and double-click **completeTask2**.

8. In the code behind, add the following:

```
private void completeTask2_MethodInvoking(object sender, EventArgs
e)
    {
        ApproveStore();
    }
```

There is one limitation to calling a WCF service from a SharePoint workflow: it is not straightforward to pass the credentials of the user to the WCF service from SharePoint. To work around this there are numerous implementations which require a fair amount of code. For simplicity in this solution, we will user a single user to communicate between Sharepoint and the MDS API. To do this add the following code to MDSServiceWrapper class:

```
public MDSServiceWrapper()
{
            service.ClientCredentials.Windows.ClientCredential.
            UserName = "{DOMAIN}\\{USER}";
            service.ClientCredentials.Windows.ClientCredential.
            Password = "{PASSWORD}";
}
```

Deploying the workflow solution

Now that the design and coding of the workflow is complete, we are ready to deploy the solution to SharePoint. Carry out the following in order to deploy:

1. Remaining within Visual Studio, click on the **Build** menu, and choose the **Build** menu item.

2. Verify that **Build Succeeded** is shown in the bottom-left hand corner, or address any errors that are shown in the **Error List**.

3. Click on the **Build** menu again and choose the **Deploy** option to deploy to SharePoint.

4. Go to Windows **Services** in **Administrative Tools** and locate the service called **SQL Server MDS Workflow Integration**. Restart this service if it's started, or start it if it is currently stopped.

5. Verify that the workflow has been successfully deployed to SharePoint by clicking on **All Site Content** and then clicking on the **Site Workflows** item. If the workflow has been deployed correctly, then it should be available in the **Start a New Workflow** section. We don't want to start it yet, instead we want MDS to start the workflow in the next section.

Running the SharePoint workflow

We are now in a position to re-test our workflow with the updates being fed back into MDS. Run the workflow as we did in *Chapter 7*, and run through the following steps:

1. To begin, go to Master Data Manager, and navigate to the **Explorer** function.

2. Click on the green plus icon to add a new leaf level member. Enter the following information for the new member:
   - **Name — AW Austin**
   - **Code — 059**

3. Click on the save button, which will cause the business rule to run.

4. Click on the edit button in the attributes section and complete the remaining attributes with appropriate values, before clicking on save.

At this point you will see your new store as you did in *Chapter 7*, however, if you now reject the new store on either task and return to Master Data Manager, you will see that the new store has been rejected. Conversely, if you approve the second task, the new store is approved.

This now completes our workflow example, and demonstrates some of the integration that a complete API can give to many applications.

Summary

In this chapter, we have discovered two methods for getting data in and out of MDS without using the supplied Master Data Manager, how to integrate MDS data into rich applications, and how to update data in MDS based on a SharePoint 2010 workflow. The following key points should be noted:

- The WCF service should be used in favor of the assemblies where possible
- The API can be encapsulated within a wrapper to enable ease of use
- The API allows retrieval, updating, and insertion of MDS data
- MDS data can be utilized in a line of business application without having to copy data around the business

10
Master Data Services Security

So far in this book we have been changing our sample master data as we wish, adding and deleting members to complete the various exercises. In contrast, in a production environment, controls need to be in place to ensure that master data is only changed by authorized users.

As we will see in this final chapter, Master Data Services contains a variety of security features to address these issues. We will cover each security feature, extending our sample model as we go.

In this chapter, we will cover the following topics:

- Master Data Services security overview
- Users and Group Administration
- User and Group Permissions

Master Data Services security overview

Master Data Services provides three ways in which security can be controlled, namely:

- Function access — Users must be assigned permissions to access the functions within Master Data Manager, for example, Explorer.
- Models — Read-only, Read/Write, and Deny permissions can be assigned for a user against the common MDS objects that we have been working with, for example, models, entities, attributes, and more as we will see in this chapter.
- Hierarchy members — Read-only, Read/Write, and Deny permissions can be assigned for a user against an individual member that exists in an Explicit or Derived Hierarchy.

These permissions take effect once the user has logged into Master Data Services.

A user is able to gain access to Master Data Services if their Windows login account, or a Windows group that they are member of, has been added to User and Group Permissions function in the Master Data Manager front-end.

A user is also able to gain access to MDS data via SQL Server Management Studio, if they have the relevant SQL Server permissions, such as being a member of the sysadmin fixed server role. The features that we will cover in this chapter address how the data can be secured for end users of the system, but care must also be taken to ensure that no unauthorized access can occur at the database level.

User and Group Administration

As the User and Group Permissions function is the starting point for all security administration, this is where we will begin. We have taken a brief look at this function in previous chapters, but will now see how we add a new user to MDS.

Adding a user

To continue with our example scenario, we need to set up a junior employee, and restrict their access to the master data. As a pre-requisite for this exercise, a new user must be added to either the domain or the computer on which MDS is running. The name of this user is not important—the following example uses a test user called User 1.

Once the above pre-requisite has been satisfied, carry out the following in order to add a new user:

1. Go to the MDS home page and click on the **User and Group Permissions** function, which will cause the following **Users** grid to be displayed:

User Name	Display Name	Description	E-Mail Address
DOMAIN\User	Jeremy Kashel	Principal Consultant	jeremy.kashel@adatis.co.uk

2. As shown, we get the same grid control that we are used to, along with the familiar buttons to add, edit, or delete users. In a vanilla MDS environment, there will be just one user, as shown. Our next step is to click the add button, in order to add our user to MDS.

3. The **Add users** page will now be shown. Enter the user into the **User names** textbox, in the form of **DOMAIN\User1**. Click the small check user icon that is highlighted in the following image, which will check that the text entered is a valid Windows login. Finally, click **OK** to add the user:

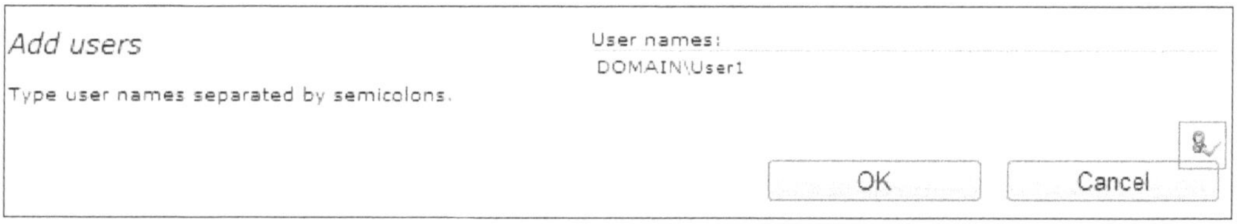

Add users	User names:
	DOMAIN\User1
Type user names separated by semicolons.	
	OK Cancel

4. The screen will now return to the **Users** page, where the new user will now be visible in the grid:

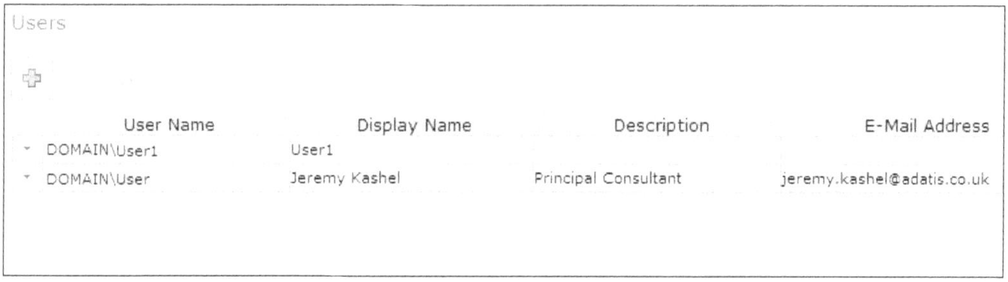

Users

User Name	Display Name	Description	E-Mail Address
DOMAIN\User1	User1		
DOMAIN\User	Jeremy Kashel	Principal Consultant	jeremy.kashel@adatis.co.uk

Editing a user

Editing a user is the process to carry out in order to change a user's details, such as name and e-mail address, in addition to changing permissions. We will now look at the process of editing the basic user details of our new user, before moving onto the permissions.

To edit the new user, carry out the following:

1. Click on the new user within the **Users** grid and then click the edit icon. This will cause the following page to display:

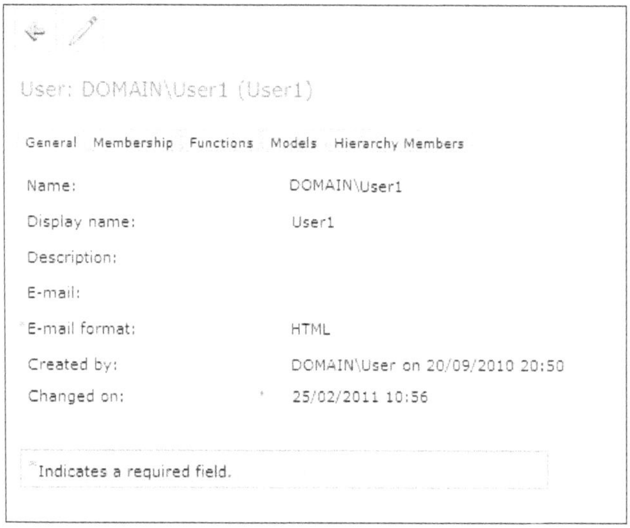

2. The tabs shown in the above screenshot allow the various different categories of permissions to be edited. For now, we will focus on the **General** tab, where we can edit the user's **E-mail** and **E-mail format**. Click on the edit icon to begin.

3. Enter an e-mail address of your choice, and choose the e-mail format of **HTML**.

4. Click on the save icon to save the changes. The user will now have an e-mail address, meaning that they can receive in the MDS notifications.

Maintaining groups

Local Windows and domain groups can also be added to MDS, meaning that any user that is part of the group at the domain or local-level will be able to gain access to MDS, once of course the group has been added to MDS.

We will now create a local Windows group, and add a local user to this group, before adding the group to MDS. Carry out the following in order to complete the example:

1. Ensure that a Windows group of your choice has been created on the computer that contains MDS. The group used in this example will be called **Group1**.

2. Create a local Windows user on the computer, and add the user to the new local Windows group. The user in this example will be called **User2**.

3. We are now ready to add the group to MDS. Ensure that you are inside the **User and Group Permissions** function, and click on the **Manage Groups** link, which at first will display a blank page, as we don't have any groups yet.

4. Click on the add button to add a group.

5. In the **Groups** textbox, enter the group in the format of **COMPUTER\Group 1,** and then click on **OK**. This will return to the **Manage Groups** page, which will now be populated with one group:

Group Name	Group Type	Description
COMPUTER\Group1	Local group	Test Group for MDS

We will log into MDS with both our new users, after we look at configuring the permissions for both the users and groups.

User and Group Permissions

We will now look at configuring permissions for:

- Functions
- Models
- Hierarchy permissions

Function permissions

The **Functions** tab on the **Edit user** page allows us to grant access for a user or group to the five functions, namely:

- **Explorer**
- **Version Management**
- **Integration Management**
- **System Administration**
- **User and Group Permissions**

Assigning user or group permissions to a function is the most basic permission level in MDS, and is a necessary step; otherwise the user would not be able to access anything in Master Data Manager.

We will now edit the user that we added to the **Manage Users** page and also the group that we added to the **Manage Groups** page:

1. Navigate to the **User and Group Permissions** page.

2. On the resulting **Manage Users** page, click on the user that we added directly to MDS, and click the edit button.

3. Click on the **Functions** tab, which will change the display as shown in the following screenshot:

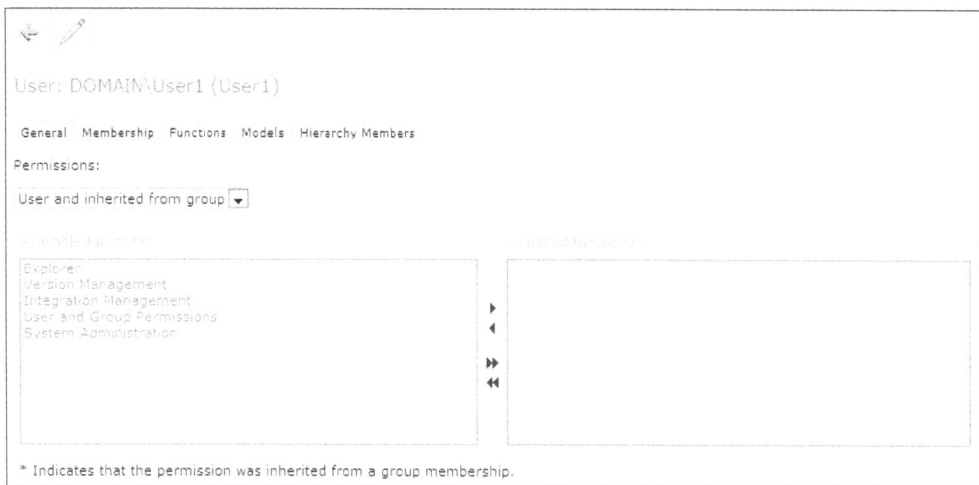

4. The **Permissions** drop-down currently shows the value **User and inherited from group**. This means that the permissions for User1 are a combination of permissions assigned directly to User1 and permissions assigned to groups that User1 belongs to. The other value in the drop-down is **User only**, which will display the permissions assigned to the user directly only. This drop-down is only for viewing the permissions, and does not affect any editing of permissions.

5. Click on the edit button.

6. Move the **Explorer** function from the **Available functions** list to the **Assigned functions** list, then click on save. The screen should look as follows when this is complete:

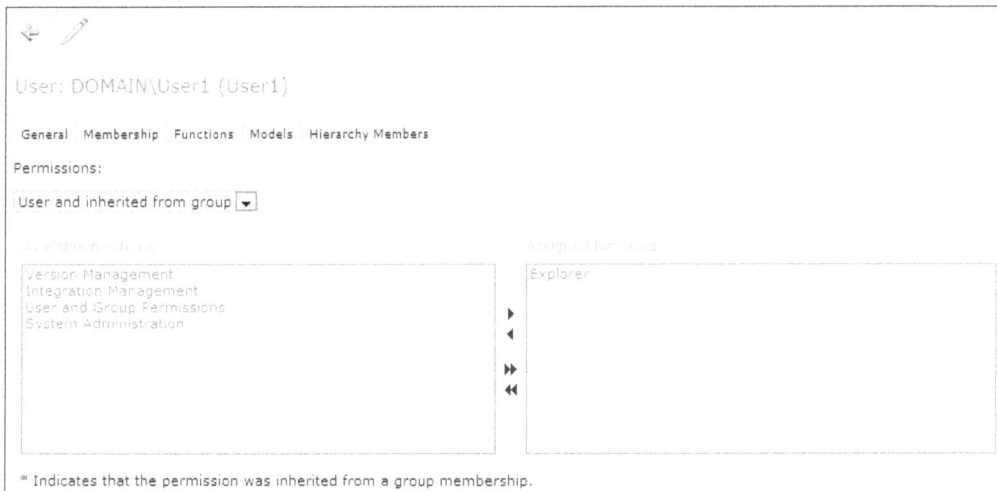

7. Repeat these steps, but with the group that we created earlier. Assign the group permission to the **Integration Management** function.

We now need to log in for the first time with our new users, in order to see our security changes in action.

> **Internet Explorer security**
>
> Logging in as another Windows user would normally require logging out of Windows and logging in again under a different user, which can be a time consuming process. An alternative option is to get Internet Explorer to prompt for a username and password while in the Local Intranet security zone. More information on Internet Explorer security zones can be found at the following link: `http://support.microsoft.com/kb/174360/en-us`.

Carry out the following steps in order to test the security changes that we have made:

1   Log out of the current browser session, or log out of Windows if you are not using Internet Explorer to prompt for a user name.

2. Log into Windows under the context of the first user that we are created, only if you are not using Internet Explorer to prompt for a user name.

3. Open a new browser session and navigate to Master Data Manager.

4. If you are prompted for a username and password, enter the credentials of the first user that we created.

5. At this point, for the first user, only the **Explorer** function should be visible, as shown:

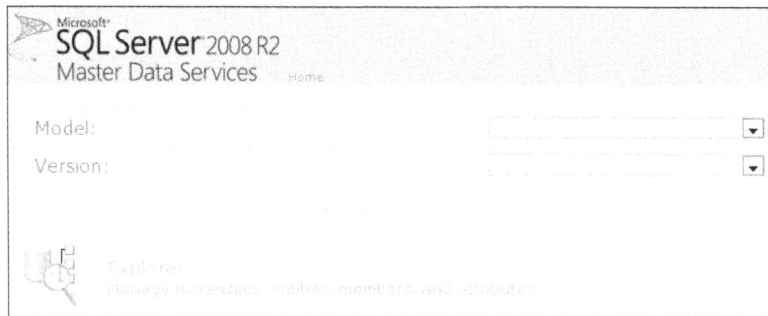

6. Notice also that the **Model** and **Version** drop-downs are both empty, as we have not given the first user permissions to any of the models yet.

7. Repeat the above process with the user that belongs to the local group that we created. At this point, only the Integration Management function should be visible, as shown in the following screenshot:

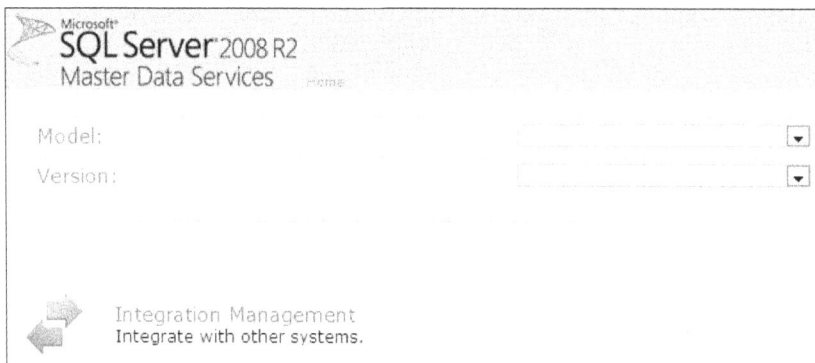

We will assign model permissions to both our user and our group, while looking at the functionality offered by the model permissions.

Model permissions

The Models tab within the User and Group Permissions function allows the following objects to be secured:

- Models
- Entities
- Attributes
- Attribute Groups
- Hierarchies (Explicit and Derived)
- Collections

For each object, the following permissions can be set:

- Update—The user can add, delete, and update data that exists against the specified object, as well as being able to view data. For example, if update permissions are assigned to an entity called Country, then the user would only be able to add, edit, and delete members within the Country entity, but would not be able to access any other Entities.
- Read-only—The user can only view data in the specified object.
- Deny—The user would be explicitly blocked from making changes to the specified object.

Administrators

If a user or group is assigned the Update permission at the model level, then they are known as a **Model Administrator**. Model Administrators must still be granted access to functions as we saw earlier, but once that is done, they can carry out the following:

- Add, delete, and update data for the model using the Explorer function
- Create, copy, lock, and validate versions using Version Management
- Import and export data using the Integration Management function
- Alter the model structure using System Administration
- Create users and groups and assign permissions for models for which they are an administrator, using the User and Group Permissions function

The only level of security within MDS that is higher than a Model Administrator is the **System Administrator**, who can access all functional areas of MDS, and can access all models, without the need for someone to specify permissions. There can only be one System Administrator for MDS, which is the user that is specified during the installation process.

> **Changing the MDS System Administrator**
>
> Although there can only be one System Administrator in MDS, the user can thankfully be changed by running the following stored procedure, as long as the new user already exists in MDS:
>
> ```
> --The @UserName parameter is for the new admin
> --The @SID parameter is for the new admin
> --The SID can be found in the mdm.tblUser table
> EXEC mdm.udpSecuritySetAdministrator @
> UserName='DOMAIN\User', @SID = '<Enter SID>', @
> PromoteNonAdmin = 1
> ```
>
> One point to note is that the old system administrator account is removed from MDS after the above stored procedure is run.

Assigning model permissions

We will now grant one of our test users access to various different objects within our model, and verify that they can only carry out a limited set of tasks.

In order to do this, carry out the following:

1. Log in to MDS as the System Administrator.
2. Navigate to the **User and Group Permissions** function.
3. Select the first user that we created, and click on the edit button.
4. Select the **Models** tab.
5. Click on the edit button at the top of the screen.
6. The **Models** hierarchy will now be enabled. Expand the **Store** node and then expand the **Entities** node.

7. Expand the **Store** node, and then click on the **Leaf** node, and choose **Update** from the pop-up menu, as shown:

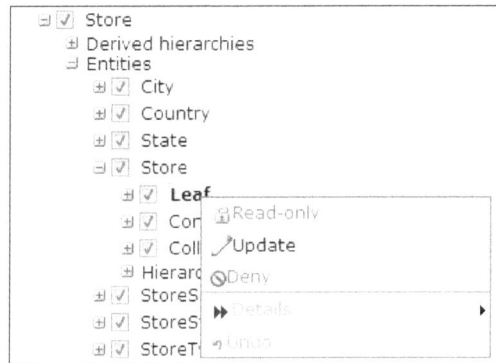

8. This will allow the user to add, edit, and delete members in the **Store** entity. It will also grant read-only access to any other entities that the **Store** is related to, for example, **City**, **StoreSize**, **StoreType**, and **StoreStatus**.

9. We want our user to be able to view the other entities, even if they are not directly related to the Store entity. Therefore, click on the **Country** entity and choose **Read-only**. Repeat this process for the **State** entity.

10. Expand the **Store** entity, then expand the **Leaf** node, then the **Attributes** node. As we granted the user update permission to the **Leaf** node, they automatically get update permissions on all attributes, unless we choose to over-ride on selected attributes, which we will now carry out.

11. Click on the **StoreStatus** attribute and choose **Read-only** from the pop-up menu. We created this attribute in *Chapter 7, Business Rules and Workflow*, but it's managed by the business rules, so we don't need a user to be changing this attribute. Once complete, the tree view on the left-hand side should look as follows:

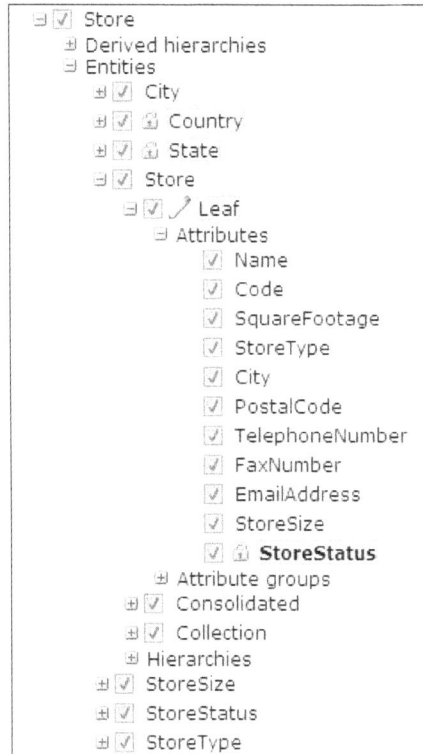

12. Click on the save button at the top of the screen.

13. The **Model Permission Summary** section should now be updated to show the following:

We now need to log in as our test user to see the effect of the permissions that we have set. In order to do this, carry out the following:

1. Log in to MDS as the first test user that was created.

2. Ensure that Store is selected from the **Model** drop-down and that **2011_ Stores** is selected from the **Version** drop-down.

3. Click on the **Explorer** function.

4. Click on the edit button to go to the **Store** entity. Notice how the Explorer grid has changed for this user, allowing editing for all attributes apart from **StoreStatus**, which is marked as read-only:

X	Name	Code▲	SquareFootage	StoreType	City	PostalCode	StoreSize	StoreStatus
☐	AW Duluth	001	2500	Mall{02}	Duluth{252}	55802	Medium{Medium}	Approved{Approved}
☐	AW Memphis	003	2500	Mall{02}	Memphis{434}	38103	Medium{Medium}	Approved{Approved}
☐	AW Detroit	004	2000	Mall{02}	Detroit{236}	48226	Small{Small}	Approved{Approved}
☐	AW Cambridge	005	2000	Mall{02}	Cambridge{228}	02139	Small{Small}	Approved{Approved}
☐	AW Baltimore	006	2000	Mall{02}	Baltimore{234}	21201	Small{Small}	Approved{Approved}
☐	AW Minneapolis	007	2000	Mall{02}	Minneapolis{255}	55402	Small{Small}	Approved{Approved}
☐	AW Clearwater 2	008	2000	Mall{02}	Clearwater{153}	33755	Small{Small}	Approved{Approved}
☐	AW Clarkston	009	2000	Mall{02}	Clarkston{170}	30021	Small{Small}	Approved{Approved}
☐	AW Woodburn	010	2000	Mall{02}	Woodburn{384}	97071	Small{Small}	Approved{Approved}
☐	AW Baytown	011	2000	Mall{02}	Baytown{440}	77520	Small{Small}	Approved{Approved}

Hierarchy Members permissions

The Hierarchy Members tab allows a user with sufficient access to set permissions on the members that exist within Explicit or Derived Hierarchies. The permissions that can be set are standard Update, Read-only, and Deny options that we have seen in previous sections of this chapter.

Hierarchy Member permissions are optional in MDS—without this in place MDS treats each member of the hierarchy exactly the same as every other member. For example, if the user has Update permission on a hierarchy (configured using the Model tab), then they will be able to update each member, whereas if they have Read-only permissions on the hierarchy then each member will be read-only.

Once Hierarchy Member permissions are saved, they are not immediately applied, meaning it may be some time before the permissions take effect from an end user perspective. Service Broker applies the permissions on a pre-defined interval, which defaults to 60 minutes. This can be changed in the system settings table called mdm. tblSystemSetting, using the Security Member Process Interval, as outlined in *Chapter 3, Installing and Confuguring Master Data Services*.

We will now work through an example of configuring Hierarchy Member permissions for one of the test users:

1. Log in to MDS as the MDS System Administrator.

2. Navigate to **User and Group Permissions**.

3. Edit the first user that we created.

4. Move to the **Models** tab and click on the edit button.

5. Expand the **Store** model node, then the **Derived Hierarchy** node. Click on the **Stores By Geography** node, and choose **Update**. This will grant the user access to the hierarchy, so that we can continue with our example.

6. Click on the save button. The **Model Permission Summary** pane should now be as follows:

Type	Name	Permission
▼ Derived Hierarchy	Derived: Store: Stores By Geography	Update
▼ Leaf Member Type	Store:Store:Leaf	Update
▼ Entity	Store:Country	Read-only
▼ Entity	Store:State	Read-only
▼ Attribute	Store:Store:Leaf:StoreStatus	Read-only

Model Permission Summary

7. We're now ready to set permissions for individual members. Move to the **Hierarchy Members** tab.

8. Ensure that **Store** is selected from the **Model** drop-down and **2011_Stores** is selected from the **Version** drop-down.

9. Pick **Derived: Stores By Geography**, which will cause the hierarchy to render in the pane below.

10. Click on the edit button.

11. Expand the **United States** node, and click on **Florida**, choosing the **Deny** option. This will prevent our user from viewing **Florida** or any of its descendant Stores, which is what we want for our example.

12. Setting **Deny** on a member will also deny any members that exist above Florida, which we don't want to happen. Thankfully we can override this behavior by clicking on the **United States** node and choosing **Update**. The hierarchy should now look as follows:

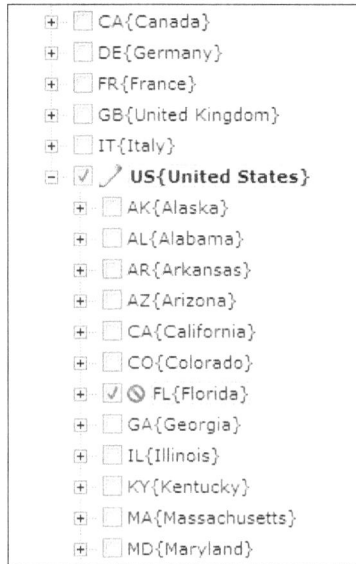

13. Click on the save button to save the permissions.

> **Applying member permissions immediately**
>
> If you do not want to wait for Service Broker to apply the member permissions, you can choose to apply the permissions immediately, by running the following piece of SQL in SQL Server Management Studio:
>
> ```
> DECLARE @ModelId INT
> SELECT @ModelId = ID FROM mdm.tblModel WHERE Name = 'Store'
> EXEC mdm.udpSecurityMemberProcessRebuildModel @ModelId, 1
> ```

Once the member security processing interval has passed, or alternatively if you have applied the permissions using SQL, we need to now log in to the MDS, and look at the changes. To do this, carry out the following:

1. Log in to MDS as the first test user that we created.

2. Navigate to the **Explorer** function.

3. Hover over the **Hierarchies** menu and click on **Derived: Stores By Geography**.

4. Expand the **United States** node and verify that **Florida** is not visible.

5. Hover over the **Entities** menu and choose the **Store** menu item. Verify that Florida and its children are not visible. If member permissions are applied for a hierarchy, they will also carry over to any other place where the members appear, such as the Store entity itself.

Summary

We have now finished this chapter and have seen that Master Data Services contains a multi-level security model that can be used to protect an organization's master data. In particular, we have learnt the following key points:

- Security is configured in the **User and Group Permissions** function of Master Data Manager

- A user can log in to MDS if their Windows account, or a Windows group that they are a member of, has been added to MDS

- Access can be restricted to each of the five functions of Master Data Manager.

- There is only one System Administrator in MDS, which is the user specified in the installation process

- A Model Administrator can access all data in the model, as well as being able to change the Model structure

- All of the objects within a model can be secured by setting a user or group's access to Update, Read-only or Deny

- Members can also be secured, but only on Explicit and Derived Hierarchies, through the use of the **Hierarchy Members** tab

Security is the final area of Master Data Services that we needed to cover, meaning that we're now at the end of the book. We hope that the content covered has been useful and will help in your own Master Data Management program.

Index

Security Member Process Interval 57
Server time out 55
Show names in hierarchy by default 56
Site Title 57
Staging batch interval 55
Validation Issue HTML 57
Validation Issue Text 57
Version Status Change HTML 57
Version Status Change Text 57
Web application time out 55
database service account 46
data access 24
data extraction, MDS
Application Programming Interface (API)
    method 235
Subscription Views method 236
data governance
about 24
change management 24
data access 24
data modification 24
data ownership 24
data privacy and retention 24
data quality standards 24
disaster recovery 24
data modification 24
data ownership 24
data privacy & retention 24
data quality, issues
complex data issues 14
data cleansing 14
data duplication 14
format issues 14
incomplete data 14
lack of consistency 13
out of range 14
data quality standards 24
data stewards
about 25
functions 25
Default Value action, MDS business rules
Defaults to 193
Defaults to a concatenated value 193
Defaults to a generated value 193
Delete Member option 92
Derived Column Transformation 177

derived hierarchies, MDS object model
about 73
creating 98, 99
exploring 100, 101
member, adding 103, 104
multiple entities, editing 102
visual representation 73
disaster recovery 24
domain attribute, attribute type 78, 79

E

Enable change tracking option 83
Enterprise Resource Planning. *See* **ERP**
entity
about 8
attributes 78
City 77
Country 78
creating 79, 80
domain attributes 78
editing 80-84
example data, importing 85, 86
relationships 78
State 78
Store 77
StoreType 77
entity data
locating 32
Entity Maintenance screen 105
ERP 10
error code, staging process 171
errors, staging process
about 170
error codes 171, 172
success codes 170
warning codes 171
ETL (Extract Transform Load) tool 39
EvalExpression 185
explicit hierarchies, MDS object model
about 74, 104
consolidated members 105, 107
creating 104
hierarchy members, moving 107-110
Explorer function 34, 112, 129, 131, 231, 327
Explorer grid view 88

F

Feature Selection window 48
features, MDS
   business rules and workflow 30
   entity maintenance 30
   hierarchy management 30
   modeling capability 30
   security 30
   version management 30
file, attribute type 77
Flags
   managing 140, 141
freeform, attribute type 77
function access 313

H

hierarchies
   about 98, 240
   derived 98
   explicit 104
hierarchy members 313
hierarchy tree structure
   Locate Parent of Selected Item 100
   Pin Selected Item 100
   Refresh Hierarchy 100
   Show/Hide Attributes 101
   Show/Hide Names 100
   View Meta Data 101
hybrid approach, MDM
   about 21-24
   data per entity 21
   overview 23
   role 22

I

implementation plan, MDM
   data, extracting 13
   data, publishing 13
   executive sponsorship, obtaining 12
   model, developing 13
   scope, defining 12
   solution, designing 13
InitExpression 185
installing
   MDS 47

sample models 66-68
installation key areas, MDS
   about 45
   administrator account 47
   database service account 46
   Distributed Configuration 46
   server topology 46
   Standalone Configuration 46
installation, MDS
   key areas 45
Integration Management function 38, 166, 238
Integration Management option 38
interface, versions
   Manage Versions page 124

L

Leaf members 86
load process, MDS
   automating, SSIS used 173-186

M

Manage Groups, menu option 42
Manage Versions page
   Manage 125
   Review 125
master data
   defining 8
   entity 8
   nouns, examples 8
   product entity 8, 9
   product entity, attributes 8, 9
   product entity, members 9
Master data delivery
   about 236
   BizTalk project, creating 248
   BizTalk Solution, deploying 263
   BizTalk Solution, testing 267
   BizTalk, using 245
   sample databases, creating 247
   scenario background, example 246
Master Data Management. *See* MDM
Master Data Manager
   about 29, 33
   accessing 33, 34
   Explorer function 34

W

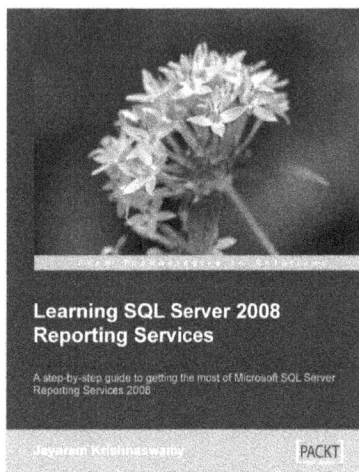

Learning SQL Server 2008 Reporting Services

ISBN: 978-1-847196-18-7   Paperback: 512 pages

A step-by-step guide to getting the most of Microsoft SQL Server Reporting Services 2008

1. Everything you need to create and deliver data-rich reports with SQL Server 2008 Reporting Services as quickly as possible

2. Packed with hands-on-examples to learn and improve your skills

3. Connect and report from databases, spreadsheets, XML Data, and more

4. No experience of SQL Server Reporting Services required

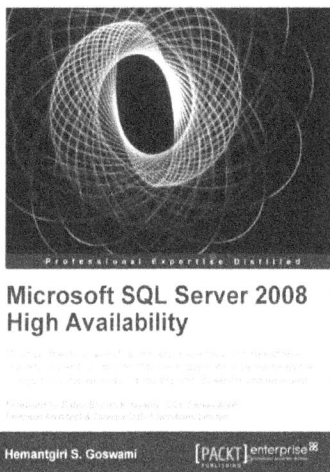

Microsoft SQL Server 2008 High Availability

ISBN: 978-1-84968-122-3   Paperback: 308 pages

Minimize downtime, speed up recovery, and achieve the highest level of availability and reliability for SQL server applications by mastering the concepts of database mirroring,log shipping,clustering, and replication

1. Install various SQL Server High Availability options in a step-by-step manner

2. A guide to SQL Server High Availability for DBA aspirants, proficient developers and system administrators

3. External references for further study

Please check **www.PacktPub.com** for information on our titles

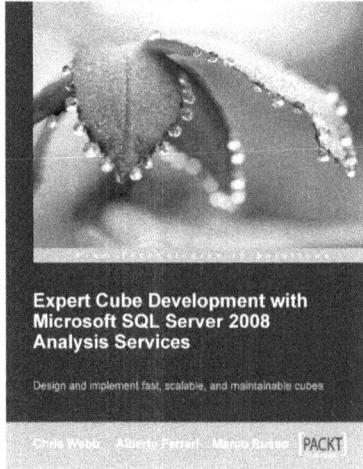

Expert Cube Development with Microsoft SQL Server 2008 Analysis Services

ISBN: 978-1-847197-22-1   Paperback: 360 pages

Design and implement fast, scalable and maintainable cubes

1. A real-world guide to designing cubes with Analysis Services 2008

2. Model dimensions and measure groups in BI Development Studio

3. Implement security, drill-through, and MDX calculations

4. Learn how to deploy, monitor, and performance-tune your cube

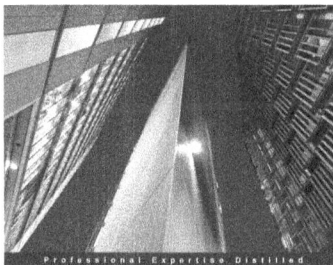

Microsoft SQL Azure Enterprise Application Development

ISBN: 978-1-849680-80-6   Paperback: 420 pages

Build enterprise-ready applications and projects with SQL Azure

1. Develop large scale enterprise applications using Microsoft SQL Azure

2. Understand how to use the various third party programs such as DB Artisan, RedGate, ToadSoft etc developed for SQL Azure

3. Master the exhaustive Data migration and Data Synchronization aspects of SQL Azure

4. Includes SQL Azure projects in incubation and more recent developments including all 2010 updates

www.ingramcontent.com/pod-product-compliance
Lightning Source LLC
Chambersburg PA
CBHW080905220326
41598CB00034B/5482